Mastering the Art of Co-Teaching
Building More Collaborative Classrooms

Nicholas D. Young
Angela C. Fain
Teresa A. Citro

Series in Education

VERNON PRESS

www.vernonpress.com

In the Americas:	*In the rest of the world:*
Vernon Press	Vernon Press
1000 N West Street,	C/Sancti Espiritu 17,
Suite 1200, Wilmington,	Malaga, 29006
Delaware 19801	Spain
United States	

Series in Education

Library of Congress Control Number: 2020931408

ISBN: 978-1-64889-029-1

Also available: 978-1-62273-916-5 [Hardback]; 978-1-62273-945-5 [PDF, E-Book]

Cover design by Vernon Press using elements designed by pressfoto / Freepik.

Table of Contents

Acknowledgement

It is with sincere appreciation that we offer this public thank you to Mrs. Suzanne (Sue) Clark for editing this tome. Sue has recently retired from a long and distinguished career in public education and her first act of "taking it easy" was to work tirelessly on this manuscript. She is a stickler for the details and has a wonderful (and kind) way of polishing draft chapters. There is no question that the final product is far better due to her efforts. We want all to know that we are grateful for her editorial work. On a more personal level, the entire team offers heartfelt congratulations to her on her retirement. Sue should be proud of what she has done to support the thousands of students who were positively impacted by her efforts over many years of service to public education.

Acknowledgement

Preface

Educators work almost exclusively alone, with only minor glimpses of others in their building with the exception of some planning time and the obligatory staff lounge lunch break. Co-teaching, however, offers educators and educational professionals a chance to do what is best for students - all students - plan, collaborate, manage and teach in tandem. In this atmosphere of togetherness, teachers become mentors, learners, leaders and followers. It is no easy feat, as there are many stumbling blocks; yet, the willing pair of teachers will find the road replete with benefits well beyond what is initially considered. *Mastering the Art of Co-Teaching: Building More Collaborative Classrooms* describes this very concept of co-teaching as a means to create a more collaborative and balanced classroom that benefits students and staff alike.

The book was written for regular and special educators, educational professionals who work within the classrooms, school administrators, guidance counselors, preservice, veteran and graduate education students. It covers a series of important topics that includes topics from how to co-plan, create a welcoming environment and how to assess students; work with a variety of service providers, paraprofessionals and families; as well as how to incorporate social-emotional learning into the co-taught classroom. Understanding that it is necessary to consider the stress of teaching in any form, professional development, relationships, mentorship and renewal are also topics of interest.

The motivation for writing this book came from several concerns:

- *Our concern that novice teachers are leaving the field within the first five years in record numbers due to stress and burnout,*

- *Our knowledge that veteran teachers who can mentor novices while teaching in tandem hold the key to more master teachers in the future,*

- *Our belief that co-teaching strengthens and encourages the best teaching practices when given the time, energy and supports needed,*

- *Our awareness that co-teaching is only possible with administrative support and professional development that honors the roles of both teachers,*

- *Our interest in promoting educational outcomes, knowing this begins within the classroom honoring all students from teachers who see every possibility in teaching and learning.*

Co-teaching, usually the pairing of a general education teacher and a special education teacher, can be traced back to 1975 and education reform (Wilson & Blednick, 2011). At its most basic level, co-teaching allows for the inclusion of students who may otherwise be separated during important learning times. This may be students with disabilities or linguistically diverse students as well as students with occupational or physical therapy needs. Teachers and educational professionals who have the opportunity to plan, collaborate and teach together give their students the opportunity to learn from others in the classroom. This is a heavy lift at first and should not be taken lightly.

Mastering the Art of Co-Teaching: Building More Collaborative Classrooms was written by a team of educators who represent preschool to the academy, all of whom are passionate about teaching and learning in the most fundamental ways. We offer this tome as a co-teaching guide to those who embrace this same passion for promoting successful educational outcomes for all students. For those willing to take the chance, or those who have been asked to co-teach, we hope you find the strategies and tools in the pages to follow as practical and useful as we have throughout our careers. For those of you who have chosen education as your profession, thank you for making a positive and productive difference in the lives of students.

References

Wilson, G.L. & Blednick, J. (2011). *Teaching in Tandem.* Alexandria, VA: ASCD

Chapter 1

Effective Co-Teaching Strategies That Work

Karen Russo, EdD, *St. Joseph's College*

Teachers occasionally express concern about 'fairness' in education. They may be anxious that one student will need an instructional or behavioral support that others do not. Some educators may question the fairness of individualized teaching or behavioral expectations (Southern Poverty Law Center: Teaching Tolerance, 2018). They may believe that all students should be treated equally. If inequity is perceived, these teachers worry that they will receive complaints from parents or even from the students themselves. Educators should know, however, that fair isn't defined as everyone getting exactly the same thing (Curwin, 2012). Fair is defined as everyone receives what they need and that everyone has the chance to be successful (Curwin, 2012).

In recent decades, a shift in education has made the inclusive classroom very much the norm. Students with special needs are often served in a general education classroom. The least restrictive environment is the most desirable placement for a student to achieve learning and behavioral goals (Morin, 2020). Congress reauthorized the Individuals with Disabilities Education Act (IDEA) in 2004 and amended IDEA through Public Law 114-95, the Every Student Succeeds Act (ESSA) in 2015 (Klein, 2016; Lee, 2020). In the law, Congress states:

> *Disability is a natural part of the human experience and in no way diminishes the right of individuals to participate in or contribute to society. Improving educational results for children with disabilities is an essential element of our national policy of ensuring equality of opportunity, full participation, independent living, and economic self-sufficiency for individuals with disabilities* (U.S. Department of Education, n.d.).

Support for inclusion can also be found from the Council for Exceptional Children (2019), which issued guidance for professional special educators' practices. Relative to inclusive classrooms, two such ethical principles seem particularly relevant and include "promoting meaningful and inclusive participation of individuals with exceptionalities in their schools and communities; [and] practicing collegially with others who are providing services to individuals with exceptionalities" (Council for Exceptional Children, 2019, n.p.).

The field of teaching has become more complex and educators must be intentional about the ways in which they meet individual student learning needs (Ricci & Fingon, 2017). It is true that some inclusive classes are taught by one general education teacher, with support personnel providing additional services throughout the school day. Those services may be offered within the classroom or in a separate location (Watson, 2019). Very often, general education and special education teachers are paired to teach a class that includes both general education students and those with special needs (Stein, 2016). They share the responsibilities for teaching and managing one class – this is known as co-teaching (Trites, 2017).

What is Co-Teaching?

Co-teaching is the partnering of a general education teacher and a special education teacher for the purpose of delivering instruction that meets the learning needs of all students in the classroom (Friend, 2019; Stein, 2016; Trites, 2017). While co-teaching does bring two teachers together, that is not the primary goal. The main purpose is to best serve students (Potts & Howard, 2011). It is "meant to provide specialized services to students with disabilities in regular classrooms, while ensuring they also get access to the same academic material as their peers" (Samuels, 2015, n.p.). Murawski and Bernhardt (2016) elaborated on this idea:

> Co-teaching requires more than just learning to "play nicely" together. It requires a paradigm shift—from teaching in silos to teaching in tandem, from owning the front of the room to sharing space, from sending students with special needs out of the classroom to thoughtfully differentiating for diverse learners. Before working on collaboration and communication skills, educators need to embrace the mindset that inclusion is an issue of both equity and social justice. Then, teachers and administrators will be more prepared for and committed to co-teaching (p. 31).

In a co-taught classroom, the general education teacher has expertise in curriculum, pacing, and class management. The special education teacher may be equally expert in these areas, with added expertise in learning processes, and the individualized needs of specific students in the class. Together, these two educators create a learning environment that benefits all students (Friend, Cook, Hurley-Chamerlain, & Shamberger, 2010).

Six Co-Teaching Models

Co-teaching often takes the form of one of six widely-accepted models to include one teach/one observe, one teach/one assist, alternative teaching, parallel teaching, station teaching, and team teaching (Cassel, 2019; Friend & Cook, 2016). Each has pros and cons and incorporates a variety of nuances to assist students.

One Teach/One Observe

In this model, co-teacher A takes the lead as the primary instructor while co-teacher B observes (Friend & Cook, 2016). The observational role is equally important to the teaching role because it demands that the observer collect data that may prove useful in future planning or meaningful in future assessments: diagnostic, formative, or summative (Cassel, 2019). The observer's job is not to critique the lesson or make a judgement about the co-teacher. Instead, the observer should collect evidence of specific behaviors to include

- Questioning: Data related to questioning can help inform the team that there is a balance in the types of questions being asked. The observer may conclude that more or fewer higher-order thinking questions are needed or that the pacing of questions and responses may be too slow or too fast (Friend & Cook, 2016).

- Student Participation: Student participation may be the result of students raising hands or from the frequency they are called upon (Friend & Cook, 2016). Is your co-teacher calling on varied students or favoring some? Are all students actively engaged? What are students saying during the lesson? These kinds of observations can be charted to note patterns over time. They can also be useful for parent conferences.

- Teacher Behavior: The observer can jot notes related to the co-teacher's facial expressions, tone of voice, or body movement and body language (Cassel, 2019).

- On-Task Behavior: The observer will note if students are engaged in active learning, if they seem focused, are they discussing the lesson, and how long is it taking them to complete tasks (Friend & Cook, 2016).

- Group Interactions: Here the observer will jot down what students are doing during the lesson and how they relate to one another and to the co-teacher. The observer will also note who is better at producing work when alone versus in a group, pair, team, or with the teacher (Cassel, 2019).

Sharma, Ali, Takhelmayum, Mahto, and Nair (2017) support the one teacher/one observer model through a study finding that noted that students in a biochemistry class "remain alert and focused, owing to presence of two teachers as one of them teaches and the other observes" (p. 97). In another study of co-teaching during a summer writing institute, the co-teachers' observations revealed that one student "sought adult approval on nearly every sentence she generated, interrupting her writing fluency" (Chandler-Olcott, 2017, p. 7). The team then reflected and brainstormed strategies that would support the student's independence. During the next lesson, the observing teacher took note of how well those strategies were working (Chandler-Olcott, 2017).

Examples of one teach/one observe in action.

- Literacy: Co-teacher A is teaching students to summarize what they have read using an excerpt from a familiar novel. At the same time, co-teacher B is jotting observational notes to determine which students are incorporating previously-learned strategies with the newly acquired ones.

- Mathematics: Co-teacher A is teaching addition of two-digit numerals with regrouping. At the same time, co-teacher B is taking note of which students are using the manipulatives effectively, which are using them ineffectively, and which are not using them at all.

One Teach/One Assist

In this model, co-teacher A leads the instruction while co-teacher B offers assistance to students who are need of support (Friend & Cook, 2016). The teacher in the assist role may clarify something that the lead teacher has said or may give additional examples to illuminate a topic. The teacher in the assist role may also bring students' questions to the larger group by asking them aloud (Cassel, 2019). In this way, the lead teacher's response will benefit the whole class. Another important job for the teacher in the assist role is to manage classroom behavior (Friend & Cook, 2016). Standing in close proximity to students who are easily distracted or have a conflict with others can help to minimize interruptions while the lead teacher is teaching.

Yopp, Ellis, Bonsangue, Duarte, and Meza (2014) found that nearly 100% of candidates in a mathematics teacher preparation program felt successful with one teach/one observe and one teach/one assist models of co-teaching, though it is worth noting that these models were also among their least favorites. Candidates shared reactions such as, "while observing and assisting are good, it feels like a teacher is being wasted [and] in one teach/one assist, I feel like I am not utilizing myself or the master teaching fellow fully" (p. 106). It is possible, however, for one teach/one and one teach/one assist to 'blur' together. Chandler-Olcott (2017) noted that once an observing co-teacher "interrupted her partner's discussion facilitation to note the 'four new voices today that we haven't heard yet' to challenge quiet students to contribute thoughts" (p. 7).

Examples of one teach/one assist in action.

- Literacy: Co-teacher A is teaching students how to use context clues to determine the meaning of unknown words. Co-teacher B thinks aloud to share a response that a student has whispered to her peer.

- Mathematics: Co-teacher A is teaching students how to measure two-dimensional shapes in inches and centimeters. Co-teacher B circles the room to support students who are having difficulty distinguishing between inches and centimeters on their rulers.

Alternative Teaching

This model allows both teachers to act as lead teacher at the same time, by teaching separate groups (Friend & Cook, 2016). The groups may be comprised of equal numbers of students or may be in a large group/small group configuration (Cassel, 2019). While the desired learning outcomes are the same for both groups, the instructional approaches each teacher uses may be quite different.

This model is the appropriate choice when teachers plan to provide specialized or intensive instruction to students. Differentiation can occur easily in this model, as methods and materials can be modified for optimal student learning. It is not meant to divide the class into homogeneous ability groups; rather, it should be seen as an opportunity to tailor instruction based on students' interests, interactions, strengths, competencies, and needs. One such example is described by Beninghof and Leensvart (2016) in which both co-teachers taught fifth-graders to sequence events of a story; however, one of the teachers modified instruction by identifying academic vocabulary words such as *plot* and *character*, as well as vocabulary from the story itself. She also incorporated visuals, oral learning, and synonyms that were easy for students to comprehend.

Examples of alternative teaching in action.

- Literacy: Both teachers are building phonological awareness skills by segmenting words into individual sounds. Co-teacher A is accomplishing this by using Elkonin Boxes (Greene, n.d.) and having students slide a colored chip into a box for each sound heard (Ex: /sh/ /ee/ /p/ = sheep). Co-teacher B is teaching students to tap out sounds on their fingers, without any visual materials.

- Mathematics: Both teachers are teaching the differences between acute, right, and obtuse angles. Co-teacher A is teaching students to use a paper right angle template to determine which angles on the worksheet are acute, right, or obtuse. Co-teacher B is working with students whose first language is not English, using the same paper right angle template. Their worksheet includes language supports such as cognates, as well as directions depicted in illustrations and words.

Parallel Teaching

This model also divides the class into two groups. Unlike alternative teaching, teachers use the same materials and the same teaching strategies. The benefits of teaching the smaller groups include that each teacher has a reduced student to teacher ratio, students have more opportunities to participate and share their learning, and teachers can focus on students' needs more effectively than in the larger group setting (Friend & Cook, 2016). This model should not be seen as an opportunity to divide the class into ability groups. Its strength lies in giving teachers the ability to work with fewer students and to bring their reflections back to the co-teaching team when planning for future groupings and instruction (Cassel, 2019).

In one study, co-teachers' success with parallel teaching of writing was attributed to the fact that "the smaller groups allowed for more intimacy with students, and the use of the same plan with different groups of learners often helped staff refine their approaches when they conferred about that plan's effectiveness during afternoon planning time (Chandler-Olcott, 2017, p. 8). This research affirms the benefits of the approach.

Examples of parallel teaching in action.

- Literacy: Both teachers are teaching students to write a persuasion essay in response to a question such as "Should homework be abolished?" Teachers would introduce a new graphic organizer for this purpose. As they are working with their groups, the teachers would be able to offer one-to-one assistance to those in need of support. They will also note the students who will likely benefit from the use of graphic organizers in their future writing. These notes will guide discussion as they co-plan an alternative teaching lesson later in the week.

- Mathematics: Both teachers are teaching students to solve two-step word problems. This is the first time such a lesson has been introduced, which is why this model of co-teaching was chosen. As they offer coaching to individual students, they are able to recognize those who are strong in computation and mathematical reasoning yet might need more support in reading. They use this information to guide discussion as they co-plan an alternative teaching lesson later in the week.

Station Teaching

This model closely resembles 'centers' in a classroom (Friend & Cook, 2016). Seating is arranged so that a few students can sit in each area at one time. Each co-teacher is stationed to a seating area, leaving one or more stations for independent activities. If desired, another adult such as a paraprofessional, a remedial teacher, or other support personnel may lead an additional station (Cassel, 2019). Specialists or special education teachers are integrated at each station so that when a student with special needs visits that station "she is simply doing what's next in her rotation" (Murdock, Finneran, & Theve, 2016, p. 45). In this way, all students are fully integrated into the station teaching routine while having their needs met.

Students spend a pre-determined amount of time at each station and visit all stations once throughout the course of the lesson (Fiend & Cook, 2016). This type of co-teaching offers the freedom to differentiate the work while engaging with smaller groups of students. It also affords educators the chance to focus on a discrete skill or strategy as a mini-lesson with each group rather than presenting a fully-developed lesson during the allotted instructional time.

Examples of station teaching in action.

- Literacy: During a butterfly life cycle unit, teachers have planned for the following stations:
  o Station 1: Co-teacher A will assist students in using their labeled butterfly life cycle diagrams to create developed sentences about the butterfly at various stages of its life. During a future lesson, these will be stretched into paragraphs for their informational books.
  o Station 2: Students work in pairs to compete in a butterfly life cycle challenge game on the Smartboard. If time allows, each pair will write at least one more question for the other team to answer as a bonus.
  o Station 3: Co-teacher B shares videos of butterfly gardens and sanctuaries around the world to further inform students'

knowledge of butterflies and the importance of protecting them at all stages of their lives. This will also increase their vocabulary knowledge within the unit.

o   Station 4: Students work independently to assemble and beautify their butterfly life cycle hanging mobiles. Mobiles will later be displayed around the classroom.

- Mathematics: During a unit on money values, teachers have planned for the following stations:

o   Station 1: Co-teacher A will act as the storekeeper and have a few simple items for sale. At first, students will pay for the items using exact change. They will then be expected to pay for items using the least appropriate dollar bill(s) and determine how much change they should expect in return.

o   Station 2: Student partners will take turns to represent the money value at least three different ways using combinations of coins and bills. To do so, they will slide pretend money onto a laminated piggy bank card while their partner will write the corresponding number sentence; for example, 1 dollar + 3 dimes + 1 nickel + 4 pennies = $1.39.

o   Station 3: Co-teacher B will distribute baggies to students, each with a different sum of money inside. Each student will count the money in their bag and record the amount on an index card. They will work as a team to arrange the index cards from least to greatest. The teacher will then scramble the cards and ask the teams to arrange them from greatest to least.

o   Station 4: Students work independently or in pairs to group pennies into 5s, 10s, and 25s. Groups of pennies will then be used to practice skip counting, as well as exchanging groups of pennies for coins of equal value.

Team Teaching

In this model, both teachers lead the lesson at the same time. Through planning, teachers actively share in all aspects of instruction, assistance, interjection, questioning, and responding (Friend & Cook, 2016). Students experience their teachers' styles and personalities, separately and as a team. This type of co-teaching can be very dynamic and engaging, as teachers bring their own energy and perspectives to the lesson. Sharma et al. (2017) report that having two teachers engaging in the lesson "reinforces the key points of the lecture through repetition or reinstatement which helps in clarifying concepts and favors long-term retention" (p. 97). For true ownership of the lesson, teachers must not simply divide the responsibilities or the work. As in all models of co-teaching, co-planning is a must (Cassel, 2019).

Examples of team teaching in action.

- Literacy: Both teachers are responsible for instructional delivery during a lesson on character traits. While co-teacher A displays picture clues on the interactive board, co-teacher B is calling on students to use multiple adjectives to describe the clue. Co-Teacher A affirms their responses and begins to type their responses into a word cloud or Wordle (Farlex, 2019). Co-teacher B facilitates a discussion about the word cloud to determine whether or not students agree it is an accurate representation of the character. Co-teacher A makes changes to the word cloud as needed while asking how these traits are similar/different than other characters in the story.

- Mathematics: Both teachers are responsible for instructional delivery during a lesson on telling time. Co-teacher A holds an analog clock while co-teacher B holds a digital clock. Students have index cards with times written in words; for example, five thirty-two. Co-teachers take turns calling on students to share a time aloud for the class. Each teacher represents that time on the analog or digital clock they are holding. Co-teachers direct student pairs to work on the next phase of the lesson. One student in each pair will represent a specific time with their two arms as if they are the hands of an analog clock, while the partner draws them on the face of a clock on the pair's worksheet. Partners work together to record the same time as it would look on a digital clock. Co-teachers move around the room to support and interact with students as they work, noting any challenges and successes students may be experiencing.

Planning for Successful Co-Teaching

Gürgür and Uzuner (2010) asserted that teachers who were new to co-teaching implementation often used the one teach/one assist model due to a lack of adequate planning that made them feel ill-equipped to try other models. They also may not yet have known how to mitigate the differences in their training, their backgrounds, their skills, and their challenges (Mielke & Rush, 2016).

Effective co-teaching cannot happen without effective co-planning. Teachers need to be good communicators, have respect for what each brings to the learning environment, and be willing to invest the time in planning together. Perhaps most importantly, they must be flexible and willing to abandon their own ideas in favor of their co-teachers' plans (Murdock et al., 2016). Due to time constraints, co-teachers may shy away from this critical co-planning process. Technology may alleviate much of the pressure in this regard; for example, using a web-based document sharing site can facilitate asynchronous co-planning.

Face-to-face interactions can be kept to a minimum, and co-teachers can read or add notes to the shared plan at any time of day. Both educator's contributions are available to the other in real time (Scruggs & Mastropieri, 2017). Face-to-face meetings can be supplemented with phone calls and email exchanges too. Ricci and Fingon (2017) detailed their protocol for teachers to engage in meaningful co-planning - that is, they met in-person for 30-90 minutes, exchanged over 40 emails, and conducted multiple phone chats a week.

Sinclair et al. (2019) reported that lack of planning time shaped teachers' roles in the classroom. The general education teacher often took the lead role as they had planned most of the lesson. Of course, special education teachers need some content knowledge in order to plan interventions and modifications for learners with needs; however, some special education teachers are assigned to several co-teaching partnerships with general education colleagues (Scruggs, Mastropieri, & McDuffie, 2007). Co-planning with multiple persons can present serious time challenges.

It is during this co-planning time that teachers can define their roles in the instructional delivery of the lesson. Scruggs (2012) describes a scenario in which a special education teacher didn't feel secure in her level of content area knowledge. She deferred to the general education teacher to take the lead role, while she assumed responsibility for modifying materials. In this way, all students in the class had access to the information presented in the lesson.

Nilsson (2015), however, found that the processes themselves of co-planning, co-teaching, and co-assessment can actually increase individual learning of both content and methods. The important step of co-planning cannot be understated. Without it, special education teachers very often assume the role of assistant teacher rather than as an equal partner in the teaching team (Gürgür & Uzuner, 2010). When the general education teacher frequently takes the lead, the special education teacher is very much underused (Beninghof & Leensvart, 2016) or functions similarly to a paraprofessional or teacher's aide (Sinclair et al., 2019).

A review of studies describing 400+ co-taught classrooms revealed that it was most common for a general education teacher to lead the whole class while the special education teacher took a subordinate role and engaged in tasks such as passing out papers (Scruggs et al., 2007). In one study, the science teacher was observed interacting with the large group twice as often as the special education teacher and presented new content nearly three times as often as the special education teacher (King-Sears, Brawand, Jenkins, & Preston-Smith, 2014).

In effective co-teaching, general education teachers and special education teachers share a sense that all students 'belong' to them; therefore, both teachers are actively engaged in every aspect of the instructional cycle from planning to reflection (Beninghof & Leensvart, 2016). The more often they can brainstorm, teach, and solve problems collaboratively, the more effective they will be. They should not function autonomously in the co-teaching environment (Murdock et al., 2016).

The Role of Teacher Preparation Programs

Approximately 62% of students with disabilities spend 80% or more of their school day in the general education setting. The statistic has increased by almost 30% in the past 20 years; thus, teacher preparation programs must provide adequate coaching, modeling, and fieldwork opportunities to teacher candidates so they will be ready to co-teach in their hired placements (McFarland et al., 2017).

In a study conducted by Ricci and Fingon (2017), 34 graduate students were enrolled in courses in which effective co-teaching was modeled by their professors; additionally, the students participated in workshops and small-group activities with resources such as videos and PowerPoint presentations to strengthen their knowledge of co-teaching. Data from student surveys and written reflections revealed positive changes in instructional practices, and a shift in thinking as a result of these experiences; for example, 'my students' became 'our students' (Ricci & Fingon, 2017).

Another study conducted by Hoppey and Mickelson (2017) explored co-teaching practices of preservice teachers and recommend that teacher preparation programs engage these teachers-to-be in shared planning to develop their collaboration skills. Professors and mentor teachers should offer multiple and varied opportunities for them to engage in authentic co-teaching activities. With such experience, preservice teachers will rise to the challenges of teaching students with disabilities in their own classrooms as either the general education teacher or the special education teacher (Hoppey & Michelson, 2017).

Pettit (2017) suggested that setting co-teaching expectations for teacher candidates' fieldwork experiences and conducting weekly discussions related to the topic produced positive outcomes for them, their cooperating teachers, and their students. Not all teacher preparation programs, however, are incorporating co-teaching strategies or practices throughout their coursework and fieldwork.

Chitiyo and Brinda (2018) studied 77 preservice teachers in the northeastern United States and asked the following questions (1) How prepared are teachers in the use of co-teaching? and (2) Is there a relationship between teachers who had co-teaching and those who had not in their preparedness? Through their research, they found that fewer than half (only 44%) of participants felt they had learned anything about co-teaching in their teacher preparation programs.

While most preservice teachers had some understanding of the foundations of co-teaching, they did not feel confident to engage in it effectively (Chitiyo & Brinda, 2018). As a result of these findings, it has been recommended that colleges and universities require students to co-teach in an inclusive setting as part of their fieldwork and that faculty model various co-teaching strategies by teaming up to teach college courses (Chitiyo & Brinda, 2018; Ricci & Fingon, 2017).

The co-teaching experience deficit is not specific to higher education in the United States alone. Frey and Kaff (2014) worked with 101 student teachers in Tanzania. They found that while special education teacher candidates viewed future co-teaching partnerships with optimism and positivity, they were not exposed to co-teaching materials, resources, or curriculum in their coursework (Frey & Kaff, 2014). As Pettit (2017) stated,

> *common sense dictates that formative co-teaching practice is critical throughout teacher training [and] meaningful experiences helped candidates to develop an early praxis about co-teaching and a strong foundation for building quality co-teaching skills, co-generative relationships, and collaboration for successful inclusive practice during their student teaching, 1st-year teaching experiences, and beyond* (p. 22).

Professional Development and Administrative Support

To co-teach successfully, partners must plan, assess, and reflect on lessons together as well as develop trust with each other as well as support given to them from leadership (Honigsfeld & Dove, 2016; Murphy & Beggs, 2010). Though lack of professional preparation and inconsistencies in co-teaching implementation still exist, administrators can help close the gaps in teacher knowledge and experiences related to co-teaching (Friend et al., 2010).

Higher education faculty in teacher preparation programs and district-level administrators share the responsibility for developing preservice and in-service teachers' skills in collaboration and co-teaching including sharing expectations of how and when students receive support, offering team-building courses and sample lesson plans, and allotting ample time for co-planning and co-reflection meetings (Gürgür & Uzuner, 2010; Krammer, Gastager, Lisa, Gasteiger-Klicpera, & Rossmann, 2018; Ricci & Fingon, 2017; Sinclair et al., 2019).

Sinclair et al. (2019) found that "teachers viewed their schools' leadership decisions as adversely affecting their ability to co-teach effectively" (p. 303). Rather than impede or undermine teachers' efforts, administrators should actively create an environment that increases teachers' knowledge and confidence in the practice of co-teaching. In their research with general education teachers and English literacy development co-teachers, Beninghof and Leensvart (2016) found that some general education teachers have difficulty "sharing instructional time, releasing control, and seeing the value of their co-teacher" (p. 72).

Honigsfeld and Dove (2016) reported similar findings in their research with general education teachers and English literacy development teachers stating, "neither classroom teachers nor secondary content-area teachers have proven eager to give up leading their lesson when a co-teacher is present, whether the co-teacher is there to support English language learners (ELLs) or students with disabilities" (p. 58). To foster more positive professional relationships among co-teachers, Beninghof and Leensvart (2016) recommended "systematic, long-term professional learning activities" for co-teachers (p. 71).

Krammer et al. (2018) compiled data from online questionnaires completed by 264 teachers. Teachers' perceptions of adequate administrative support included such practices as training, positive feedback, and assisting them in the development of specific skills within the context of co-teaching. Seglem, VanZandt, and Fink (2010) described one school district in which the general education teacher was referred to as the lead teacher and the special education teacher as the supporting teacher. The teachers felt this message undermined their collective efforts to help all students succeed (p. 41).

It is a mistake to assume that only general education teachers are well-versed in curriculum and class management. Both general education teachers and special education teachers can contribute greatly in these areas. Special education teachers have additional expertise in the highly individualized needs of some students in the class (Friend et al., 2010). Together, these co-teachers are a strong force for learning and advocacy in their classroom.

Final Thoughts

Federal legislation has inspired policy changes in our educational system. In response to these changes, co-teaching has emerged as a way to ensure that students with special needs have "access to the same curriculum as other students while still receiving the specialized instruction to which they are entitled" (Friend et al., 2010, p. 9). Like all educational strategies, co-teaching must be utilized with increased student learning and participation in mind. As Mackey, Reilly, Jansen, and Fletcher (2018) stated, "good teaching results in improved outcomes for students and the impact on children's learning should be at the heart of any consideration to adopt co-teaching in flexible learning environments" (p. 466).

The six models of co-teaching, one teach/one observe, one teach/one assist, alternative teaching, parallel teaching, station teaching, and team teaching, have distinct features but can benefit students equally when facilitated in appropriate ways (Friend & Cook, 2016). No matter the model, it is critically important that both teachers are actively engaged and working together throughout the instructional cycle, which includes planning, teaching, assessing, and reflection (Cassel, 2019). Teacher roles must be clearly defined so that neither teacher struggles to secure their place in the co-teaching dyad.

Teacher preparation programs and school administrators play important roles in the development and support of co-teaching strategies. Providing pre-service and in-service teachers with modeling, mentoring, practice, experience, and common time together strengthens co-teaching skills and relationships. Co-teachers should be involved in all aspects of the decision-making process to ensure success for all.

Points to Remember

- *All students have the right to meaningful participation in school and co-teaching is one way to teach everyone in an inclusive setting.*

- *Co-teachers share responsibility for academic content and pacing as well as class management. The special educator takes responsibility for individualizing instruction for students with specific learning needs.*

- *There are six widely-accepted models for co-teaching: one teach/one observe, one teach/one assist, alternative teaching, parallel teaching, station teaching, and team teaching.*

- *Co-teachers should be actively engaged in all aspects of the instructional cycle to include planning, teaching, management, assessment, and reflection.*

- *Teacher preparation programs have a responsibility to provide adequate modeling, mentoring, and experiences so that preservice teachers are fully prepared to co-teach in their schools.*

- *School administrators should provide clear expectations, mentoring, professional development, and time for in-service teachers to hone*

> their co-teaching skills and strengthen their co-teaching relationships. They should welcome teacher voices and feedback in all aspects of co-teaching decision making.

References

Beninghof, A., & Leensvaart, M. (2016). Co-teaching to support ELLs. *Educational Leadership, 73*(5), 70-73. Retrieved from http://www.ascd.org/publications/educational_leadership/feb16/vol73/num05/Co-Teaching_to_Support_ELLs.aspx

Cassel, S. (2019). How to choose a co-teaching model. *Edutopia.* Retrieved from https://www.edutopia.org/article/how-choose-co-teaching-model

Chandler-Olcott, K. (2017). Co-teaching to support early adolescents' writing development in an inclusive summer enrichment program. *Middle School Journal, 48*(1), 3-12. DOI:10.1080/00940771.2017.1243916

Chitiyo, J., & Brinda, W. (2018). Teacher preparedness in the use of co-teaching in inclusive classrooms. *Support for Learning, 33*(1), 38-51. https://onlinelibrary.wiley.com/doi/abs/10.1111/1467-9604.12190

Council for Exceptional Children. (2019). *Professional standards and practice: Policies and positions.* Retrieved from https://cec.sped.org/Standards/Professional-Policy-and-Positions

Curwin, R. (2012). *Fair isn't equal: Seven classroom tips.* Retrieved from https://www.edutopia.org/blog/fair-isnt-equal-richard-curwin

Farlex. (2019). *Wordle.* Retrieved from https://www.thefreedictionary.com/Wordle

Frey, L., & Kaff, M. (2014). Results of co-teaching instruction to special education teacher candidates in Tanzania. *Journal of the International Association of Special Education, 15*(1), 4-15. Retrieved from https://eric.ed.gov/?id=EJ1058232

Friend, M. (2019). *Co-teach! Building and sustaining classroom partnerships in inclusive schools* (3rd ed). Greensboro, NC: Marilyn Friend, Inc.

Friend, M. & Cook, L. (2016). *Interactions: Collaboration skills for school professionals.* New York, NY: Pearson

Friend, M., Cook, L., Hurley-Chamberlain, D., & Shamberger, C. (2010). Co-Teaching: An illustration of the complexity of collaboration in special education. *Journal of Educational & Psychological Consultation, 20*(1), 9-27. https://doi/org/10.1080/10474410903535380

Greene, K. (n.d.). *Evidence-based literacy strategy: Elkonin sound boxes.* Retrieved from https://www.understood.org/en/school-learning/for-educators/teaching-strategies/evidence-based-literacy-strategy-elkonin-sound-boxes

Gürgür, H., & Uzuner, Y. (2010). A phenomenological analysis of the views on co-teaching applications in the inclusion classroom. *Kuram Ve Uygulamada Egitim Bilimleri, 10*(1), 311-331. Retrieved from https://files.eric.ed.gov/fulltext/EJ882729.pdf

Honigsfeld, A., & Dove, M. (2016). Co-teaching ELLs: Riding a tandem bike. *Educational Leadership, 73*(4), 56-60. Retrieved from

http://www.ascd.org/publications/educational_leadership/dec15/vol73/nu
m04/Co-Teaching_ELLs@_Riding_a_Tandem_Bike.aspx

Hoppey, D. & Mickelson, A.M. (2017). Partnership and coteaching: Preparing
preservice teachers to improve outcomes for students with disabilities.
Action in Teacher Education, 39(2), 187-202, doi:
10.1080/01626620.2016.1273149

King-Sears, M., Brawand, A., Jenkins, M., & Preston-Smith, S. (2014). Co-
teaching perspectives from secondary science co-teachers and their
students with disabilities. *Journal of Science Teacher Education, 25*(6), 651-
680. doi:10.1007/s10972-014-9391-2

Klein, A. (2016). *The Every Student Succeeds Act: An overview.* Retrieved from
https://www.edweek.org/ew/issues/every-student-succeeds-
act/index.html

Krammer, M., Gastager, A., Lisa, P., Gasteiger-Klicpera, B., & Rossmann, P.
(2018). Collective self-efficacy expectations in co-teaching teams: What are
the influencing factors? *Educational Studies, 44*(1), 99-114.
doi:10.1080/03055698.2017.1347489

Lee, A.M.I. (2020). *Individuals with disabilities act (IDEA): What you need to
know.* Retrieved from
https://www.understood.org/en/school-learning/your-childs-
rights/basics-about-childs-rights/individuals-with-disabilities-education-
act-idea-what-you-need-to-know

Mackey, J., Reilly, N.O., Jansen, C., & Fletcher, J. (2018) Leading change to
coteaching in primary schools: a "Down Under" experience. *Educational
Review, 70*(4), 465-485, doi: 10.1080/00131911.2017.1345859

McFarland, J., Hussar, B., de Brey, C., Snyder, T., Wang, X., Wilkinson-Flicker,
S., . . . Hinz, S. (2017). *The Condition of Education 2017* (NCES 2017-144).
Washington, DC: U.S. Department of Education, National Center for
Education Statistics. Retrieved from https://eric.ed.gov/?id=ED574257

Mielke, T.L. & Rush, L.S. (2016). Making relationships matter: Developing co-
teaching through the concept of flow. *English Journal, 105*(3), 49–54.
https://jstor.org/stable/26359395

Morin, A. (2020). *Least restrictive environment (LRE): What you need to know.*
Retrieved from
https://www.understood.org/en/school-learning/special-services/special-
education-basics/least-restrictive-environment-lre-what-you-need-to-
know

Murawski, W., & Bernhardt, P. (2016). An administrator's guide to co-
teaching. *Educational Leadership, 73*(4), 30-34. Retrieved from
http://www.ascd.org/publications/educational_leadership/dec15/vol73/nu
m04/An_Administrator's_Guide_to_Co-Teaching.aspx

Murdock, L., Finneran, D., & Theve, K. (2016). Co-teaching to reach every
learner. *Educational Leadership, 73*(4), 42-42. Retrieved from
http://www.ascd.org/publications/educational_leadership/dec15/vol73/nu
m04/Co-Teaching_to_Reach_Every_Learner.aspx

Murphy, C. & Beggs, J. (2010). A five-year systematic study of coteaching
science in 120 primary school. In C. Murphy & K. Scantlebury, *Coteaching in*

International Contexts: Research and Practice, Culture Studies of Science Education (pp. 11-34). Dordrecht: Springer.

Nilsson, P. (2015). Catching the moments: Coteaching to stimulate science in the preschool context. *Asia-Pacific Journal of Teacher Education, 43*(4), 296-308. doi:10.1080/1359866X.2015.1060292

Pettit, S. (2017). Preparing teaching candidates for co-teaching. *Delta Kappa Gamma Bulletin, 83*(3), 15-23.

Potts, E.A. & Howard, L.A. (2011). *How to co-teach: A guide for general and special educators.* Baltimore, MD: Brookes Publishing.

Ricci, L.A. & Fingon, J.C. (2017). Faculty modeling co-teaching and collaboration practices in general education and special education courses in teacher preparation programmes. *Athens Journal of Education 4*(4), 351-362. Retrieved from https://www.athensjournals.gr/education/2017-4-4-4-Ricci.pdf

Samuels, C.A. (2015). Challenge of co-teaching a special education issue. *Education Week.* Retrieved from https://www.edweek.org/ew/articles/2015/06/10/hurdles-in-pairing-general-special-education-teachers.html

Scruggs, T.E. (2012). Differential facilitation of learning outcomes: What does it tell us about learning disabilities and instructional programing? *International Journal for Research in Learning Disabilities, 1,* 4-20. Retrieved from http://www.iarld.com/home/the-journal-thalamus

Scruggs, T.E., & Mastropieri, M.A. (2017). Making inclusion work with co-teaching. *Teaching Exceptional Children, 49*(4), 284-293. https://doi.org/10.1177/0040059916685065

Scruggs, T.E., Mastropieri, M.A., & McDuffie, K.A. (2007). Co-teaching in inclusive classrooms: A metasynthesis of qualitative research. *Exceptional Children, 73,* 392-416. https://doi.org/10.1177/001440290707300401

Seglem, R., VanZant, M., & Fink, L. S. (2010). Privileging students' voices: A co-teaching philosophy that evokes excellence in all learners. *English Journal, 100*(2), 41-47. DOI: 10.2307/25790030

Sharma, S., Ali, A., Takhelmayum, R., Mahto, M., R., & Nair, R. (2017). Co-teaching: Exploring an alternative for integrated curriculum. *Journal of the National Medical Association, 109*(2), 93-97. doi:10.1016/j.jnma.2017.02.002

Sinclair, A.C., Bray, A.E., Wei, Y., Clancy, E.E., Wexler, J., Kearns, D.M., & Christopher, J.L. (2019). Coteaching in content area classrooms: Lessons and guiding questions for administrators. *NASSP Bulletin 102*(4), 303-322. https//:doi.org/10.1177/0192636518812701

Southern Poverty Law Center: Teaching Tolerance. (2018). *Critical practices for anti-bias education.* Retrieved from https://www.tolerance.org/sites/default/files/2019-04/TT-Critical-Practices for Anti bias Education.pdf

Stein, E. (2016). *Elevating co-teaching through UDL.* Wakefield, MA: CAST

Trites, N. (2017). *What is co-teaching? An introduction to co-teaching and inclusion.* Retrieved from http://castpublishing.org/introduction-co-teaching-inclusion/

U.S. Department of Education. (n.d.). *About IDEA*. Retrieved from
https://sites.ed.gov/idea/about-idea

Watson, S. (2019). *Supports for special education students*. Retrieved from
https://www.thoughtco.com/supports-for-special-education-students-3110276

Yopp, R., Ellis, M., Bonsangue, M., Duarte, T., & Meza, S. (2014). Piloting a co-teaching model for mathematics teacher preparation: Learning to teach together. *Issues in Teacher Education, 23*(1), 91-111. Retrieved from https://eric.ed.gov/?id=EJ1045811

Chapter 2

Communicating with Your Teaching Partner

Micheline S. Malow, PhD, *Manhattanville College*
Vance Austin, PhD, *Manhattanville College*

Successful co-teaching requires the camaraderie of two professionals as it is an interactive endeavor that brings together individuals with different experiences, personality traits, and areas of expertise (Fitzell, 2018). Some researchers suggest that the co-teaching relationship is similar to a marriage, where there must be open and honest communication (Sileo, 2011; Tomlinson, 2015); yet, others discount that analogy as co-teaching is a professional relationship (Mastropieri & Scruggs, 2017; Stivers, 2008). Regardless of the stance, co-teaching is predicated on effective communication between a pair of professional educators.

Twenty-two years ago, not long after the educational movement toward serving students in inclusive settings was popularized, a study was conducted that investigated co-teaching in elementary and secondary schools in Bergen County, NJ (Austin, 2001). Ten years after that, the same author replicated the study in the greater Nashville, Tennessee vicinity to learn about the perceptions of teachers relative to co-teaching (Austin, 2010). Both studies found that co-teaching was regarded by the educators engaged in the practice as generally effective (Austin, 2001; Austin 2010). Teachers were also unanimous in their selection of the team teaching or parity approach over the consultant approach as the preferred model of implementation (Austin, 2001; Austin 2010). In this popular model, both the special and general educator share equally in the duties of planning curriculum, implementing the instructional practices, and evaluating student progress (Friend & Cook, 2016).

The two studies about co-teaching confirmed several things about effective co-teaching; namely, the need for administrative support in providing sufficient planning time, the need for greater parity in the distribution of labor and teaching responsibilities between the special and general educator (findings from both studies conveyed that both special education and general education teachers believed that general education teachers frequently took on more teaching responsibility) and, lastly, the need for authentic co-teaching training and experiences prior to and during student teaching (Austin, 2001;

Austin, 2010). The following vignette illustrates the differences between co-teaching experiences.

A certified special education and social studies teacher had been a co-teacher in a public school in the early 1990s. In need of quick assimilation of grade 11 biology curriculum, he received the patient mentoring of a co-teaching partner. The high school biology teacher he was fortunate to have been paired with was warm, communicative, and generous in sharing both materials and subject knowledge.

As much of the research described in this chapter confirms, the keys to the success of this co-teaching assignment were attributable to several things (1) the easy rapport established early on between the special educator and general educator, (2) while the pair were not allotted shared planning time, they met three times a week, after class, on their own time, to evaluate their co-teaching and plan for the following week's lessons, and (3) the co-teachers used humor to defuse tensions and soften potentially acerbic feedback, frequently sublimating cherished teaching ideas for the sake of the lesson objective.

The net result proved successful; a special education teacher who knew little to nothing about biology was complimented on his subject knowledge by the school's principal during an observation, and a general education biology teacher who had never heard of differentiated instruction deftly incorporated that technique into all her lesson plans. Both teachers had not volunteered for a co-teaching position and were initially skeptical about its effectiveness as a teaching model; however, at the end of that first year, both teachers requested to co-teach together again the following year.

Fast forward ten years, the special education teacher becomes a newly minted assistant professor, who volunteered to co-teach an introductory special education class to graduate students. Flush with the success of co-teaching in high school and eager to try out the model in a college setting, the new co-teaching pair, both former special education teachers with co-teaching experience, were convinced of the potential for successful application in a postsecondary classroom. After all, both reasoned, their students were preservice special educators who would invariably be assigned to co-teach at some point in their careers.

Unfortunately, things didn't go as expected. The professors had very different teaching philosophies and evaluation standards. One of the professors was accused of being "too generous" with grading, while the other was reluctant to equitably share instructional time. To complicate matters further, both had scheduling conflicts and planning time suffered. The result was that two assistant professors who enjoyed each other's company prior to the co-teaching experiment, became estranged and hardly spoke to each other.

The situation became so untenable that a colleague suggested mediation, which helped restore the relationship, but could not resurrect the co-teaching experience. At the end of the semester, the course evaluations reflected the concerns: an inconsistent quality of instruction, the lack of parity, uneven grading, and perceived tension between the instructors (Austin & Pace, 2003).

Research on Communication

The vignette illustrated perhaps the single most important guarantor of the success of co-teaching or impediment to it; that is, the quality of communication between the partners (Bacharach, Heck & Dalberg, 2008; Murawski & Dieker, 2004; Stivers, 2008). In support of the primacy of communication skills in co-teaching, a study conducted by Brinkmann and Twiford (2012) found that 23 percent of general education teachers and 26 percent of special education teachers polled identified these skills as the most important for effective co-teaching. By way of contrast, however, only 15 percent of general education teachers and 7 percent of special education teachers said they received training in the acquisition of these skills (Brinkmann & Twiford, 2012).

It is instructive to consider studies conducted on the efficacy of co-teaching and the importance of effective communication instruction in teacher preparation classes, as preservice special education teachers will likely be asked to co-teach in inclusive K-12 classrooms at some point in their careers (Casey, 2019). Counter to their preparation, special educators find that much of their day is spent navigating adult-adult communications for which they are not prepared (Wysocki, 2016). The lack of preparation may lead some educators to experience resistance, stress, and uncertainty when confronted with the task of co-teaching, increasing the likelihood of conflict (Wysocki, 2016).

In their evaluation of several co-taught teacher preparation classes, Bacharach et al. (2008) noted the importance of good communication and recommended the following strategies to facilitate it (a) always communicate honestly with your partner, even when uncomfortable, (b) attentively listen to your partner's suggestions and feedback, (c) share ideas for feedback prior to implementing them, (d) address communication strategies, and (e) pay attention to your partner's affect, non-verbal cues, and body language to enhance understanding.

Similarly, Devlin-Scherer and Sardone (2013) noted that preservice teacher candidates reported in their instructor/course evaluations that their greatest concerns relative to their experience were the lack of effective co-teacher communication and organization. As a result of this feedback, several suggestions were given to future co-teachers. The suggestions included (a) select a co-teaching partner with different skills, interests, and strengths, (b) be confident in your teaching abilities, (c) take inventory of your and your partner's strengths and weaknesses, (d) don't be too critical of each other as perfect doesn't exist, (e) be genuinely receptive to feedback, (f) engage each other socially by taking time to share non-professional interests, and (g) share constructive ideas, not gossip (Devlin-Scherer & Sardone, 2013).

Graziano and Navarrete (2012) suggested that co-teachers of teacher preparation courses, like their K-12 counterparts, dismiss misperceptions about each other through honest, open dialogue. Co-teachers do not have to share the same teaching philosophy to be effective; rather, they must establish trust, mutual respect, and accountability from the outset to ensure a successful co-teaching experience (Graziano & Navarrete, 2012). The researchers contend that co-teaching enriches pedagogy but is predicated on effective communication that addresses teaching styles, preconceptions, fears, and ideas to enhance the professional growth of both partners (Graziano & Navarrete, 2012).

Barriers to Communication in Co-Teaching Relationships

There are many barriers to an effective co-teaching relationship; some may seem obvious as they are difficult conditions for all teachers to manage, whether in a co-teaching situation or not. These barriers, including issues of time, grading practices, student and teacher readiness, and more recently, high stakes testing, complicate circumstances for everyone in the teaching profession (Friend & Cook, 2016; Beninghof, 2012). When co-teaching, however, the ability to mitigate conflict around these issues is a necessity. Conflict can occur between co-teaching pairs when there are unresolved differences in regard to needs, values, goals and personalities (Dettmer, Thurston, Knackendoffel & Dyck, 2009).

Educational researchers, Friend and Cook (2016), defined conflict in regard to co-teaching as the struggle experienced when it is perceived that there is interference with the ability to accomplish set goals. Although conflict can occur between individuals who voice the same goals, the approach used to attain those goals may be different (Beninghof, 2012). Complicating the approach to goal attainment is the difference in the perceived power between individuals in the co-teaching pair. If one teacher is more experienced than the other, decision- making authority may not be shared equally (Beninghof, 2012; Friend & Cook, 2016).

A framework for understanding conflict in the co-teaching relationship was presented by Conderman (2011b). This framework was built on the idea that conflict typically occurs around three components to include co-planning, co-instructing, and co-assessing. With co-planning, barriers to effective co-teaching can occur throughout the preparation of lessons; for example, both educators must be prepared and attend scheduled lesson planning sessions in order to set the foundation for teamwork (Beninghof, 2012). This may mean using personal time in order to plan, or the need to get creative in arranging opportunities for planning. Planning time is often not allotted by administrators despite the recognition that it is a necessary step for effective practice. If one or both partners cannot come to terms with the mechanics of arranging for co-planning, the team will not be able to get to the content and instructional sequences that will allow for smooth co-instruction (Conderman, 2011b; Friend & Cook, 2016).

Co-instruction becomes a barrier when teaching philosophy, classroom management, and content knowledge are not shared (Stein, 2016). Conflict can result when one of the co-teaching pair continually takes on the role of the lead teacher for instructional purposes, when setting up classroom management policies, or when providing the assessment and feedback to students (Friend & Cook, 2016). In this situation, students may come to view the other teacher to be in a supportive role; as an assistant to the teacher instead of as an equal co-teacher in the classroom. The inequality on display to the students, as well as to the other educational professionals in the building, will not further the professional reputation or growth of either teacher, leading to resentment by one or both teachers if not addressed (Conderman, 2011b).

Barriers to co-assessment in a paired relationship can occur when co-teachers have different philosophies and procedures for grading. While one teacher may rely on rubrics and strictly defined criteria for grading, the other may base assessment practices on more of a gestalt approach, using their subjective opinion (Stein, 2016). This can lead to both teacher and student resentment if one co-teacher is seen as an easy grader and another is viewed as stricter in regard to grading practices; students may begin to favor one teacher over the other and express this perception to parents further complicating the situation (Austin, 2010).

Mastropieri and Scruggs (2017) acknowledged several challenges to the co-teaching relationship and offered viable solutions. If, for example, the teaching pair experience control issues, they should look for common ground and consider what is in the best interests of the students, not what serves their egos. Next, if co-teachers are stymied by differences in teaching philosophy, they should identify common goals and ensure that any instructional or behavior management decisions they make are evidence-based (Mastropieri & Scruggs, 2017). Finally, in the case of disagreements about behavioral or classroom management issues, they should agree to explore positive behavioral interventions and employ scientifically validated techniques (Mastropieri & Scruggs, 2017).

Knowing where the barriers to effective co-teaching can occur is an important first step in addressing conflict; however, personality and conflict style also factor into whether or not communication between co-teachers is positive or problematic. Conderman (2011b) explicitly described the five approaches to communication based on the work of Thomas and Kilmann (1974) that individuals engage in when a conflict in a relationship is present (1) avoidance, (2) accommodation, (3) compromising, (4) collaborating, and (5) dominating.

Adapted for co-teaching communication, Conderman (2011b) applied personality trait communication factors to an individual's preferred approach for managing conflict (Copley, 2008 as cited in Conderman 2011b). Although each individual may engage in their preferred style of communication most often, Conderman (2011b) recommended that individuals entering into co-teaching situations should know, understand and be able to utilize all five methods to manage conflict. Within the co-teaching relationship, there may be a time and situation that calls for any one of the five-conflict management styles and choosing a style to utilize based on a particular situation can produce the most constructive outcome (Conderman, 2011b; Fisher, Ury, & Patton, 2011; Thomas & Kilmann, 1974).

An avoidant conflict management style is often utilized if someone is afraid to discuss important information with their partner, or alternatively if they possess poorly developed conflict resolution skills (Thomas & Kilmann, 1974). This circumstance may be observed in relationships that have an uneven power distribution; typically seen when an experienced teacher is paired with a novice teacher (Conderman, 2011b). In an effort to keep the peace, one individual may avoid communication conflict in an effort to not make the situation worse; however, not wanting to discuss a difficult situation does not lead to resolution. Using an avoidant style can only be considered beneficial when the concern is minor or trivial to both parties (Fisher et al., 2011).

The accommodating style is often utilized by individuals who hold others in higher regard than they hold themselves (Thomas & Kilmann, 1974). When working from this style, an individual may choose to look for commonalities, emphasizing areas where the pair are in agreement (Conderman, 2011b). In this way, a stable relationship is maintained as long as peaceful interpersonal communication is viewed as more valuable than the issue causing conflict. Using an accommodating style may be beneficial if the disagreement is of little consequence; however, similar to that of overreliance on an avoidant style, if the same individual accommodates to the other's needs repeatedly, resentment and a power differential in the relationship will emerge (Fisher et al., 2011).

The give and take approach that is the hallmark of the compromising style, demonstrates to self and others that the co-teaching pair have parity; they are equally situated in the relationship (Thomas & Kilmann, 1974). In this approach to conflict management, the individual has some resolution skills and values themselves as well as the other person. When using a compromising approach, however, neither individual may have their needs met or their values represented as each member of the pair sacrifices something in order to reach a mutually acceptable agreement (Conderman, 2011b). Compromise is best used in situations where time is of the essence and there is no easy solution or pre-determined path forward (Fisher et al., 2011).

Unlike in the compromising style, the collaborative style of conflict management frequently is viewed as a winning situation for all individuals (Thomas & Kilmann, 1974). Collaboration is viewed as part of a problem-solving process where multiple solutions are conceived through content-area techniques in an attempt to identify the best path forward. In this approach, the goal is to think outside of the box, allowing both individuals to freely express their needs and values relative to the source of conflict (Conderman, 2011b). In this way, both members of the team are held in high regard and work toward a solution that embodies everyone's values. Collaborative approaches are most successful when it is important to merge the ideas of the co-teaching team; this is an important process for long-range planning and relationship building (Fisher et al., 2011).

The final conflict management approach is not typically effective for relationship building between co-teachers (Thomas & Kilmann, 1974). In the forced or dominating style, a decision is imposed on the pair either by a third party in charge, such as an administrator, or by the more dominant of the co-teaching pair (Conderman, 2011b). This is a last step approach and should only be used if teaching, learning, or behavior is severely undermined if a decision is not implemented. This approach should only be used when a quick decision must be made or if an unpopular course of action must be taken (Fisher et al., 2011).

Planning for Co-Teaching with Effective Communication

Although evidence that confirms the benefits associated with co-teaching on teaching diverse students in inclusive settings is somewhat elusive, the practice remains strongly supported (Beninghof, 2012; Casey, 2019). Along with the documented benefits of co-teaching, researchers have identified and strongly support the need for better preparation in effective communication prior to beginning to co-teach (Fitzell, 2018). Mastropieri and Scruggs (2017) underscore the importance of sound communication skills for co-teachers noting that co-teachers must listen carefully and clearly communicate their perceptions and suggestions during planning time. Co-teachers benefit when using active listening techniques; taking a sincere interest in what their partner has to say and avoid interjecting or interrupting with advice or commentary (Friend & Cook, 2016; Mastropieri & Scruggs, 2018).

Communication between co-teachers is predicated on mutual respect as well as to parity of roles and responsibilities. Sileo (2011) urged co-teachers or those preparing to co-teach to become acquainted with their partners and commit the time to develop a sound professional relationship, further noting that "effective communication is key to navigating professional relationships" (p. 32). Sileo (2011) further urged co-teachers to communicate openly about issues that challenge the quality of their instruction and share their understanding of what constitutes good co-teaching as well as their respective philosophies of education.

The process of engaging in effective communication practices extends to considering cultural differences in the practice of communication and accepting the interpersonal style of each individual in the relationship while engaging in communication pre and post instruction (Ploessl, Rock, Schoenfeld & Blanks, 2010). Like many researchers on co-teaching communication, Ploessl et al. (2010) suggested that co-teachers engage in ongoing shared reflections employing ongoing, clear and open communication.

Conderman (2011a) encouraged co-teachers to engage in open communication and interaction as well as to discuss beliefs and expectations about teaching and learning. Teaching partners should know each other's areas of expertise and agree upon shared and individual responsibilities relative to planning, instructing, and assessing students' work (Beninghof, 2012; Fitzell, 2018). As co-teaching is a joint venture, use language such as the plural pronouns 'we,' 'us,' and 'ours' rather than the singular, 'I,' 'me,' and 'mine' when communicating about co-teaching classroom concerns (Conderman, 2011b).

Murawski and Dieker (2004) provided several recommendations to improve communication between teachers assigned to co-teach to include (a) share hopes, attitudes, responsibilities, and expectations (SHARE), (b) establishment of private signals to let the partner know to advance the discussion, change the topic, or if one partner needs to leave the room, (c) model civil discourse in order to show students how to respectfully disagree and offer constructive feedback to others, (d) discuss evaluation standards and the provision of alternative assignments upfront, and (e) engage in reflective practices to determine if the planning and implementation is working for the teaching pair as well as the students.

Conderman, Johnston-Rodriguez and Hartman (2009) extended the notion of partner knowledge in co-teaching. Conderman et al. (2009) suggested that knowing what their co-teaching partner is doing, thinking, and feeling, as well as what skills and experiences they bring into the classroom makes for a strong connection. This intimate professional knowledge can only be acquired through open and honest communication and for that reason, the authors note that co-teachers frequently requested training in effective communication skills.

According to Conderman et al. (2009), some of the more popular communication skills sought were how to effectively discuss teaching and learning goals, classroom management plans, instructional noise and other distractions, as well as sharing personal 'pet peeves.' Co-teachers should always treat others the way they want to be treated (Alessandra, & O'Connor, 1996). This is called the Platinum Rule, and it shifts the focus of communication to understanding what the other individual wants and needs (Alessandra & O'Connor, 1996; Conderman, 2011a). This rule captures the notion that not all individuals in a relationship will need the same thing and that effective communication will be based on giving others what they need.

Additional suggestions to improve co-teachers' communication include (a) ensure their verbal and non-verbal signs are congruent, (b) use the appropriate venue for communicating, such as cell phone, text, email, face-to-face conference calls, (c) use open-ended questions, (d) use of "I" statements, (e) paraphrase or summarize responses of your colleague, and (f) employ parallel communication techniques such as using similar vernacular, vocabulary, and communication styles (Austin, 2001; Conderman, 2011b; Fisher et al., 2011; Friend & Cook, 2016).

Conderman et al. (2009) also recommended that when personal disagreements arise, co-teachers should reflect on their motive for the need to confront their partners. If confrontation is unavoidable, do so caringly and sparingly using humor to defuse tension, as appropriate - or better yet - try to share the problem and allocate sufficient time to develop the relationship (Fisher et al., 2011).

In a similar vein, Friend and Cook (2016) offered sets of questions for co-teachers to ask each other before, during, and after a co-taught lesson.

- Before questions might include (a) are we willing to try something new? (b) how many of our students have a disability? and (c) how can we equitably share teaching responsibilities?

- During questions might include: (a) what can the other do while one is lecturing or leading? (b) what are some non-verbal signals we can use to signal the need for a break or a transition? and (c) do any students need pre-teaching, reteaching, or enrichment?

- After (reflection) questions might be: (a) have we reviewed assessment data to improve student performance? (b) how do you prefer to receive feedback? and (c) what are we doing that we both enjoy and feel is effective?

Final Thoughts

Communication in co-teaching is key to success. Teaching pairs who have constructive two-way conversations are more likely to have classrooms in which students receive instruction and learning with positive outcomes. Unfortunately, most preservice teachers are not given instruction on how to manage a co-teaching situation and in-service teachers are given little to no training as well. Administrators would be well-advised to offer professional development in this area as good communication benefits staff and students in all classrooms, but especially a co-taught academic setting.

Keeping in mind, the conflict resolution types will assist teaching pairs in communicating issues and finding solutions. Better still, putting the Platinum Rule into action at all times will save time and energy for co-teachers. Creating a common language and set of signals will ensure that co-teachers have a way to communicate. When teaching pairs can speak respectfully to each other and work through potential issues, they are more likely to feel successful in tandem teaching and students will ultimately benefit in terms of academics as well as social and emotional behaviors.

Points to Remember

- *Honest communication between co-teaching partners, which, at times, can be awkward and uncomfortable, ensures transparency of motives and intentions.*

- *Practice active listening techniques such as: not interjecting ideas or interrupting a colleague when they're providing feedback, listening attentively to their suggestions or comments before respectfully sharing yours, and paying close attention to body language and similar non-verbal cues.*

- *Co-teachers should engage in ongoing debriefing and shared reflection on their instruction, employing clear, open communication as vital elements in the successful planning and implementation of lessons.*

- *Teaching pairs should consider cultural differences in communication, resolve minor issues before they escalate, think first and act later, and see differences in thinking as beneficial to the co-teaching practice.*

- *Co-teachers should celebrate their differences as well as their similarities. Good co-teaching might be compared to singing a duet or when two jazz musicians take turns riffing. Teaching pairs should be encouraged to develop a common vernacular.*

- *In the event that relational problems arise, co-teachers are encouraged to (a) identify the problem, (b) develop an alternative course of action, (c) analyze the effectiveness of each intervention, (d) select a course of action, (e) implement the intervention, (f) assess the results, and (g) take responsibility for the outcomes.*

- *The ability to mitigate conflict in co-teaching relationships is key. Communication conflict typically occurs around three components to include co-planning, co-instructing, and co-assessing. Using one of the five conflict management styles – avoid, accommodate, compromise, collaborate, dominate – will help to successfully navigate conflict.*

References

Alessandra, T. & O'Connor, M.J. (1996). *The platinum rule: Discover the four basic business personalities-and how they can lead you to success.* New York, NY: Warner Books

Austin V. L. (2001). Teachers' beliefs about co-teaching. *Remedial and Special Education, 22*(4), 245-255. https://doi.org/10.1177/074193250102200408

Austin, V. L. (2010). Inclusive practices in Tennessee: An investigation of co-teaching in Middle Tennessee schools. *Electronic Journal for Inclusive Education, 2*(5), http://corescholar.libraries.wright.edu/cgi/viewcontent.cgi?article=1118&context=ejie

Austin, V. L. & Pace, D. (2003). Collaborative teaching: Reflections of general and special education co-teachers. *Academic Exchange Quarterly, 7*(3).

Bacharach, N. L., Heck, T. W., & Dalberg, K. R. (2008). What makes co-teaching work? Identifying the essential elements. *College Teaching Methods and Styles Journal, 4*(3), 43-40. https://doi.org/10.19030/ctms.v4i3.5534

Beninghof, A.M. (2012). *Co-teaching that works: Structures and strategies for maximizing student learning.* San Francisco, CA: Jossey-Bass

Brinkmann, J. & Twiford, T. (2012). Voices from the field: Skill sets needed for effective collaboration and co-teaching. *Connections Module, Creative*

Commons Attribution License, 1(8), 1-13. Retrieved from
https://files.eric.ed.gov/fulltext/EJ997467.pdf

Casey, B. (2019). *When special and general educators collaborate, everybody
wins.* Retrieved from
http://www.ascd.org/ascd-express/vol14/num25/when-special-and-
general-educators-collaborate-everybody-wins.aspx

Conderman, G. (2011a). Middle school co-teaching: Effective practices and
student reflections. *Middle School Journal, 42*(4), 24-31. doi:
10.1080/00940771.2011.11461771

Conderman, G. (2011b). Methods for addressing conflict in cotaught
classrooms. *Intervention in School and Clinic, 44*(4), 221-229.
doi:10.1177/1053451210389034

Conderman, G., Johnston-Rodriguez, S., & Hartman, P. (2009).
Communicating and collaborating in co-taught classrooms. *Teaching
Exceptional Children Plus, 5*(5), 2-16. Retrieved from
https://files.eric.ed.gov/fulltext/EJ967751.pdf

Dettmer, P., Thurston, L., Knackendoffel, A., & Dyck, N. (2009). *Collaboration,
consultation, and teamwork for students with special needs* (6th ed).
Columbus, OH: Pearson.

Devlin-Scherer, R. & Sardone, N. B. (2013). Collaboration as a form of
professional   development: Improving learning for faculty and students.
College Teaching, 61, 30–37. https://doi.org/10.1080/87567555.2012.714815

Fisher, R., Ury, W.L. & Patton, B. (2011). *Getting to yes: Negotiating agreement
without giving in.* New York, NY: Penguin Books

Fitzell, S.G. (2018). *Best practices in co-teaching & collaboration: The HOW of
co-teaching –implementing the models.* Manchester, NH: Cogent Catalyst
Press

Friend, M. & Cook, L. (2016). *Interactions: Collaboration skills for school
professionals* (8th ed.). New York, NY: Pearson

Graziano, K. J. & Navarrete, L. A. (2012). Co-teaching in a teacher education
classroom: Collaboration, compromise, and creativity. *Issues in Teacher
Education, 21*(1), 109-126. Retrieved from https://eric.ed.gov/?id=EJ986819

Mastropieri, M. A., & Scruggs, T. E. (2017). Making inclusion work with co-
teaching. *Teaching Exceptional Children, 49*(4), 284-293.
https://doi.org/10.1177/0040059916685065

Mastropieri, M.A. & Scruggs, T.E. (2018). *The inclusive classroom: Strategies for
effective differentiated instruction* (6th ed.). New York, NY: Pearson

Murawski, W. W., & Dieker, L. A. (2004). Tips and strategies for co-teaching at
the secondary   level. *Teaching Exceptional Children, 36*(5), 52-58. Retrieved
from
http://citeseerx.ist.psu.edu/viewdoc/download?doi=10.1.1.453.3368&rep=r
ep1&type=pdf

Ploessl, D., Rock, M. L., Schoenfeld, N. A., & Blanks, B. (2010). On the same
page: Practical   techniques for enhancing co-teaching interactions.
Intervention in School and Clinic, 45 (3), 158-168. Retrieved from
https://eric.ed.gov/?id=EJ874396

Sileo, J. M. (2011). Co-teaching: Getting to know your partner. *Teaching Exceptional Children, 43*(5), 32-38. DOI: 10.1177/004005991104300503

Stein, E. (2016). *Elevating co-teaching though UDL.* Wakefield, MA: CAST

Stivers, J. (2008). Strengthen your co-teaching relationship. *Intervention in School and Clinic, 44*(2), 121-125. https://journals.sagepub.com/doi/abs/10.1177/1053451208314736

Thomas, K. W., & Kilmann, R. H. (1974). *Thomas-Kilmann Conflict MODE Instrument.* DOI: 10.1037/t02326-000

Tomlinson, C.A. (2015). One to grow on/Teaching in tandem: A reflection. *Educational Leadership,* 73(4), 90-91. Retrieved from http://www.ascd.org/publications/educational-leadership/dec15/vol73/num04/Teaching-in-Tandem@-A-Reflection.aspx

Wysocki, C.D. (2016). *The collaboration of general and special education in a teacher preparation program design: A case study.* Retrieved from https://etd.ohiolink.edu/!etd.send_file?accession=osu1460893938&disposition=inline

Chapter 3

Working with Paraprofessionals in the Classroom

Angela C. Fain, PhD, *University of West Georgia*

Paraprofessionals also commonly referred to as teaching assistants (TAs), teacher aides, educational support personnel, paraeducators, and classroom assistants are used in general education classrooms to support the inclusion of students with disabilities (Butt, 2016; Douglas, Chapin, & Nolan, 2016; Radford, Bosanquet, Webster, & Blatchford, 2015). They are also used in more restrictive educational classroom settings primarily serving students with disabilities to ensure high quality teacher-student interactions (Curby, Rudasill, Edwards, & Pérez-Edgar, 2011). Paraprofessionals are employed to provide a range of non-instructional roles (Harris & Aprile, 2015) and appropriately trained and supervised paraprofessionals can offer supplementary instructional services (Salend, 2016). According to the U.S. Department of Labor (2017), just over one million teacher assistants are employed in elementary and secondary schools.

Due to increased educational testing and demands to support student learning, shortages in special educators, and changing roles of the classroom teacher, the presence and reliance of paraprofessionals in the classroom has changed (Boe & Cook, 2006; Council for Exceptional Children, 2012). According to the U.S. Department of Education (2004), paraprofessionals are employees who provide instructional support, including those who:

(1) *provide one-on-one tutoring if such tutoring is scheduled at a time when a student would not otherwise receive instruction from a teacher,*

(2) *assist with classroom management, such as organizing instructional and other materials,*

(3) *provide instructional assistance in a computer laboratory,*

(4) *conduct parental involvement activities,*

(5) *provide support in a library or media center,*

(6) *act as a translator, or*

(7) *provide instructional support services under the direct supervision of a teacher* (p. 1).

Traditionally, paraprofessionals assumed clerical duties such as grading papers, taking roll, and managing classroom behaviors to allow teachers to focus more time on academic instruction; however, the role of the paraprofessional has evolved to spending more time with individual students and small groups of students to provide academic, behavioral, social and physical support to help students succeed in school (Nevin, Villa & Thousand, 2009).

The Individuals with Disabilities Education Act (IDEA) of 2004 specified that paraprofessionals may assist in the delivery of services to students; however, they should not be the primary service providers, highlighting the fact that paraprofessionals must be supervised while assisting students in the delivery of instruction (Council for Exceptional Children, n.d.; National Center for Learning Disabilities, 2014). Research suggests that paraprofessionals who are trained and supervised in specific instructional models can promote the success of students; therefore, it is of great importance that teachers take the time and effort needed to invest in building a positive and productive relationship with their paraprofessional (Bingham, Hall-Kenyon, & Culatta, 2010; Lushen, Kim, & Reid, 2012).

Paraprofessional Roles and Responsibilities

Paraprofessionals generally serve in one of two ways (1) as a one-on-one assistant to a student with exceptional needs or (2) as support for special education programs to assist different students (Friend & Cook, 2017; Villa, Thousand & Nevin, 2013). As one-on-one assistants, paraprofessionals can assist students who have academic, behavioral, and/or physical disabilities during part or all of the day, while as support for teachers or programs, paraprofessionals may be assigned to a classroom, a grade level, or work across grade levels based on the needs of students (Friend & Cook, 2017; Villa et al., 2013). Specific roles and responsibilities are often based on the qualifications needed for the job and the number of hours the individual is needed to work; however, the student population and needs of the classroom will ultimately determine the duties of the paraprofessional.

Non-instructional and instructional tasks can be allocated to paraprofessionals. Non-instructional tasks include making copies, laminating materials, collecting money for field trips, taking attendance, and corresponding with parents regarding upcoming meetings and conferences (Conderman, 2011). Paraprofessionals can also assist in entering grades, updating notes on progress reports, and entering data on behavior intervention plans. Some paraprofessionals may be assigned to provide individual services to students for their personal care (Nevin et al., 2008). This may involve helping the student transition from one place to another, assisting in feeding, providing procedures such as catheterization, changing diapers, or assisting a student to use the toilet (Villa et al., 2013).

Paraprofessionals can help with a number of instructional tasks to work with students in the classroom to assist the teacher. Instructionally based tasks include direct lesson instruction and answering student questions, enforcing rules and routines, and providing reinforcements (Friend & Cook, 2017; Friend, Cook, Hurley-Chamberlain, & Shamberger, 2010; Giangreco, Halvorsen, Doyle, & Broer, 2004).

For students who need additional support in the classroom, paraprofessionals can assist with instructional activities such as reading individually with students or in small groups, reviewing prior instruction, reading tests to students, assisting students to find resources, and helping students maintain organized notebooks and materials (Friend & Cook, 2017). Paraprofessionals may assist students in following directions, staying on task, completing multiple-step directions, or serving as a "partner" to the student in an activity (Nevin et al., 2008). For students with more significant needs, paraprofessionals may assist students in alternative curriculum while participating in the general education classroom (Villa et al., 2013).

Collaborating with Your Paraprofessional

Research has shown that paraprofessionals generally perform a variety of roles in the classroom that are viewed positively by teachers, students, and parents. However, literature on the relationship between teachers and paraprofessionals remains sparse, despite increased roles and responsibilities for paraprofessionals (Cipriano, Barnes, Bertoli, Flynn & Rivers, 2016). When educators take the time to train and supervise paraprofessionals, meet regularly, delegate tasks, and demonstrate respect for paraprofessionals, they maximize the learning potential of students and create a more collaborative learning environment (Cipriano et al., 2016).

As an important part of the classroom environment, and under the direction of the teachers in the special education and general education classroom, paraprofessionals are a key component of an effective learning environment (Friend & Cook, 2017). As leaders of the classroom, teachers should consider the many roles their paraprofessionals can play in the classroom and how they will work with and manage their paraprofessional. When teachers delegate responsibilities it allows the teacher to maximize time for instruction with students (Conderman, 2011). It is essential that teachers consider approaching the relationship with an open and collaborative attitude. Teaching plans, classroom expectations and routines, classroom management, and student progress are just a few of the things that will need to be shared and discussed with the paraprofessional (Villa et al., 2013).

Effective communication is essential to any effective co-teaching relationship (Nevin et al., 2008). First and foremost, it is important to clearly communicate the paraprofessional's assigned tasks. The special education and general education teachers should provide actionable feedback to the paraprofessional regarding work with students (Friend & Cook, 2017). This can include acknowledging strategies that are being implemented correctly, redirecting ineffective strategies, modeling effective techniques, and problem-solving.

When conflict arises, teachers should be professional and demonstrate respect for one another. Research has shown that teachers who are respectful engage in more productive relationships than teachers who do not (Clarke, Embury, Jones, & Yssel, 2014; Friend et al., 2010). Collaboration is viewed to be easier and individuals are more likely to be willing to engage in collaborative efforts when respect is present (Friend et al., 2010). Respect between teachers is demonstrated by using the other's name, making eye contact, and using a warm tone when speaking (Conderman, 2011; Friend et al., 2010). Teachers and paraprofessionals who are engaged in these actions are modeling prosocial behaviors for their students as well (Lunenberg Korthagen, & Swennen, 2007).

Research shows that paraprofessionals feel more valued when there is effective communication and collaboration with the teacher (Brown & Stanton-Chapman 2014; Cockroft & Atkinson, 2015; Docherty, 2014; Wasburn-Moses et al., 2013). Effective collaboration occurs when teachers and paraprofessionals feel supported by each other, share information regarding students and teaching, have clearly defined roles, and are respectful (Devecchi & Rouse, 2010).

Clarification of roles, time for planning, and feedback are factors that have been found to improve effectiveness (Nevin et al., 2008). Research shows that when roles are unclear, there is limited supervision and feedback, and communication is limited regarding students and lesson planning paraprofessionals feel their performance is hindered (Cockroft & Atkinson, 2015; Docherty, 2014; Fisher & Pleasants, 2012; Lehane, 2015).

Numerous studies have found that paraprofessionals can have a positive impact on academic achievement and social and behavioral performance if they receive training and supervision in research-based practices (Bingham et al., 2010; Cooke, Galloway, Kretlow, & Helf, 2011; Feldman & Matos, 2013; Lane, Fletcher, Carter, Dejud, & Delorenzo, 2007; Lushen et al., 2012; Moore & Hammond, 2011).

Final Thoughts

As the number of paraprofessionals in the classrooms continues to grow it is important to consider how their role will impact student learning. Paraprofessionals who have significant roles in the classroom and execute a variety of important tasks are viewed positively by teachers, parents, and students. It is important that teachers work on building positive relationships with their paraprofessionals in the classroom through training and supervision, planning, communication, delegation of tasks, and a demonstration of respect.

Points to Remember

- *Paraprofessionals are also referred to as teaching assistants (TAs), teacher aides, paraeducators, and are used in classrooms to support the learning of students.*

- *Paraprofessionals generally serve in one of two ways: as a one-on-one assistant to a student with exceptional needs or as support for special education programs to assist different students.*

- *Paraprofessionals work with individual students and small groups of students to provide academic, behavioral, and physical support to help students succeed.*

- *Effective collaboration occurs when teachers and paraprofessionals feel supported by each other, share information regarding students and teaching, have clearly defined roles, and are respectful.*

- *Research shows that when roles are unclear, there is limited supervision and feedback, and communication is limited regarding students and lesson planning paraprofessionals feel their performance is hindered.*

- *Teachers who show solidarity and respect towards the paraprofessional can expect to find paraprofessionals who are happy and engaged in the learning process, which leads to positive student outcomes.*

- *When educators take the time to train and supervise paraprofessionals, meet and plan regularly with paraprofessionals, and delegate tasks to paraprofessionals they maximize the learning potential of students and create a more collaborative learning environment.*

References

Bingham, G., Hall-Kenyon, K. M. & Culatta, B. (2010). Systematic and engaging early literacy: Examining the effects of paraeducator implemented early literacy instruction. *Communication Disorder Quarterly, 32*(1), 38-49. http://dx.doi.org/10.1177/1525740109340796

Boe, E. E., & Cook, L. H. (2006). The chronic and increasing shortage of fully certified teachers in special and general education. *Exceptional Children, 72*, 443-460. Retrieved from http://repository.upenn.edu/cgi/viewcontent.cgi?article=1148&context=gse _pubs

Brown, T. S. & Stanton-Chapman, T. L. (2014). Experiences of paraprofessionals in US preschool special education and general education classrooms. *Journal of Research in Special Educational Needs, 17*(1). http://dx.doi.org/10.1111/1471-3802.12095

Butt, R. (2016). Teacher assistant support and deployment in mainstream schools. International *Journal of Inclusive Education, 20*(9). http://dx.doi.org/10.1080/13603116.2016.1145260

Cipriano, C., Barnes, T. N., Bertoli, M. C., Flynn, L. M., & Rivers, S. E. (2016). There's no "I" in team: Building a framework for teacher-paraeducator interactions in self-contained special education classrooms. *Journal of Classroom Interaction, 51*(2), 4-19. Retrieved from https://eric.ed.gov/?id=EJ1117458

Clarke, L. S., Embury, D. C., Jones, R., & Yssel, N. (2014). Supporting students with disabilities During school crises: A teacher's guide. *TEACHING Exceptional Children, 46*(6), 169-178. doi:10.1177/0014402914534616

Cockroft, C., & Atkinson, C. (2015). Using the wider pedagogical role model to establish learning support assistants' views about facilitators and barriers to effective practice. *Support for Learning, 30*(2), 88-104. http://dx.doi.org/10.1111/1467-9604.12081

Conderman, G. (2011). Middle school co-teaching: Effective practices and student reflections. *Middle School Journal, 42*, 24-31. doi:10.1080/00940771.2011.11461771

Cooke, N. L., Galloway, T. W., Kretlow, A. G., & Helf, S. (2011). Impact of the script in a supplemental reading program on instructional opportunities for student practice of specified skills. *The Journal of Special Education, 45*(1), 28-42. http://dx.doi.org/10.1177/0022466910361955

Council for Exceptional Children (2012). The Council for Exceptional Children's position on Special education teacher evaluation. Arlington, VA: Author. Retrieved from http://www.cec.sped.org/~/media/Files/Policy/CEC%20Professional%20Po licies%20and%20Positions/Position_on_Special_Education_Teacher_Evalua tion_Background.pdf

Council for Exceptional Children. (n.d.). *A primer on the IDEA 2004 regulations.* Retrieved from https://www.cec.sped.org/Policy-and-Advocacy/Current-Sped-Gifted-Issues/Individuals-with-Disabilities-Education-Act/A-Primer-on-the-IDEA-2004-RegulationsIDEA

Curby, T. W., Rudasill, K. M., Edwards, T., & Pérez-Edgar, K. (2011). The role of classroom quality in ameliorating the academic and social risks associated with difficult temperament. *School Psychology Quarterly, 26*(2), 175. doi:10.1037/a0023042

Devecchi, C. & Rouse, M. (2010). An exploration of the features of effective collaboration between teachers and teaching assistants in secondary schools. *Support for Learning, 25*(2), 91-99. http://dx.doi.org/10.1111/j.1467-9604.2010.01445.x

Docherty, R. (2014) A complete circuit: The role of communication between class teachers and support staff and the planning of effective learning opportunities. *Educational Psychology in Practice: Theory, Research and Practice in Educational Psychology, 30*(2), 181-19. http://dx.doi.org/10.1080/02667363.2014.899997

Douglas, S. N., Chapin, S. E., & Nolan, J. F. (2016). Special education teachers' experiences supporting and supervising paraeducators: Implications for special and general education settings. *Teacher Education and Special Education, 39*(1), 60-74. http://dx.doi.org/10.1177/0888406415616443

Feldman, E.K., & Matos, R. (2013). Training paraprofessionals to facilitate social interactions between children with autism and their typically developing peers. *Journal of Positive Behavior Interventions, 15*(3), 169-179. http://dx.doi.org/10.1177/1098300712457421

Fisher, M. & Pleasants, S. L. (2012). Roles, responsibilities and concerns of paraeducators: Findings from a statewide survey. *Remedial and Special Education, 33*(5), 287-297. http://dx.doi.org/10.1177/0741932510397762

Friend, M., & Cook, L. (2017). *Interactions: Collaboration skills for school professionals* (8th ed.). Boston, MA: Pearson.

Friend, M., Cook, L., Hurley-Chamberlain, D., & Shamberger, C. (2010). Co-teaching: An illustration of the complexity of collaboration in special education. *Journal of Educational and Psychological Consultation, 20*, 9-27. doi:10.1080/10474410903535380

Giangreco, M. F., Halvorsen, A. T., Doyle, M. B., & Broer, S. M. (2004). Alternatives to overreliance on paraprofessionals in inclusive schools. *Journal of Special Education Leadership, 17*, 82-90. Retrieved from https://pdfs.semanticscholar.org/615c/dfd5aaf506ddbcbf570a0f2e0e4d9dc dd02d.pdf

Harris, L. R., & Aprile, K. T. (2015). 'I can sort of slot into many different roles': Examining teacher aide roles and their implications for practice. *School Leadership & Management, 35*(2), 140-162. http://dx.doi.org/10.1080/13632434.2014.992774

Lane, K.L., Fletcher, T., Carter, E., Dejud, & Delorenzo, J. (2007). Paraprofessional-led phonological awareness training with youngsters at-risk for reading and behavioral concerns. *Remedial and Special Education, 28*(5), 266 276. http://dx.doi.org/10.1177/07419325070280050201

Lehane, T. (2015). Cooling the mark out: Experienced teaching assistants' perceptions of their work in the inclusion of pupils with special educational needs in mainstream secondary schools, *Educational Review, 68*(1), 4-23. http://dx.doi.org/10.1080/00131911.2015.1058753

Lunenberg, M., Korthagen, F., & Swennen, A. (2007). The teacher educator as a role model. *Teaching and Teacher Education, 23*, 586-601. doi: 10.1016/j.tate.2006.11.001

Lushen, K., Kim, O., & Reid, R. (2012). Paraeducator-led strategy instruction for struggling writers. *Exceptionality, 20*(4), 250-265. http://dx.doi.org/10.1080/09362835.2012.724626

Moore, W. & Hammond, L. (2011). Using education assistants to help pave the road to literacy: Supporting oral language, letter-sound knowledge and phonemic awareness in the preprimary year. *Australian Journal of Learning Difficulties, 16*(2), 85-110. http://dx.doi.org/10.1080/19404151003763029

National Center for Learning Disabilities. (2014). *IDEA parent guide: A comprehensive guide to your rights and responsibilities under the Individuals with Disabilities Act (IDEA 2004)*. Retrieved from https://www.ncld.org/wp-content/uploads/2014/11/IDEA-Parent-Guide1.pdf

Nevin, A.I., Villa, R.A. & Thousand, J.S. (2009). *A guide to co-teaching with paraeducators: Practical tips for K-12 educators.* Thousand Oaks, CA: Corwin

Radford, J., Bosanquet, P., Webster, R., & Blatchford, P. (2015). Scaffolding learning for independence: Clarifying teacher and teaching assistant roles for children with special educational needs. *Learning and Instruction, 36*, 1-10. http://dx.doi.org/10.1016/j.learninstruc.2014.10.005

Salend, S. J. (2016). Creating inclusive classrooms: Effective, differentiated and reflective practices (8th ed.). Columbus, OH: Pearson.

U.S. Department of Education. (2004). *Title I Paraprofessionals: Non-regulatory guidance.* Retrieved from https://www2.ed.gov/policy/elsec/guid/paraguidance.pdf

U.S. Department of Labor. (2017). Bureau of labor statistics: Occupational employment statistics. Retrieved from https://www.bls.gov/oes/2017/may/oes259041.htm#nat

Villa, R.A., Thousand, J.S., Nevin, A.I. (2013). *A guide to co-teaching: New lessons and strategies to facilitate student learning* (3rd ed.). Thousand Oaks, CA: Corwin

Wasburn-Moses, L., Chun, E., & Kaldenberg, E. (2013). Paraprofessional roles in an adolescent reading program: Lessons learned. *American Secondary Education, 41*(3), 34-49. Retrieved from https://jstor.org/stable/43694166

Chapter 4

Keys to Effective Collaboration
with Other Professionals

Elizabeth J. Bienia, EdD, *Endicott College*
Nicholas D. Young, PhD, EdD, *American International College*
Amy S. Amico, EdD, *Pentucket Public Schools, MA*

Co-teaching is defined as two or more professionals sharing their instructional responsibility and intellectual expertise to develop a classroom culture conducive to educator success and positive student outcomes (Stein, 2016). This model benefits students and teachers through the integration of specialized skills that positively support all students (Friend, 2019). Beyond the relationship between two general education teachers or a general education teacher and a special education teacher, the model for co-teaching is also used successfully between a generalist and other educational professionals (Friend, 2019). This extension of co-teaching supports the academic, social-emotional, physical, and occupational needs of students through the use of specialized instruction, strategies, teaching methods and other techniques. There are key elements for co-teaching with other professionals that support students in the face of challenges.

Professional Roles and Skill Sets

Each educator contributes a unique skill set, outlook and strengths to the instructional process, which ultimately assists in the academic achievement of students (Friend, 2019). Co-teaching between a general educator and other professionals offers an opportunity to share intellectual abilities and pedagogical responsibility to develop a classroom culture useful for positive student outcomes and educator success (Friend, 2019).

Multiple co-teacher pairs have acknowledged that they discovered effective and creative methods that combined their expertise through various co-teaching approaches as they taught diverse student populations (Friend, 2019). These co-teachers established collaborative skills through the communication of their strengths, interests, challenges, and environmental needs, as well as the roles and responsibilities needed for a successful working relationship (Friend, 2019).

Each professional contributes a unique perspective and set of strengths to the educational process and these combined perspectives result in more success with student learning (Darling-Hammond, Flook, Cook-Harvey, Barron & Osher, 2019). Co-teaching with any professional should result in a more fulfilling and less stressful professional life. When these professionals engage in explicit conversations to determine how to divide and conquer the teaching tasks needing completion, they are expanding their roles to provide stronger services to their students (Kluth & Causton, 2016).

There are multiple combinations for co-teaching partnerships. Although the most common pairing is a general education teacher with a special education teacher, the generalist may also partner with speech and language pathologists (SLP), physical and/or occupational therapists (PT or OT), teachers whose focus English language learning (ELL) or English to speaker of other languages (ESOL), adaptive physical education teachers, reading or math specialists and Title I teachers (Beninghof, 2012; Dove & Honigsfeld, 2018).

Successes and Challenges for Common Planning Time

Benjamin Franklin was known to have said that by failing to prepare, you are preparing to fail (Friend, 2019). The foundation for compelling instruction is having co-teachers plan together to integrate each professional's expertise while meeting individual student needs (Friend, 2019). Co-planning happens when both educators collaborate to blend their expertise while planning the lesson content, method for instructional delivery, intermittent checks for understanding and completion of assessments (Friend, 2019).

During planning time educators can consider student data, concentrate on reaching targeted levels for academic achievement, select the approach for each lesson with necessary materials and accommodations/modifications, and the division of responsibilities (Waldron & McLeskey, 2010). They can also review content, determine roles within each lesson, identify and include technology tools and evaluate previous plans and implementation (Friend, 2019). It is vital that co-teachers have predetermined, uninterrupted common planning time daily to discuss their students and instruction needs (Murawski & Bernhardt, 2016; Stein, 2016). Co-planning for co-teachers should incorporate a positive, supportive, and safe environment where they can share knowledge, expertise, student needs and data to drive instruction and create differentiated activities for students based on personalized needs and, when applicable, IEPs (Dove & Honigsfeld, 2018).

Even when genuine attempts are made to provide educators with a chance to meet, the conundrum of overseeing all the time-consuming details of educating has no simple solution. After analysis of any current profession in our fast-paced society, a shortage of time is a key component (Friend, 2019).

The most common dilemma communicated among teachers and administrators is the challenge of organizing common planning time (Pearl, Dieker & Kirkpatrick, 2012; Pratt, Imbody, Wolf & Patterson, 2017).

No matter how much time is found, most co-teaching teams continually have to do more with less (Kluth & Causton, 2016; Scruggs & Mastropieri, 2017). Creative approaches to this challenge may include electronic planning such as shared documents, shared electronic calendars, and sometimes less effective email and text message communications (Arnold, 2017; Friend & Cook, 2016). On-the-spot planning may be necessary if plans or scheduling are changed at the last minute, teachers are behind in their pacing, or when clearly developed plans fall through (Friend, 2019; Friend & Cook, 2016; Stein, 2016).

Teachers may also request macro-planning sessions in larger chunks of time if administrators can offer cover to their regular schedule using a plainly articulated agenda so that the cherished mutual time is spent on targeted topics (Embury & Dinnesen, 2012). Another approach is to think about co-planning time in a three-part model with intermittent face-to-face planning, on-the-spot planning and electronic planning combined (Arnold, 2017).

The intermittent face-to-face planning is critical for effective communication while recognizing the feasibility of efficiently used time available (Friend, 2019). Whenever face-to-face planning time is able to occur, effective co-planning duos can benefit from a tremendous collection of supporting tools including digital and virtual documents, do-not-disturb signs, role cards, chart paper and markers, a timer and food to support effective time together (Friend & Cook, 2016). When these moments occur, it is recommended to start co-teachers time together with something positive about their week, and at the end of the time together something positive about their meeting (Kluth & Causton, 2016).

Administrative Support

It is essential that administrators comprehend what co-teaching is as well as what it is not, and that they mentor and coach their staff in a productive and positive manner (Fitzell, 2018). Research demonstrates that administrative support is an essential factor in co-teaching effectiveness (Kamens, Susko & Elliot, 2013). Administrators should value an actively supported, collaborative school culture (Waldron & McLeskey, 2010).

For co-teaching to be advantageous in a high-stakes testing environment, a school administrator's commitment to foster a culture that supports co-teaching and entrusts educators to make needed enhancements, adjustments and non-critical modifications to their lesson plans while supporting their students is required (Fitzell, 2018). When staffing levels are high and funding supports the required, frequently scheduled co-planning time, co-teachers have a safe and secure base from which to begin (Friend, 2019).

It is best for administrators to begin modestly when a new co-teaching initiative begins in a district (Dove & Honigsfeld, 2016). Administrators may be apprehensive concerning their roles in co-teaching initiatives and the methods to best support the school community. It is vital for teachers to be willing to commit to this arrangement and for administrators to recognize and acknowledge a level of anxiousness before the initiative begins (Dove & Honigsfeld, 2016). This can be exacerbated if a program begins too aggressively without proper preparation or training. In certain situations, schools have no choice but to select educators for co-teaching roles even when unwilling; therefore, it is most helpful for administrators to align personalities for the best possible success (Fitzell, 2018).

Professional Development

Data indicates that there is a substantial divergence in administrator knowledge and practices surrounding co-teaching practices and that professional development for both administrators and educators is justified (Kamens et al., 2013). Both training in the form of embedded coaching and in-service opportunities are key to the success of co-teaching initiatives. Instruction that was an explicit result of coaching offered to educators resulted in increased outcomes for students with disabilities (Walsh, 2012). Educators experiencing more frequent in-service opportunities directed towards being strong co-teaching and planning partners displayed stronger confidence in their practice opportunities (Pancsofar & Petroff, 2013). Higher levels of interest and positive attitudes regarding co-teaching were demonstrated than were for those teachers with fewer in-service opportunities (Pancsofar & Petroff, 2013).

Other educators can often be a quality professional learning resource, which can start the process for general education teachers to implement the practices taught by other professionals to more precisely meet the needs of their students (Rouleau, 2019). An effective approach to instructional coaching is one that is focused on "inside-out," strengths-based peer coaching that guides small teams of teachers together to build on the bright spots while growing and learning as professionals and peers (Dempsey, Gutierrez, Lewis, Rouleau, & Stone, 2017). This method of professional development for educators can incorporate the belief that personal and collective growth are achievable through building current strengths with an asset-based approach and using data to drive decisions on what student skills need to be developed (Dempsey et al., 2017).

Including Professionals in the Co-Teaching Equation

All students, parents and colleagues should recognize each professional in the classroom as an equal and appreciated participant who is responsible for the education of all students (Beninghof, 2012). When other professionals co-teach with general educators, it is beneficial for them to develop a stronger understanding of content knowledge, specially-designed instruction and classroom management routines and rituals of the classroom (Friend, 2019).

It is common for other specialists to work only with students on their caseload, rather than being invited to participate in a collaborative role, which maximizes the talents of both professionals and supports the success of all students (Darling-Hammond et al., 2019; Dove & Honigsfeld, 2018; Friend & Cook, 2016). Often the general education teacher does not acknowledge the presence of supporting professionals when they arrive in the classroom, and they attempt to pull 'their students' aside to deliver the needs outlined on their IEP, as extraneous members of the classroom rather than an equal contributor (Fitzell, 2018).

For students in a classroom with a general educator who co-teaches with other professionals, the benefits of their learning experience are many (Fitzell, 2018). Appropriate support leads to achievement gains as students access the curriculum with greater ease (Friend, 2019). Specially-designed instruction offerings, reduced student-teacher ratios and increased interaction time with teachers also benefits each student regardless of need (Friend & Cook 2016). A variety of co-teaching relationships can exist between other professionals and the generalist that bring unique expertise and experiences into the classroom.

Co-teaching relationships with specialists and professionals can apply the same approaches to pairings of a generalist and a special education teacher including one teaching-one observing, station teaching with learning centers, parallel teaching with both teachers leading the same lesson concurrently in separate areas of the classroom, alternative teaching when students need additional attention in a small group, teaming as instruction is delivered together and one teaching-one assisting (Ftizell, 2018; Friend, 2019).

Title I Specialists and Reading and/or Math Specialists

Most Title I specialists and other reading/math specialists are educating students in elementary schools. A strong benefit of co-teaching with reading/math specialists is the opportunity for them to model strategies to benefit students that can be implemented by general education teachers at other times (Friend, 2019). In an interview, Fitzell (2018) found that one interventionist believed that before she used a co-teaching model, she was often playing catch-up to the main lesson plan, rather than inserting strategies proactively. Once co-teaching began, she inserted herself in the discussion and development of lesson plans to assure the needs of struggling learners were met, while benefiting all student learning and increasing her appreciation of the daily challenges of classroom needs (Fitzell, 2018).

The goal for co-teaching with the reading/math specialist is to enhance instruction and remediate students' skill weaknesses, while avoiding the removal of students from their general education classroom. This may be organized with short co-teaching times daily or longer co-teaching times one to three times weekly. Reading/math specialists are challenged with extensive other responsibilities often including collection and analysis of student data, development of professional development and large caseloads (Friend, 2019).

Occupational and Physical Therapists

The inclusion of occupational and physical therapy in the classroom enables students to participate in school activities and remain in the least restrictive environment (Morin, 2019; Silverman, 2011). Therapy services in the classroom provide for the student's greatest freedom of movement in the school setting, facilitates their ability to interact with basic sensorimotor information to develop motor skills and for the organization of attention and behavior while preserving the student's best position to optimize learning (Kushich, 2019).

Occupational Therapy (OT) provides indispensable support for the successful inclusion of OT services in general education classrooms through the co-taught model (Silverman, 2011). In most cases, providing co-taught services with an OT offers greater opportunities to generalize and apply skills in a general education setting, better opportunities to collaborate and consult with general education teachers, allows an improved understanding of how their suggested strategies impact actual participation, and gives therapists an opportunity to demonstrate the use of techniques to be applied later (Friend & Cook, 2016; Silverman, 2011). Students requiring OT services may not feel singled out when services are provided in the classroom as other classmates who may need extra support can benefit from the presence of an OT (Smith, Weaver & Holland, 2014) Classmates can also act as peer models to support new skills or behaviors (Heffron, 2015).

Speech Language Pathologist

The general education classroom is the natural setting for many students to have their speech and language needs productively met. Co-teaching between the speech-language pathologist (SLP) and a generalist promotes the sharing of materials, reduction of scheduling concerns as students are not removed from their general education class, and an extension of services as many SLP strategies are used throughout the day after being modeled (Friend, 2019). This co-teaching relationship is more beneficial for students as it gives the SLP clarity over what is being taught and how concepts on both sides can be reinforced in the classroom.

Preset curriculum maps can be a challenge if the topics covered do not seem to support the SLP skills to be taught (Fitzell, 2018). As with other supporting professionals, large caseloads can also be a challenge to determining co-teaching time, which is also impacted by the schedule of the SLP when they are required to support more than one school (Friend, 2019). Overall the benefits outweigh the concerns as it offers an opportunity to provide scaffolding, while keeping the rigor and content steady, and offering flexibility and the sharing of physical space (Fitzell, 2018).

English Language Learner Teachers

Educators who teach English language learners (ELL) or English to speakers of other languages (ESOL) often face challenges different from other educators. It's important for them to begin by ensuring all teachers have a consistent understanding of the overall goals for ELL/ESOL students (Friend, 2019). The goal is for ELL/ESOL students to learn and observe English in a more natural setting (Dove & Honigsfeld, 2018).

Alternative teaching approaches with a general education teacher leading an activity and an ELL/ESOL teacher running a small group vocabulary lesson to encourage background knowledge can lead to success. (Fritzell, 2018). In some schools, the ELL/ESOL teacher is seen as remedial and only offering translation services, which is completely inappropriate and unfortunate when an ELL/ESOL teacher essentially can function as a teaching assistant (Friend, 2019).

The inclusion of novels and picture books with cultural relevance can be included in lessons and the classroom library as a way to encourage co-ownership of the classroom. When the ELL/ESOL teacher offers explicit instruction in the language of reading, math and writing to decrease the language gap, they are able to benefit all learners (Fitzell, 2018). Occasionally, differences between a general education teacher and an ELL/ESOL educator develop due to cultural differences, most likely if services are relatively new or needed for a small population which undermines a unified culture (Dove & Honigsfeld, 2018). ELL/ESOL educators can also be challenged by dividing time across several schools. Communication and collaboration are the key to the pairing of general educators and their ELL/ESOL counterpart in order to develop a positive and productive relationship (Friend, 2019).

School Adjustment Counselors

School adjustment counselors (SAC) are an indispensable resource and tremendous partner for teachers. Professional counselors today are proactively searching for innovative methods to maximize academic achievement by meeting the needs of all students (Ferlazzo, 2014). There are multiple methods for teachers to utilize counselors, including co-teaching lessons in the general education classroom (Brodie, 2012). A school counselor can co-teach lessons that integrate academic and counseling standards, social-emotional topics and character development through

- guided reading/book clubs,
- fact and opinion lessons that can be related to teasing,
- writer's workshop where students write about memories of emotions,
- math to graph how they spend their day and how they can lessen stressful times each day, and
- a study of diversity in social studies where students learn about people from different cultures to recognize how all people are unique (Brodie, 2012).

Time is valuable to teachers, and it's often challenging to find time for guidance lessons while still complying with other rigorous requirements, so it is helpful when school counselors collaborate with regular education teachers (Carden, 2014).

Gifted & Talented Specialists

The purpose of co-teaching with a gifted and talented educator is somewhat different from that of other professionals as their goal is to foster deeper skill development to achieve differentiated instruction. Many students who may not qualify for this type of instruction can still benefit from these lessons (Friend, 2019). A gifted and talented co-teacher also may have multiple challenges for successful pairing experiences. These challenges may include adhering to the schedules of the general education teacher, adjusting to their teaching styles and plans, having to share the classroom space, and justifying their pedagogy to educators who often have little or no training for educating a gifted and talented population (Haberlin, 2016).

Co-teaching with gifted and talented educators is more likely to take place in an elementary setting as upper grades often have honors programs, but by no means is it widespread. The law doesn't require that schools offer a gifted and talented program making this co-teaching experience extremely rare (Friend, 2019).

Response to Intervention/Multi-Tiered System of Supports Specialist

Response to Intervention (RTI) or Multi-Tiered System of Supports offers a cooperative path by which a team of educators can be successful (Metcalf, 2019). These educators use the RTI/MTSS process to increase students' ability to reach their goals through differentiated support, which can also be through a co-teaching model (Whitten, Esteves & Woodrow, 2019).

The RTI/MTSS specialists focus on academic, communication, cognitive, physical, or behavioral delays or gaps in learning and implement specific plans for students who have been identified. When developing lesson plans together with general education teachers, these co-teachers need to define their overall responsibilities and teaching techniques prior to lesson implementation, including various seating arrangements and educational strategies (Friend, 2019). Effective co-teaching is a critical component to success for students of all ability levels in the regular education classroom.

Final Thoughts

The work to be done between a general education teacher and non-classroom oriented educational professionals has the ability to change how students learn in the least restrictive setting. From setting up schedules to finding common planning time, and especially specifically designed professional development that focuses on key areas of co-teaching success, students are the winners when this process is followed with fidelity and care. Administrators play an important role in matching teachers and educational professionals in order to promote the co-teaching model.

Each educational professional brings something different to the classroom and it is possible that the primary teacher may pair with more than one professional during the course of the day or week. This is where the planning process is vital. It may be that the ELL/ESOL educator and the SLP share space during the reading block, or the Title I and reading specialist may each take a group during guided reading. Regardless of what the schedule looks like, the ability of the staff members to create a co-teaching model that works for them and is considerate of everyone's strengths and interests within the classroom setting is of the utmost importance.

Using the RTI/MTSS support teacher and the Title 1 educator as integral members of the co-teaching team ensures that students who may have deficits or gaps in learning will find success and those who may be able to serve as peer models are readily available. It is also possible that students who do not need official plans, but would benefit from some support, are able to find it when the co-teaching model is used. Whatever the configuration, ongoing clear communication can support a positive culture of collaboration, resulting in educators who develop a connection to a teaching team for student success (Whitten, Esteves & Woodrow, 2019).

Points to Remember

- *Co-teaching is defined as two or more professionals sharing their instructional responsibility and intellectual expertise to develop a classroom culture conducive to educator success and positive student outcomes.*

- *Beyond the relationship between a general education teacher and a special education teacher, the model for co-teaching is also used successfully between a generalist and other educational professionals including, but not limited to, OT, PT, ELL/ESOL, SAC, Title 1, SLP, and gifted and talented educators.*

- *This extension of co-teaching has the opportunity to support academic achievement through specialized instruction when the co-teaching educators can find methods to be successful through the student challenges that surface.*

- *Clarity around professional roles and skill sets is critical between paired teachers. While co-teaching, two or more professionals share their unique skill set and pedagogical responsibility to develop an educational environment that promotes positive student achievement and teacher accomplishment.*

- *Co-planning happens when both educators collaborate to blend their expertise while planning the lesson content, method for instructional delivery and completion of assessments. The greatest challenge is finding time to co-plan and being open to new planning strategies including technology tools, or macro-planning.*

- *Educators experiencing more frequent co-teaching in-service opportunities displayed stronger confidence in their co-teaching practice and higher levels of interest and positive attitudes about co-teaching were demonstrated than were for those teachers with fewer in-service opportunities.*

- *It is essential that administrators comprehend what co-teaching is, what it isn't, and that they mentor and coach their staff in a productive and positive manner. Research demonstrates that administrative support is an essential factor in co-teaching effectiveness.*

- *Co-teaching relationships with other educational professionals apply the same approaches to co-teaching as are used with a generalist and a special education teacher including one teaching-one observing, station teaching with learning centers, parallel teaching with both teachers leading the same lesson concurrently in separate areas of the classroom, alternative teaching when students need additional attention in a small group, teaming as instruction is delivered together and one teaching-one assisting.*

References

Arnold, C. (2017). *Using technology to facilitate planning for the co-taught classroom.* Retrieved from http://inservice.ascd.org/using-technology-to-facilitate-planning-for-the-co-taught-classroom%E2%80%A8/

Beninghof, A.M. (2012). *Co-teaching that works: Structures and strategies for maximizing student learning.* San Francisco, CA: Jossey-Bass.

Brodie, I. (2012). The top 10 ways school counselors can support teachers. *Ed. Homeroom: The Official Blog of the U.S. Department of Education.* Retrieved from https://blog.ed.gov/2012/06/the-top-10-ways-school-counselors-can-support-teachers/

Carden, A. (2014). Co-teaching lessons with counselor and teachers. *The Inspired Counselor.* Retrieved from http://theinspiredcounselor.blogspot.com/2014/07/co-teaching-lessons-with-counselor-and.html

Darling-Hammond, L., Flook, L., Cook-Harvey, C., Barron, B. & Osher, D. (2019). Implications for educational practice of the science of learning and development. *Applied Developmental Science.* DOI: 10.1080/10888691.2018.1537791

Dempsey, J. R., Gutierrez, K., Lewis, G., Rouleau, D., & Stone, B. (2017). *Peer coaching that works: The power of reflection and feedback in teacher triad teams.* Denver, CO: McREL International. 20170920

Dove, M.G. & Honigsfeld, A. (2018). *Co-teaching for English learners: A guide to collaborative planning, instruction, assessment and reflection.* Thousand Oaks, CA: Corwin

Embury, D.C., & Dinnesen, M.S. (2012). Planning for co-teaching in inclusive classrooms using structured collaborative planning. *Kentucky Journal of Excellence in College Teaching and Learning,* 10 (31), 36-52.

Ferlazzo, L. (2014). *Response: A teacher-counselor partnership is 'essential' for student success.* Retrieved from http://blogs.edweek.org/teachers/classroom_qa_with_larry_ferlazzo/2014/05/response_a_teacher-counselor_partnership_is_essential_for_student_success.html

Fitzell, S.G. (2018). *Best practices in co-teaching & collaborating: The how of co-teaching – implementing the models.* Manchester, NH: Cogent Catalyst Publications.

Friend, M. (2019). *Co-teach! Building and sustaining effective classroom partnerships in inclusive schools.* Greensboro, NC: Marilyn Friend Publishing.

Friend, M. & Cook, L. (2016). *Interactions: Collaboration skills for school professionals.* New York, NY: Pearson

Haberlin, S. (2016). Teaching in circles: Learning to harmonize as a co-teacher of gifted education. *The Qualitative Report, 21*(11), 2076-2087. Retrieved from http://nsuworks.nova.edu/tqr/vol21/iss11/5

Heffron, C. (2015). Inclusion: How to provide OT services in the classroom. *The Inspired Treehouse*. Retrieved from https://theinspiredtreehouse.com/inclusion-how-to-provide-ot- services-in- the-classroom/

Kamens, M.W., Susko, J. P., Elliot, J. S. (2013). Evaluation and Supervision of Co-Teaching: A Study of Administrator Practices in New Jersey. *NASSP: National Association of Secondary School Principals*, 97(2), doi: 10.1177/0192636513476337

Kluth, P. & Causton, J. (2019). *30 Days to the co-taught classroom*. Baltimore, MD: Paul H. Brookes Publishing Company Inc.

Kushich, K. (2019). Physical Therapy & Occupational Therapy (OT & PT). *Midwestern Intermediate Unit IV: Making a Difference in Education*. Retrieved from https://www.Miu4.org /Page/305

Metcalf, T. (2019). *What's your plan? Accurate decision making within a multi-tier system of supports: Critical areas in Tier 1*. Retrieved from http://www.rtinetwork.org/essential/tieredinstruction/tier1/accurate-decision-making-within-a-multi-tier-system-of-supports-critical-areas-in-tier-1

Morin, A. (2020). *Least restrictive environment (LRE): What you need to know*.

Murawski, W.W., & Bernhardt, P. (2016). An administrator's guide to co-teaching. *Educational Leadership*, 73 (4), 30-34.

Pancsofar, N. & Petroff, J.G. (2016). Teachers' Experiences with co-teaching as a model for inclusive education. *International Journal of Inclusive Education*, 20 (10), 1043-1053. DOI: 10.1080/13603116.2016.1145264.

Pearl, C., Dieker, L.A., & Kirkpatrick, R.M. (2012). A five-year retrospective on the Arkansas Department of Education co-teaching project. *Professional Development in Educational Leadership*, 73 (4), 30-34.

Pratt, S. M., Imbody, S.M., Wolf, L.D. & Patterson, A.L. (2017). Co-planning in co-teaching: A practical solution. *Intervention in School and Clinic*, 52, 243-249.

Rouleau, K. (2019). *Professional development: Tapping into the expertise in the building. The triad model of peer coaching takes advantage of a powerful professional learning resource available to teachers—their colleagues*. Retrieved from https://www.edutopia.org/article/tapping-expertise-building

Scruggs, T.E., & Mastropieri, M.A. (2017). Making inclusion work with co-teaching. *Teaching Exceptional Children*, 49, 284 - 293.

Silverman, F. (2011) Promoting inclusion with Occupational Therapy: A co-teaching model. *Journal of Occupational Therapy, Schools, & Early Intervention*, 4(2), 100-107. DOI: 10.1080/19411243.2011.595308

Smith, J.C., Weaver, L., Holland, T. (2014). Effects of a classroom-embedded Occupational Therapist–Teacher handwriting program for first-grade students. *American Journal of Occupational Therapy*, 68, 690-698. DOI:10.5014/ajot.2014.011585

Stein, E. (2016). *Elevating co-teaching through UDL.* Wakefield, MA: CAST Professional Publishing

Waldron, N.L. & McLeskey, J. (2010). Establishing a collaborative school culture through comprehensive school reform. *Journal of Educational and Psychological Consultation, 20,* 58-74. DOI: 10.1080/10474410903535364

Walsh, J. (2012). Co-teaching as a school system strategy for continuous improvement. *Preventing school failure: Alternative education for children and youth,* 56(1), 29-36. DOI: 10.1080/1045988X.2011.555792.

Whitten, E., Esteves, K.J. & Woodrow, A. (2019). *RTI success: Proven tools and strategies for schools and classrooms.* Minneapolis, MN 55427-3674

Chapter 5

How to Plan for Success
in Co-Teaching Environments

Ellen L. Duchaine, PhD, *Texas State University*

Planning together begins the moment educators agree to co-teach. Often, casual discussions start the process as teachers informally discuss the benefits of co-teaching; yet, sometimes, teachers are brought together by the administration without warning. Once educators are in a co-teaching situation, however, planning becomes more formal. This formal planning includes personal preferences and student expectations, ideas as practical as how to handle pencil sharpening and as important as student academic expectations (Fitzell, 2018). The planning process becomes more organized and focused as co-teachers discuss the scope and sequence of the curriculum, state standards, and unit plans (Friend, 2019).

Co-teaching is an efficient and effective means of increasing the achievement of students with and without disabilities across all grade levels and content areas within inclusive classrooms (Mastropieri & Scruggs, 2018; Ronfeldt, Farmer, McQueen, & Grissom, 2015; Scruggs & Mastropieri, 2017). Diversity among students within a classroom increases student knowledge of differences and sets the stage for building acceptance of others with varying strengths, abilities, interests, cultures, backgrounds, and needs (Scruggs & Mastropieri, 2017).

Being inclusive of students with a variety of educational needs at an early age breaks the cycle of 'unable-ness' (Baglieri, Bejoian, Broderick, Connor & Valle, 2011). Like any other relationship, co-teachers must agree to work toward a sense of unity and when co-teaching, both teachers must agree to believe all children can learn. This unity is achieved only through various phases of collaborative planning and open communication, as well as valuing the expertise of one another (Mastropieri & Scruggs, 2018; Potts & Howard, 2011; Scruggs & Mastropieri, 2017).

Making Plans to Co-Teach

Decisions and assignments for co-teaching partnerships occur through a vast number of progressions. In some schools, teachers envision the benefits and request to co-teach, sometimes parents request their child learn in a co-taught classroom rather than being pulled from the classroom for remediation, and in some schools, the leadership team asks for volunteers or may assign teachers to paired teaching situations without choice (Friend & Cook, 2016). Some schools have the autonomy to implement co-teaching and move forward on their own, while other schools are part of a districtwide initiative to build co-taught classrooms across grade levels to support the educational needs of their student body as well as building communities that accept diverse learners (Beninghof, 2012; Fitzell, 2018).

Regardless of the way in which co-teaching originates, the process for individual, independent teachers to become effective and efficient collaborative teachers, sharing the same space and students, requires multiple phases of planning (Schwarz, 2006). The key focus, however, is on student learning. In a co-taught class, students learn from both teachers and from other students who are both similar and different from themselves (Stein, 2016). To be successful, the special education teacher and the general education teacher must be open to learning from one another (Cassel, 2019).

Embarking on the Co-Teaching Adventure

One of the most crucial elements of successful co-teaching is the ongoing planning process. Successful co-teaching is a responsibility in which educators are expected to impart measurable skills and knowledge on every child in the classroom; therefore, the effectiveness of how lesson plans will be executed must be investigated at each planning session (Beninghof, 2012). Efficient and tenacious educators evaluate their own performance, overall class performance, and individual student performance in order to adapt both the lesson plans and the teaching process regularly (Fitzell, 2018).

Co-teaching requires the ongoing cycle of joint planning, equal instructional activities, and collaborative analysis of learning in order to adapt future planning, instruction, and assessment. As Schwarz and Kluth proclaimed (2007), "We collaborate because it forces us to grow as educators and because it will ultimately result in better outcomes for our students" (p. vii).

Collaborative planning should begin as soon as educators agree to become co-teachers. There are five 'phases of co-planning' with ideas to incorporate best practices during each phase. Casual discussions commence the process of planning as teachers informally discuss the benefits of teaching as a team. Once teams are established, planning becomes more prescribed, covering teaching strengths, preferences, student expectations, planning processes, the scope and sequence of the content standards, unit planning, teaching approaches, the six methods of co-teaching, and role responsibilities (Beninghof, 2012; Fitzell, 2018; Friend & Cook, 2016).

Phases of Collaborative Planning

Co-teaching cannot exist without collaborative planning (Fitzell, 2018). Efficacious co-teaching necessitates that both parties a) accept the challenge, b) believe in one another, c) commit to the process, d) devote the time, and e) expect success (Case, 2017; Kottler, 2017; Peery, 2017; Wilson, 2016). This list can be applied to co-teaching in general; however, these phases must first reference the planning process, which preempts the teaching process.

Comparing co-teaching to an adventurous journey with a friend means progressing from acknowledging individuality to detailed plans, knowing plans change as trips progress and unexpected factors unfold. During the journey, planning phases reoccur time and again to refine the venture for optimum satisfaction (Wilson, 2016).

Accept the Challenge

The second phase, 'accept the challenge,' may not seem apropos for some as there are teachers who are eager to co-teach, have co-taught in the past, or are currently co-teaching; however, with each new partnership and each new set of students, this phase resurfaces. Regardless of how or when the co-teaching partnerships were formed, once the assignment is made, as professionals, teachers must 'accept the challenge' to plan for success (Potts & Howard, 2011).

This phase begins with casual discussions between partners or within school teams about beliefs in student learning, inclusion, equity in co-teaching, the joy of learning, preferences and pet peeves, career history and aspirations, and even outside interests (Case, 2017). These are the conversations that begin to build personal relationships to support co-teaching (Cantu, 2015). It is difficult, if not impossible, to share responsibilities and tasks equitably without first knowing who the person is that is sharing the workload and classroom space (Cantu, 2015).

Conversations can then move to educational topics that will disclose teaching styles, personal philosophies of education, individual teaching strengths, time management skills, and personal planning preferences (Scruggs & Mastropieri, 2017). Discussions of expertise may indicate the need for the special education teacher to review specific grade/course level content and/or for the general education teacher to investigate how the characteristics of various disabilities influences student learning, before officially joining forces. Educators who take the time to familiarize themselves with these topics demonstrate a necessary understanding of and an agreement to co-teach (Lindermann & Magiera, 2014; Sileo, 2011).

After casual discussion and educational topics, co-teaching partners must address non-negotiables and parity (Wilson, 2016). This list includes student expectations, beliefs regarding student abilities, instructional practices, organization of materials, grading, and forms to use in lesson planning that clearly define not only the activities, but the who, what, and how of each lesson activity (Friend, 2019). It is important for the teaching pair to decide how the classroom might be arranged, giving each teacher equal work areas. Co-teachers should also discuss classroom management, teaching, and assessment philosophies (Conderman, 2016).

It is vital to place both names on the classroom door, paperwork and newsletters sent home, listed alphabetically as co-teachers, without delineating who holds which position. Approaching sensitive matters such as parity and other topics close to the heart can be handled by agreeing to reflect on personal preferences before the next meeting, writing down questions and listing important ideas (Potts & Howard, 2011). This meeting should be held at a time when co-teaching partners will not be interrupted by other obligations or visitors to the classroom, in order to provide uninterrupted discussion (Conderman, 2016). Sensitive conversations are difficult enough. An interruption during delicate topics or points of view may result in misunderstanding or lost thoughts and ideas.

Team-building activities provide valuable insight and can be included at the beginning of each meeting. Co-teaching partners simply agree to prepare one team-building activity for each meeting as a light-hearted way to learn about one another (Fulford, n.d.). Some ideas include bringing three favorite songs to share, writing three personal facts or two truths and one lie and let the other person guess the lie, or preparing a set of story starters or questions such as, "I remember a time when I was 12…" or "I have never…" or "In the little spare time I have, I like to…." These activities are used as ice-breakers to open conversations, fostering comfort through nonsense chit-chat (West, 1997). An additional suggestion is to meet with co-teachers from different classrooms for team-building activities and educational discussions to generate a co-teaching support system (Casserly & Padden, 2018).

The overall purpose of the 'accept the challenge' phase is to begin building trust between co-teaching partners and to ease into the process of setting up the physical classroom, defining student expectations, and creating a unified front for the students and school community (Wilson, 2016). This planning phase should be revisited periodically as situations arise that challenge the status quo, indicating changes may need to be made (Friend & Cook, 2016).

Believe in One Another

The 'believe in one another' phase may seem a fanciful philosophy, but not all professionals have insight into the countless disciplines within the field of education resulting in misconceptions of unknown specialties (Blanton, Pugach & Florian, 2011; McKinney, 2017). For some individuals, it is easy to have faith in the expertise of any other teacher. For others, it is a most difficult task to be certain of another's value; yet, the only way to plan collaboratively is to believe in one another. Because most co-teachers are initially individual and independent teachers, it can be less than comfortable to share the room and release some of the responsibility for instructional decisions (Wilson, 2016).

Teachers who take the time to build community and share teaching ideas develop stronger co-teaching relationships (Casserly & Padden, 2018). These strong relationships build trust, making it easier to accept ideas and share responsibility for the many tasks of planning to co-teach. Communication established during this original phase fosters a working relationship essential to successful co-planning (Friend, 2019).

When partners purposefully plan to communicate, they are more likely to begin to believe in one another and be better able to share the roles and responsibilities of educating a classroom filled with diverse learners (Beninghof, 2012). Building trust and respect through effective communication encourages partners to state their own views and make suggestions during planning (Scruggs & Mastropieri, 2017). To get to this point, however, partners must be active listeners, who can accept constructive feedback while remaining focused on the lesson planning (Schilling, 2012).

Acknowledging and respecting the talents of one another and understanding each teacher brings expertise to the table makes for a smoother planning process. Both teachers maintain a responsibility for classroom structures and procedures; therefore, using a pre-planning checklist (Cantu, 2015), a planning agenda (Nevin, Villa & Thousand, 2009), and a structured co-teach lesson plan form that clearly structures the work, leaves no question as to what will be accomplished in the classroom (Beyers-Brown, Howerter, & Morgan, 2013; Conderman, 2016). In doing this, both educators become comfortable enough to release control and be flexible in the co-planning process to allow equity between them (Murawski & Dieker, 2008).

Invariably, problems will arise. No classroom is without occasional disruption; no relationship is without communication difficulties or discomfort periodically because each person brings a different set of skills, perspectives and experiences to the relationship (Conderman, 2016). Relationships take time to build. Co-teaching partners need to give one another the benefit of the doubt, that actions come from a place of true compassion for and commitment to student learning (Peery, 2017).

Early in the partnership, the paired educators should plan for the inevitable conflict. This makes the realization that a problem will occur easier to accept. Co-teachers who plan for conflict are prepared and ready to look at problems when they arise as an expected opportunity to further build rapport. Schwarz (2006) suggested a simple problem-solving technique coined SODA

S = Situation - Clearly define the situation;

O = Options - Generate a list of options;

D = Decision - From the list, make a decision; and

A = Assess- Determine how well it worked.

If this simplistic approach does not work, co-teachers can try the structured 7-step problem solving by Sileo (2011):

(1) identify the issues;

(2) develop alternative courses of action;

(3) analyze the risks and benefits of each possible course of action;

(4) [together] choose a course of action;

(5) take action;

(6) evaluate results of the action; and

(7) assume responsibility for the consequences, correcting potentially negative consequences, or re-engaging in the decision-making process.

Solving problems before they expand will result in a better and smoother co-planning and co-teaching partnership.

The overall purpose of the 'believe in one another' phase is to discuss and recognize how difficult it can be to release total control of the planning process for classroom instruction, management, and student achievement (Beninghof, 2012). Knowing how qualified another teacher is, this trust is built by actually sharing responsibility for student success through consistent team planning, providing instruction as planned, then evaluating the success of the planned lessons. This phase definitely needs to be reflected on and revisited periodically until co-teaching partners are comfortable with each other and the process.

Commit to the Process

The 'commit to the process' phase seems obvious, as teachers know the need for planning; yet, this task becomes complicated when it adds the extra layer of finding time in an extremely busy schedule to meet with one or more additional professionals for planning (Friend & Cook, 2016). Depending on the co-teaching assignment, both teachers may already have grade level and/or content level professional learning communities that meet regularly to address state standards and key ideas for instruction (Friend, 2019). Many teachers work across grade levels and/or in different content areas, particularly special education teachers and secondary level teachers (Scruggs & Mastropieri, 2017). Considering extracurricular duties, school committees, special education paperwork, and family obligations, the idea of committing even more time to planning with another teacher for every detail of your co-taught class(es) can seem overwhelming.

Effective collaboration for paired educators who will teach students with disabilities sometimes means getting more than two professionals together, it could mean multiple service providers in a room at the same time to plan for individuals with more complicated needs such as language or physical therapy, interpreters, or orientation/mobility consultation (Blanton et al., 2011; Blask, 2011; Casey, 2019). Specialists generally travel among schools, which makes finding common planning time even more difficult; however, teachers have deemed the extra effort worthwhile (Altieri, Colley, Daniel, & Dickenson, 2015; Casserly & Padden, 2018; Lindermann & Magiera, 2014). Meetings may not occur weekly; yet, it is vital to meet at least monthly to collaborate instruction across services to maximize instruction and extend learning outcomes (Blask, 2011).

Some educators are fortunate enough to work in a district and/or school that fully supports true co-teaching with actions that demonstrate an understanding of time commitments necessary to make it happen. In these situations, administrators prioritize and purposely plan, so co-teachers have planning periods scheduled at the same time (Nierengarten & Hughes, 2011; Solberg, 2017). When this isn't feasible, school administrators can work with co-teachers to find creative ways to offer consistent, uninterrupted weekly planning.

Some administrators are able to provide substitute teachers weekly to allow various co-teaching partners to plan together, while others allow planning on teacher workdays, some allow co-teachers to accumulate comp time to use within the workday but outside of the instructional times, others provide dinner for co-teachers working late, and still, others pay a stipend for the extra time needed to co-plan outside of the typical workday (Nierengarten & Hughes, 2011; Solberg, 2017). If these options are not available, co-teachers committed to the process will find the time necessary to collaborate, ensuring plans are thorough and there is equity in creating the plans and preparing materials for the lessons (Austin, 2001).

While finding available times for co-teachers to plan regularly is important, it is only the first consideration in demonstrating a commitment. Collaborative planning is a complex endeavor that began with accepting the challenge and moved into the difficult process of believing in one another (Nierengarten & Hughes, 2011; Solberg, 2017). With the previous two phases underway, committing to the process has already begun. But there are many parts to this phase of planning.

Planning to co-teach is most effective when discussion begins before the end of the previous school year, allowing partners to process co-teaching ideas during the summer break, gradually mulling over the tentative planning ideas while away from the school (Wilson, 2016). The early stage of planning is revisited in the weeks before school starts, looking with fresh eyes and new ideas (Wilson, 2016).

Partners need to agree on a lesson plan form with a co-teach format before the school year begins. The use of a planning tool allows for seamless lessons with equitable roles and responsibilities leaving no portion of the teaching undetermined (Beyers-Brown et al., 2013; Fitzell, 2018). Quality lesson planning requires attention to detail, which is essential for the success in a co-taught classroom (Stein, 2016). Lesson plans delineate not only learning objectives and activities, but the co-teaching approach for each portion of each lesson, and who will do which tasks. Detailed plans avoid confusion and ensure student success (Beyers-Brown et al., 2013).

During this discovery phase of co-planning, co-teachers organize the classroom design using Universal Design for Learning (UDL) to differentiate the physical environment (Conderman & Hedin, 2015; Stein, 2016). Co-teachers can use UDL to intentionally provide designated areas for specific use to include an area for whole group instruction, two teacher zones, small group instruction zones, a silent work zone, partner work zones, a technology zone, a class library, a creative zone, and a calm down zone (Stein, 2016). Organizing the room through UDL principles incorporates the ability to easily differentiate instruction (Dieker, Finnegan, Grillo, & Garland, 2013; Rimpola, 2014; Strogilos, Stefanidis, & Tragoulia, 2016).

The list shown below outlines considerations co-teaching partners must address and agree on. The list appears finite; however, it will quickly be viewed as only the start when individual teachers commence a true co-teaching partnership sharing all duties of lesson plans, instruction, and assessment. The emphasis here is that all teachers who embrace the opportunity to co-teach need to commit to planning together. Joining forces to increase achievement for all children is a different type of process. This list is intended to guide the conversation and the planning process. A plethora of researchers (Beninghof, 2012; Fitzell, 2018; Friend, 2019; Stein, 2016; Wilson, 2016) agree that the following actions reflect a commitment to the collaborative planning process and include, but is not limited to

- Work as equals.

- Start communicating early.

- Before summer break begins, schedule several planning sessions for the summer break.

- Plan the full scope and sequence for grade-level state standards & IEP goals.

- Design the classroom with the Principles of UDL.

- Generate unit plans with a UDL foundation and intention to differentiate instruction.

- Develop classroom procedures to include furniture arrangement, material storage, where to submit assignments, and how grading will be handled.

- Outline a schedule for proactive parent phone calls and structured parent conferences.

- Commit to both teachers being present and actively teaching from bell to bell.

- Create the daily/class schedule and plan for regular data collection/progress monitoring.

- Formulate clear student expectations for participation, recognition, and consequences.

- Agree on regular co-plan appointments. Block the times on personal and work calendars.

- Schedule monthly planning sessions to assess growth and plan for upcoming weeks.

- Invite any other service providers to the monthly planning meetings.

- Schedule weekly lesson plan sessions to evaluate progress and adapt plans accordingly.

- Investigate and agree on a lesson plan form to detail individual teacher obligations.

- Plan procedures for unexpected teacher absences. What if one or both of you are absent?

- Plan a time and/or procedure for daily touch-ups on lesson plans.

- Consider how to differentiate instruction for individual students with disabilities.

- Organize accommodations and IEP goals on an easy-access form to use while planning.

With the exception of the first item on the list, to work as equals, all the items on this list are typically considered by any teacher each year; nevertheless, the beginning of the year process is made more difficult when working as a team with the intent to display a unified front with the students, which may or may not require some compromises along the way.

Devote the Time

The phase 'devote the time' may seem redundant once teams have already accepted the challenge, started to believe in one another, and committed to the process of planning; however, this phase moves beyond simply devoting time to plan. This phase refers to devoting the time to be in the classroom and engaged with teaching the students (Wilson, 2016). In many co-teaching situations, this is often the most difficult phase because it requires both teachers to be completely present in the moment (Mielke, 2015). It requires both individuals to resist the temptation of paperwork, collaborating with other specialists, covering classes when no substitute is available, or attending to duties outside of the classroom.

A successful co-teaching partnership is rooted in prioritizing time to plan and reflect (Friend, 2019; Mielke, 2015). "How is what the two of you are doing together substantially different and better for students than what one teacher would do alone?" (Kramer & Murawski, 2017, p. 154) should guide all planning sessions and teaching conversations. It is worth noting that when co-teach partners plan lessons and devote the necessary time to the processes, the results are easy to observe; the question above easily answered. It is imperative that the teaching pair co-plan to co-teach, so the day cannot work without both educators (Kramer & Maurawski, 2017).

It is also important to devote the time to understand the potential difference in the knowledge of teaching philosophies and practice as well as culture and upbringing, general likes and dislikes, and life experiences (Friend, 2019). It cannot be underscored enough that devoting the time to accomplish these tasks makes a considerable difference in co-teaching. They have the potential power to make the classroom come to life.

Teachers should periodically conduct an individual self-assessment on their collaboration and contributions to the partnership in the areas of co-planning, lesson preparation, co-teaching, and grading procedures (Fitzell, 2018). This should be followed with time to compare and discuss self-assessment results and highlight similarities, differences, and areas to work on. This ongoing process opens the door to implement goals for new teaching structures and practices.

This dedication to become more familiar with one another and to the co-teaching process opens the door to investigate options for different teaching methods. Co-teaching is not intended to be the same as teaching solo; therefore, partners need to participate in a bit of give and take on ideas, trusting one another to have the best interest of the class and student learning at heart (Wilson, 2016).

Both the special education teacher and the general education teacher must 'devote the time' to plan together using a variety of materials and teaching approaches in order to successfully accomplish effective instruction in their co-taught classroom (Murawski, & Lochner, 2018). A supportive alliance helps avoid bias and judgement, while using evidence-based instruction leads to shared responsibility and accountability (Hamilton-Jones & Moore, 2013; Pancsofar & Petroff, 2016).

It is vital to reserve and maintain the planning time and the teaching time as co-planning is critical to successful co-teaching (Kramer & Murawski, 2017; Murawski & Lochner, 2018). It must be scheduled, honored, and respected. The scheduled time for planning needs to stay focused on planning (Pratt, Imbody, Wolf, & Patterson, 2016). Teaching pairs decide to enact a few ground rules to ensure the success of planning time to include bringing a snack, turning off cell phones, and not scheduling meetings or events (Kramer & Murawski, 2017).

Grading papers can be completed before or after planning sessions. Planning time is to be devoted to planning together and all materials can be created after the session is over as well (Murawski & Lochner, 2018). Kramer and Murawski (2017) suggest following an agenda as it keeps both educators accountable and alleviates off-task discussions that often pop up when two people get together. The agenda should include what will be taught, how it will be taught, and who will teach it.

Reflective educators are most effective; therefore, include a discussion of previous lessons and how well students are advancing in the curriculum (Mielke, 2015). This means coming prepared to the planning meeting with knowledge of the latest grades and progress monitoring, rather than waiting until the meeting to look at scores (Kramer & Murawski, 2017). Planning sessions should be about planning upcoming lessons and teacher duties only.

'Devote the time' to teach together. The lesson plans written with a co-teach format will delineate the decisions made about the what, how, and who in the lesson (Friend, 2019). Be consistent. Both teachers need to know and understand the content and each class period should begin and end with both educators (Fitzell, 2018). When delivering instruction, it is important that both educators deliver substantive instruction; therefore, when planning, consider who has the best grasp for the original teach and who will conduct small group re-teach (Murawski & Lochner, 2018).

On occasion, one teacher may find their knowledge is not as strong. The confident teacher presents the new content with the other contributing on a smaller scale until both teachers are comfortable (Beyers-Brown et al., 2013). This should not happen frequently as it will result in a situation that resembles teacher and helper, which should be avoided at all costs. Teacher equity must be honored and viewed as integral to the class environment.

Both teachers should also teach all students equitably, in whole group, small group, and individual tutoring. The special education teacher is not intended to only teach students with disabilities (Potts & Howard, 2011). On the contrary, the co-planning should ensure both educators are on the same page devoted to knowing the content well enough to teach all students.

Finally, 'devote the time' to discuss the process of evaluation and to the progress the students are making so that co-teaching partners adapt the curriculum and instruction accordingly. Lindermann and Magiera (2014) point out that "co-teaching professionals need time to ask questions and compare strategies while they plan together" (p. 42). Planning allows collaborative instruction to evolve in a positive direction with professional respect and confidence (Friend, 2019).

Expect Success

The phase 'expect success' is the ultimate purpose of co-teaching. This phase is the basis for co-planning and co-teaching, going beyond the idea that all students will learn to the belief that all children will excel, mastering grade-level standards (Friend, 2019). Two trained, qualified teachers in one classroom increases the learning of all students in the class. This begins with planning when teachers adamantly oppose the concept of planning for the 'general education students' then adding supports and accommodations for students with special education needs (Baglieri et al., 2011). Plan for all learners at the onset.

Plan to know your students. This level of planning begins in the early phase when ideas and expectations of co-teaching are being explored. Co-teaching partners getting to know one another should lament on the concept of getting to know their future students as well (Fitzell, 2018). They should investigate topics of diversity before the year begins and during the year.

Planning lessons that teach how people are more alike than different, yet celebrating differences will teach acceptance (Southern Poverty Law Center: Teaching Tolerance, 2018). It is important for educators to find, adapt, or create interest inventories to understand the students' experiences, families and what they like to learn. Celebrating diversity and acknowledging similarities and differences by bringing it to the forefront of the classroom benefits all students (Southern Poverty Law Center: Teaching Tolerance, 2018).

Let students discover ways they look alike, things liked and disliked, favorites and pet peeves, who does math fast and who reads fast, who writes well and who draws well. Paired educators should teach acceptance of self as well as others (Southern Poverty Law Center: Teaching Tolerance, 2018). Teaching students that the expectation is to accept and value others who learn, look, speak, behave, or believe differently provides invaluable learning that goes beyond what is in any book (Duchaine, 2019). Co-teachers must plan to recognize differences among students and plan to teach the students to recognize and understand that differences are amazing and wonderful! Acceptance leads to student success (Friend, 2019).

Co-teachers should plan with the belief that all students learn. The success of inclusion depends on the teachers' attitudes that all students can learn when lessons are well-designed and teachers are comfortable differentiating instruction based on student needs (Dimitrova-Radojchikj & Chichevska-Jovanova, 2015). Consequently, successful inclusive environments begin with lesson planning grounded in student ability at the onset, rather than adjusting lessons as an afterthought. This allows each child to be fully included, rather than being an add on in the lesson plan (Rusanescu, Sora, & Stoicescu, 2018; Young & Luttenegger, 2014).

Paired educators should realize that instead of blaming students who are not succeeding, good teaching means revising lesson plans based on student struggles to increase the success of the students (Sumrall & Sumrall, 2018). When observed by an outsider, a well-planned co-taught classroom should flow smoothly without indication of which teacher represents special education and which teacher represents the general content area. Well-planned classes should flow smoothly as students move between whole-class instruction, small group lessons, collaborative learning tasks and independent work (Potts & Howard, 2011). It should not be obvious which students have special education needs as instruction and learning activities are planned to differentiate, providing remediation for weaker skill areas while offering other activities that challenge the students and elevate their strengths (Friend, 2019).

This phase, 'expect success,' requires a strong sense of inclusion, which means that all students are valued as equals. Every child is regarded as capable academically, socially, and behaviorally within the classroom, the school, the community, and society (Scruggs & Mastropieri, 2017). Although some students will learn at a different pace or through a different process, they are learning grade-level skills (Friend, 2019). Co-taught classrooms with high expectations for all learners exhibit a welcoming community and increase academic achievement for all students (Wilson, 2016). True co-teaching, where equity of roles and responsibilities are planned for demonstrate inclusion and prepare children and adolescents to experience a community where everyone can learn, and a community that values everyone (Fitzell, 2018).

Final Thoughts

Like the phases of the moon, one phase of planning gradually evolves into the next phase, cycling through over and over. Comparable to the moon's role in astronomy, the role of co-planning in co-teaching is an ongoing and complex process encompassing the full entity, while focusing on one visible phase. At any given time, the entire moon is present, even though the focus from earth is on the portion of the moon momentarily lit by the sun. Likewise, the phases of co-planning will cycle through with teachers focusing on one aspect, while understanding all other aspects must be present continuously to support the current phase being addressed.

Points to Remember

- *Co-teaching requires co-planning. One cannot occur without the other.*

- *'Accept the challenge' to get to know one another, to differentiate between solo-teaching and co-teaching, and to fully engage to teach all students.*

- *'Believe in one another' to share a respectful relationship with teacher equity, dividing all roles and responsibilities equally, and trusting in each other's expertise.*

- *'Commit to the process' dedicating energy to co-planning and co-teaching consistently, begin with UDL for the success of all students.*

- *'Devote the time' to being where you are supposed to be, when you are supposed to be there. No exceptions!*

- *'Expect success' to realize that this model, implemented as defined, will produce classes where all students excel.*

References

Altieri, E. M., Colley, K. M., Daniel, L. S., & Dickenson, K. W. (2015). Merging expertise: Preparing collaborative educators. *Rural Special Education Quarterly, 34*(1), pp 17-22. https://doi.org/10.1177/875687051503400105

Austin V. L. (2001). Teachers' beliefs about co-teaching. *Remedial and Special Education, 22*(4), 245-255. https://doi.org/10.1177/074193250102200408

Baglieri, S., Bejoian, L. M., Broderick, A. A., Connor, D. J., & Valle, J. (2011). [Re]claiming "inclusive education" toward cohesion in educational reform: Disability studies unravels the myth of the normal child. *Teachers College Record, 113*(10), 2122-2154. Retrieved from https://eric.ed.gov/?id=EJ951089

Beninghof, A.M. (2012). *Co-teaching that works: Structures and strategies for maximizing student learning.* San Francisco, CA: Jossey-Bass

Beyers-Brown, N., Howerter, C. S., & Morgan, J.J. (2013). Tools and strategies for making co-teaching work. *Intervention in School and Clinic, 49,* 84–91. https://doi.org/10.1177/105345121349174

Blanton, L.P., Pugach, M.C., & Florian, L. (2011). *Preparing general education teachers to improve outcomes for students with disabilities.* Retrieved from https://www.ncld.org/wp-content/uploads/2014/11/aacte_ncld_recommendation.pdf

Blask, F. (2011). *Collaboration between general education teachers and related service providers.* Retrieved from https://files.eric.ed.gov/fulltext/ED518582.pdf

Cantu, D. A., (2015). Role of general educators in a multidisciplinary team for learners with special needs. *Interdisciplinary Connections to Special Education: Important Aspects to Consider Advances in Special Education, 30,* 35-57. https://doi.org/10.1108/S0270-40132015000030A003

Case, M. (2017). *A qualitative case study of coteaching relationships.* Retrieved from https://dc.etsu.edu/cgi/viewcontent.cgi?article=4788&context=etd

Casey, B. (2019). When special and general educators collaborate, everybody wins. *ASCDExpress, 14*(25). Retrieved from http://www.ascd.org/ascd-express/vol14/num25/when-special-and-general-educators-collaborate-everybody-wins.aspx

Cassel, S. (2019). How to choose a co-teaching model. *Edutopia.* Retrieved from https://www.edutopia.org/article/how-choose-co-teaching-model

Casserly, A. M., & Padden, A. (2018). Teachers' views of coteaching approaches in addressing pupils with special educational needs (SEN) in multi-grade classrooms. *European Journal of Special Needs Education, 33*(4), 555-571. https://doi.org/10.1080/08856257.2017.1386315

Conderman, G. (2016). Methods for addressing conflict in cotaught classrooms. *Intervention in School and Clinic, 44*(4), 221-229. https://doi.org/10.1177/1053451210389034

Conderman, G. & Hedin, L. (2015). Differentiating instruction in co-taught classrooms for students with emotional/behaviour difficulties. *Emotional and Behavioural Difficulties, 20*(4), 349–361. https://doi.org/10.1080/13632752.2014.976918

Dieker, L., Finnegan, L., Grillo, K., & Garland, D. (2013). Special education in the science classroom: A co-teaching scenario. *Science Scope*, 18-22. DOI: 10.2505/4/ss13_037_04_18

Dimitrova-Radojchikj, D., & Chichevska-Jovanova, N. (2015). Teacher's acceptance of students with disability. *Bulgarian Journal of Science Education, 24*(5), 647-656.

Duchaine, E. L. (2019). Advancing the social standing of students from educationally at-risk populations: Students who learn, look, speak, behave, or believe differently. In N. Young, E. Jean & T. Citro, *Acceptance, Understanding, and the Moral Imperative of Promoting Social Justice Education in the Schoolhouse* (pp. 75-92). Wilmington, Delaware: Vernon Press.

Fitzell, S.G. (2018). *Best practices in co-teaching & collaboration: The HOW of co-teaching – implementing the models.* Manchester, NH: Cogent Catalyst Press

Friend, M. (2019). *Co-teach! Building and sustaining classroom partnerships in inclusive schools* (3rd ed). Greensboro, NC: Marilyn Friend, Inc.

Friend, M. & Cook, L. (2016). *Interactions: Collaboration skills for school professionals* (8th ed.). New York, NY: Pearson

Fulford, G. (n.d.). *Quick guide to teacher team building.* Retrieved from https://www.teachhub.com/quick-guide-teacher-team-building

Hamilton-Jones, B., & Moore, A. (2013). Ensuring high-quality inclusive practices: What co-teachers can do. *Kappa Delta Pi Record, 49*(4), 156-161. https://doi.org/10.1080/00228958.2013.845503

Kottler, E. (2017). *Co-planning for co-teaching.* Retrieved from https://corwin-connect.com/2017/06/co-planning-co-teaching/

Kramer, A., & Murawski, W. W. (2017). Beyond just "playing nicely": Collaboration and co-teaching. In W. Murawski & K.L. Scott, *What Really Works with Exceptional Learners* (pp. 169-187). Thousand Oaks, CA: Corwin.

Lindermann, K., W., & Magiera, K. (2014). A Co-teaching model: Committed professionals, high expectations, and the inclusive classroom. *Odyssey*, 40-45. Retrieved from https://files.eric.ed.gov/fulltext/EJ1030993.pdf

Mastropieri, M.A. & Scruggs, T.E. (2018). *The inclusive classroom: Strategies for effective differentiated instruction* (6th ed.). New York, NY: Pearson

McKinney, A. (2017). *What special education teachers wish general ed teachers knew.* Retrieved from https://www.teachervision.com/blog/morning-announcements/what-special-ed-teachers-wish-general-ed-teachers-knew

Mielke, C. (2015). *Staying present in the classroom: Practicing mindful teaching.* Retrieved from https://www.weareteachers.com/staying-present-in-the-classroom-practicing-mindful-teaching/

Murawski, W.W. & Dieker, L. (2008). 50 ways to keep your co-teacher: Strategies for before, during, and after coteaching. *Teaching Exceptional Children 40*(4): 40–48. Retrieved from http://laspdg.org/files/50ways.pdf

Murawski, W.W. & Lochner, W.W. (2018). *Beyond co-teaching basics: A data-driven, no-tail model for continuous improvement.* Alexandria, VA: ASCD

Nevin, A.I., Villa, R.A. & Thousand, J.S. (2009). *A guide to co-teaching with paraeducators: Practical tips for K-12 educators.* Thousand Oaks, CA: Corwin

Nierengarten, G.M. & Hughes, T. (2010). *What teachers wish administrators knew about co-teaching in high schools.* Retrieved from https://corescholar.libraries.wright.edu/cgi/viewcontent.cgi?article=1122&context=ejie

Pancsofar, N., & Jerry G. Petroff, J. G. (2016). Teachers' experiences with coteaching as a model for inclusive education, *International Journal of Inclusive Education, 20*(10), 1043-1053. https://doi.org/10.1080/13603116.2016.1145264

Peery, A. (2017). *Co-teaching: How to make it work.* Retrieved from https://www.cultofpedagogy.com/co-teaching-push-in/

Potts, E.A. & Howard, L.A. (2011). *How to co-teach: A guide for general and special educators.* Baltimore, MD: Brookes Publishing.

Pratt, S. M., Imbody, S. M., Wolf, L. D., & Patterson, A. L. (2016). Co-planning in co-teaching: A practical solution. *Intervention in School and Clinic, 52*(4) 243–249. https://doi.org/10.1177/1053451216659474

Rimpola, R. C. (2014). Collaborative planning and teacher efficacy of high school mathematics co-teachers. *Educational Planning, 21*(3), 41-53. Retrieved from https://files.eric.ed.gov/fulltext/EJ1208552.pdf

Ronfeldt, M., Owens Farmer, S., McQueen, K., & Grissom, J. A. (2015). Teacher collaboration in instructional teams and student achievement. *American Educational Research Journal, 52*, 475– 515. https://doi.org/10.3102/0002831215585562

Rusanescu, A. G., Sora, A. M., & Stoicescu, M. (2018). Comparative study on approaching inclusive physical education from the perspective of alternative pedagogies. *Revista Romaneasca pentru Educatie Multidimensionala, 10*(1), 123-135. https://doi.org/10.18662/rrem/23

Schilling, D. (2012). *10 steps to effective listening.* Retrieved from https://www.forbes.com/sites/womensmedia/2012/11/09/10-steps-to-effective-listening/#22617d053891

Schwarz, P. (2006). *From disability to possibility: The power of inclusion.* Allyn & Bacon.

Schwarz, P., & Kluth, P. (2007). *You're welcome: 30 innovative ideas for the inclusive classroom.* Portsmouth, NH: Heinemann.

Scruggs, T.E., & Mastropieri, M.A. (2017). Making inclusion work with co-teaching. *Teaching Exceptional Children, 49*(4), 284-293. https://doi.org/10.1177/0040059916685065

Sileo, J. M. (2011). Co-teaching: Getting to know your partner. *Teaching Exceptional Children, 45*(5), 32-38. Retrieved from https://sites.newpaltz.edu/ncate/wp-content/uploads/sites/21/2014/06/Example-Sileo.pdf

Solberg, H.P. (2017). *A recipe for success: Essential administrative and interpersonal considerations of co-teaching in secondary settings.* Retrieved from

https://pdfs.semanticscholar.org/5881/c8b957cd53dc6586ae6ba2a4084409
191aa8.pdf

Southern Poverty Law Center: Teaching Tolerance. (2018). *Critical practices for anti-bias education.* Retrieved from
https://www.tolerance.org/sites/default/files/2019-04/TT-Critical-
Practices-for-Anti-bias-Education.pdf

Stein, E. (2016). *Elevating co-teaching though UDL.* Wakefield, MA: CAST

Strogilos, V., Stefanidis, A., & Tragoulia, E. (2016). Co-teachers' attitudes towards planning and instructional activities for students with disabilities. *European Journal of Special Needs Education, 31*(3), 344-359. https://doi.org/10.1080/08856257.2016.1141512

Sumrall, W. & Sumrall, K. (2018). Understanding by design. *Science and Children, 56*(1), 48-54. Retrieved from https://eric.ed.gov/?id=EJ1187970

West, E. (1997). *201 icebreakers: Group mixers, warm-ups, energizers, and playful activities.* New York, NY: McGraw-Hill

Wilson, G.L. (2016). *Co-planning for co-teaching: Time-saving routines that work in inclusive classrooms.* Alexandria, VA: ASCD

Young, K., & Luttenegger, K. (2014). Planning "lessons for everybody" in secondary education. *American Secondary Education 43*(1), 25-32. Retrieved from https://eric.ed.gov/?id=EJ1047044

Chapter 6

Assessment in a Co-Teaching Environment

Nicholas D. Young, PhD, EdD, *American International College*
Elizabeth J. Bienia, EdD, *Endicott College*
Doris Buckley, EdD, *Northern Essex Community College*

As discussed throughout this book, co-teaching is an exciting endeavor that brings positive educational outcomes for students across grade spans. Assessment serves as a critical tool, with the goal of guiding teachers as they plan lessons (Aviles, & Grayson, 2017). Teachers must have a clear understanding of their students' current levels of mastery in order to provide instruction that will scaffold them to increasingly more complex content and understanding (Fisher & Frey, 2010; Stein, 2016). Assessment must always be approached with this end goal in mind and the process itself should be as meaningful and engaging as possible (Black & Wiliam, 2018).

High-stakes assessments have been a part of the educational climate since the passing of the No Child Left Behind Act (Klein, 2015). It has led to a negative view of assessment by many teachers, students, and their families (Dee & Jacob, 2010). The No Child Left Behind Act of 2001 (NCLB) was a United States Act of Congress that was signed into law by George W. Bush in 2002 (Cortiella, 2019; Klein, 2015). This version of the reauthorized Elementary and Secondary Education Act (ESEA) from 1965 required that all public schools receiving federal funds administer a statewide standardized test annually to all students (Klein, 2015; Young, Jean & Mead, 2018).

The goals of this latest version of the ESEA were to ensure that all students were given access to qualified teachers that were then held accountable for student outcomes (Klein, 2015). The act further identified schools that were failing to make adequate yearly progress (AYP) and instituted sanctions and rewards based on each school's AYP status (Dee & Jacob, 2010). It supported standards-based education reform based on the idea that setting high standards and establishing measurable goals could improve individual outcomes in education. The next reauthorization was known as the Every Student Succeeds Act (ESSA), which replaced NCLB in 2015, and modified the requirements of periodic standardized tests given to students as well as gave more authority to the state level (Dee & Jacob, 2010; Young, Jean & Mead, 2018).

These acts created an educational system that quickly became more data-driven and focused on ensuring students' progress from grade to grade with the necessary skills and aptitudes deemed as appropriate for each stage on the educational continuum and according to the common core (Common Core State Standards Initiative, 2018). Educators are much more aware of the need for data-driven classroom assessments that can measure a child's progress and provide a guide for instruction (Mertler, 2014). Although it would be easy to have a negative view of assessment as a result of these mandates, it is important to remember that long before this age of high-stakes accountability, intentional teachers were developing and using assessments as powerful resources to guide learning in their classrooms (Blessing, 2019).

Understanding the Differences Between
Traditional Evaluation and Classroom Assessment

There is an important distinction to be made between classroom assessment and traditional evaluation. Traditional evaluation is content centered, passive, and content-specific (British Columbia Institute of Technology [BCIT], 2010). Classroom assessment is student-centered, active, and content-specific (McMillan, 2018; Popham, 2017). Today's classroom environment, regardless of the educator's instructional approach, should strive to include classroom assessment that is authentic and linked to measurable competencies of students' knowledge (McMillan, 2018; Popham, 2017).

For the purposes of this chapter, assessment refers to a systematic process of gathering information about what a student knows, is able to do, and is learning to do. All three of these components are necessary and provide the foundation for solid decision-making and planning for learning and instruction that is both high-quality and differentiated (McMillan, 2018). Assessment is an integral part of the instructional process, which, when done effectively enhances and empowers student learning (Popham, 2017).

Using a variety of assessment techniques allows teachers to most effectively obtain information about what students know and are able to do while providing positive and supportive feedback. Assessment should guide instructional programs and techniques to help students learn more effectively (Popham, 2017). Instructional methods and approaches will vary among teaching teams. In the co-teaching classroom, it is important for both teachers to come to an agreement on the theoretical foundations that will guide their work together (Grant, 2014).

Teachers must decide how to approach teaching and assessment; for example, they may choose to have students learn and assess on a more personalized basis using one of three types of frameworks/approaches to include

- a multiple intelligence-based approach, which would provide a classroom environment where instructional methods will strive to target students' strengths through a variety of activities (Armstrong, 2017);

- the Universal Design for Learning (UDL) approach, which provides a framework for understanding that there are multiple ways for a student to demonstrate mastery of a particular concept (CAST, 2019; Stein, 2016); or

- the project-based learning approach is a creative and deeply rigorous way for co-teachers to create projects and assessments that are meaningful to students (Boss & Larmer, 2018; Larmer, Mergendollar & Boss, 2015).

These personalized learning situations can be a unit of study dependent or co-teachers can choose to use only one and make all assignments meet those guidelines (Chappuis, & Stiggins, 2019). These are important considerations when teaching with a partner. Students should know what is acceptable and be able to expect a high level of cohesiveness in regard to teacher and classroom expectations.

Multiple Intelligences

Educators who use a multiple intelligences framework in the classroom may teach to students' stronger elements or they may choose to engage students in their less developed intelligences as a way to strengthen them (Armstrong, 2017). Using a variety of pathways to ensure rigorous learning and academic awareness take place, co-teachers have the ability to mix and match intelligences for individual students or groups of students (Hendron, 2018). Placing two students together who each have a different strong intelligence will force each to work as a team to increase knowledge and understanding.

Academic activities can push students to assess their multiple intelligences in such a way that it expands all intelligences. According to Terada (2018), giving students multiple ways to assess information means they will be more likely to remember it. When students are able to receive information that has been personalized, or uses their dominant intelligences, their interests and needs are being met and, thus, they will likely work harder (Terada, 2018). Allowing students to express themselves in a variety of ways will increase their ability to show their knowledge as they feel that they are being taken seriously and what they know is important (Armstrong, 2017).

Universal Design for Learning

Universal Design for Learning (UDL) as a teaching and learning technique is a prime example of how two educators may teach together to benefit students. This framework is "based on scientific insights into how humans learn" (CAST, 2019, n.p.). Using a three-part system that examines why (engagement), what (representation), and how (action and expression), educators can create instructional goals, lessons, and assessments that can be "customized and adjusted to meet individual needs" (CAST, 2019, n.p.).

Co-teachers who use UDL as a learning and assessment tool mix and match specific guidelines to match the topic, the instructional outcomes required and the student needs in their classroom (Stein, 2016). This means that students have multiple ways to engage with the material, multiple ways to represent or approach the content, and multiple means to express or show their understanding (Meyer, Rose, Gordon, 2014). Through this process, co-teachers and students turn each assessment into a personalized experience.

Gold Standard Project-Based Learning

Project-based learning, or PBL, is an interactive teaching and learning technique in which students solve meaningful and current world problems (Boss & Larmer, 2018; Larmer, Mergendoller, & Boss, 2015). It differs from UDL in that the students, in conjunction with the educator, are responsible for coming up with the problem, determining the artifacts necessary to demonstrate understanding and creating a public display or presentation to display their solution. The project may take anywhere from a week to a month to a semester to complete; however, students are engaged in collaborative exercises that encourage critical thinking, communication, and creativity (Boss & Larmer, 2018).

Gold Standard PBL has a set of seven specific essential project design elements that include challenging problem or question, sustained inquiry, authenticity, student voice and choice, reflection, critique and revise, and public product (Buck Institute for Education, n.d.; Larmer et al., 2015). In addition, there are project-based teaching practices that ensure the educator remains as the guide during the learning process. These seven teaching practices include design and plan, align to standards, build the culture, manage activities, scaffold student learning, assess student learning, and engage and coach (Buck Institute for Education, n.d.; Larmer et al., 2015).

Using a combination of the design elements and the teaching practices, co-teaching teams can guide individual students or student teams through scaffolded lessons and strategies that help them find the solutions they seek (Boss & Larmer, 2018). At the end of the project time, students are required to present their problem/solution to a public audience, further ensuring understanding and creating an ability to speak publicly with confidence and clarity (Larmer et al., 2015).

Other Assessment Techniques

In addition to MI Theory, UDL, and PBL, classroom assessment should include a combination of teacher-made tests, technology-based testing and classroom-based assessments all with appropriate testing accommodations to assure that students with diverse needs are given the opportunity to achieve (McMillan, 2018; Spencer, 2009). There are many assessment strategies and techniques; some include observation, anecdotal records, RTI, peer conferencing, learning progressions, and student conferencing (McMillan, 2018; Popham, 2017).

Observations

Systematic observations of students allow for a more informal yet highly valuable method of gaining insights into student learning (Alber, 2017; White, 2016). It involves observing children throughout the day in the natural learning environment. In the co-teaching classroom, this type of assessment becomes much more possible; one teacher is able to focus their attention on an individual pupil, while the other teacher is focused on the other students in the class (Popham, 2017). Valuable insights can be obtained that will then allow for specific targeting of different needs (McMillan, 2018). Informal checklists can help assess basic skill levels for things such as rote counting, ability of alphabet cognition in the early grades, and skills such as mastery of multiplication facts and sight work recognition for students in later grades (Konen, 2017).

Informal observations of children also allow an educator to look at each child as a whole, looking specifically at a child's approaches to learning, their language and communication skills, cognitive development, emotional and social development, and health and physical development (Alber, 2017; Konen, 2017). Careful reflection of this data requires that the teacher collecting data be given the opportunity to record and document what is being observed. The co-teachers can then evaluate the data together as a guide for differentiating instruction (Blessing, 2019).

Anecdotal Records

Anecdotal records are notes taken based on close observations of students (McFarland, 2008). The notes can record a range of student behavior, including approaches to the learning process, specific skill mastery in a variety of subjects such as literacy, mathematics, social studies and science, as well as social, emotional, and physical development (McMillan, 2018). One of the most important considerations when using anecdotal records is assuring that documentation provides a clear description and enough details to inform future instruction (Bates, Schenck & Hoover, 2019). The co-teaching classroom offers a unique opportunity for one of the teachers in the co-teaching team to regularly take on the role of observer. This allows one teacher to closely observe students' behaviors and conversations in writing while the co-teacher is leading the classroom activities or lessons (Bates et al., 2019).

The quality of anecdotal records depends largely on the teacher's ability to be a neutral observer while consciously setting aside assumptions and biases one may have (McFarland, 2008). There are many systems available for organizing one's anecdotal records so that they can be of best use. In a co-teaching environment, notes should be managed in such a way that both teachers have reviewed them together and they can serve as a point of reference used in goal setting for specific students and overall instructional plans (Bates at al., 2019).

Developing a manageable system for taking and using anecdotal notes is critical if they are then ideally going to be a tool for intentional instruction. Notes with clear language that both co-teachers can understand provide concrete documentation of students' emerging behaviors, skills, and competencies while also giving teachers a foundation for reflective practice (Bates et al., 2019).

Learning Progressions

Learning progressions, sometimes called learning trajectories, emphasize the goal that an individual student is moving towards and are an important feature of high quality, holistic assessment repertoires (Mangione, Osborne & Mendenhall, 2019; Shepard, 2018; Taylor et al., 2018). Progressions define sequences of learning and development from less challenging to more challenging. Research-based progressions incorporate data gathered on thousands of children and enable educators to better understand the development and learning of their specific students (Mangione et al., 2019). These can then be used to focus assessment outcomes on smaller groups of students.

These progressions use what students know as the starting point and help to inform curriculum and supports that will guide each student to progressively higher levels of learning and development (Shepard, 2018). Learning progression assessment in the co-teaching classroom can focus on specific skills such as a student's understanding of gravity or a more general progression in the social skills appropriate for a student of a specific age.

A balance is required when completing learning progression assessments (Taylor et al., 2018). With too much focus on specific skills, the teacher may lose sight of a child's holistic development. For learning progressions focused on more general skills, particularly in the social-emotional domain, the number of specific learning progressions that one may create can become overwhelming (Taylor et al., 2018). As with any assessment, specific targets should be decided upon within the co-teaching team with plenty of time for joint reflection and discussion in planning future instruction and goal setting for specific students (Sztajn, & Wilson, 2019).

Response to Intervention

Response to Intervention (RTI) is a set of scientifically-based processes that can be utilized to help make educational decisions for a student (Metcalf, 2019). This approach incorporates screening, progress monitoring, a multi-level prevention system, and data-based decision making and has led to a significant decrease in special education referrals (Young, Mumby & Rice, 2019). RTI teams meet regularly and are focused on short-term goal attainment (VanDerHeyden, 2019).

Once an RTI referral has been initiated, observations of the child take place by various personnel in the school. Depending on the specific concern, observations may take place by a reading specialist, math interventionist, occupational therapist, physical therapist, guidance counselor, behavior specialist, school nurse, or speech and language pathologist. Student work is also evaluated and a meeting, that usually includes the parent/guardian, takes place (Metcalf, 2019).

In many cases, RTI significantly decreases the need for a full special education referral, allowing a team to target specific gaps in a child's achievement gaps relatively quickly and effectively. For students who do not respond to the RTI supports implemented, the team makes the decision that a special education referral is warranted (Metcalf, 2019). A breadth of data is already available for that student through RTI which provides the necessary justification for special education services (Young, Mumby & Rice, 2019).

Peer Conferencing

Peer conferencing is an effective assessment strategy that allows peers to respond to another peer's work (Villa, Thousand, & Nevin, 2013). This process can be as structured or as informal as the teaching team decides. In the co-teaching team, it becomes invaluable as there are two teachers who can oversee the peer conferencing process and provide coaching to teams as needed throughout the process (Villa et al., 2013).

Peer conferencing, sometimes referred to as peer assessment, has been shown to help promote self-assessment through a cycle of peer feedback, analysis and revision of one's work (Reinholz, 2016). Peer conferencing allows students to provide feedback to one another with proper structure provided by the co-teaching team. As the school year progresses, peer conferencing can become a routine that needs a decreasing amount of instructor support and increasing amount of value to student work, revisions, and learning (Villa et al., 2013).

Teacher-Student Conferencing

Assessment can, and should, be an active process where students and teachers work together continually to gather evidence of learning (Moss & Brookhart, 2009; Villa et al., 2013). Classrooms that use this approach are guided by three major questions (1) Where am I now? (2) Where am I going? (3) What methods or strategies can get me where I need to go or be? (Moss & Brookhart, 2009). These questions help to guide both teachers and students in continual scaffolding and increasing understanding of course concepts and skill development (Moss & Brookhart, 2009; Spencer, 2009).

Teacher-student conferencing is an underutilized tool in today's classrooms (McMillan, 2018; Villa et al., 2013). Effective conferencing should incorporate several key components that include the teacher(s) asking effective questions, student self-assessment, feedback that leads forward to the next steps in goal attainment and student goal setting (Moss & Brookhart, 2009; Spencer, 2009).

Feedback to Students

The increased diversity present in today's classrooms further adds to the challenges of assuring that assessment strategies are culturally responsive and adequately guide teachers in their approaches to student learning and feedback (Lew & Nelson, 2016). Regardless of the type of assessment used by co-teachers, it should provide sound feedback on student learning (McMillan, 2018; Popham, 2017; Stein, 2016; Villa et al., 2013). Feedback characteristics include that it should provide encouragement, take place in frequent intervals, and it should give students a clear picture of their progress as well as overall areas in need of improvement and specific next steps (Marzano, 2006).

Use of Rubrics to Guide Assessment

Co-teachers would be wise to devise a rubric system for all assessments. These rubrics can vary depending on need; however, they must always guide the student and offer examples of what each tier of compliance would look like (Brookhart, 2013). When creating rubrics it is important to choose three or four specific measures and give detailed information on each one. Students will need to know, for example, that in the writing convention section, a perfect score means that all sentences have capital letters and proper punctuation, while a single point would be given for multiple mistakes (Roell, 2019). Likewise, when students use specific information from the text to respond to a question, they will receive more credit than a student who does not identify anything from the text that proves the point to be made (Brookhart, 2013; Roell, 2019).

Rubrics can be used to structure observations, written assignments, oral assignments, and physical projects, as well as technology-based projects (Brookhart, 2013). Co-teachers who can create and use rubrics offer students a relatively easy and consistent way to assess work prior to submission. This lessens the chance that work will be subpar or that teachers will ask students to try again, although some teachers may use the rubric intentionally to give students a second chance at success (Brookhart, 2013).

Final Thoughts

Any discussion of assessment must be embedded within a larger theoretical field of an educator's pedagogical views. Co-teachers must explore pedagogical practices that should then inform the functions of specific assessment techniques and protocols in their classrooms (Black & Wiliam, 2018). Co-teaching provides an ideal environment for high-quality assessment that will give a snapshot of a student's current level of mastery as well as provide a clear trajectory for curriculum planning and targeted supports.

Regardless of the type of assessment used, it is vital that co-teachers are consistent in the way the appraisals are used and the way in which feedback is provided. If peer coaching is used, students must be taught the specific protocols to ensure that their peers do not become frustrated or perceive the situation to be uncomfortable. Educators, as well as students, benefit from clear expectations and rubrics that further ensure student success.

Points to Remember

- *Assessment techniques that are varied allows teachers to most effectively obtain information about what students know and are able to do while providing positive and supportive feedback.*

- *Learning progressions or learning trajectories define sequences of learning and development from less challenging to more challenging and emphasize the goal that an individual student is moving towards.*

- *The use of multiple intelligences, universal design for learning, and project-based learning are three specific models of instruction that offer assessments designed for students that specifically target the area of study and are most often created through a union of co-teachers and students.*

- *RTI plans help to meet short-term gaps in student achievement and significantly decreases the need in many cases for a full special education referral.*

- *Student conferencing with one teacher or both teachers in a co-teaching classroom as well as peer-to-peer conferencing offer supportive structures for student learning.*

- *The use of anecdotal notes can provide a foundation for reflective practice and collaboration in the co-teaching classroom environment.*

References

Alber, R. (2017). *3 ways student data can inform your teaching.* Retrieved from https://www.edutopia.org/blog/using-student-data-inform-teaching-rebecca-alber

Armstrong, T. (2017). *Multiple intelligences in the classroom* (4th ed.). Arlington, VA: ASCD

Aviles, N. & Grayson, K. (2017). *Backwards planning-how assessment impacts teaching and learning.* Retrieved from https://www.idra.org/resource-center/backward-planning-assessment-impacts-teaching-learning/

Bates, C., Scheneck, S. & Hoover, H. (2019). Anecdotal records: Practical strategies for taking meaningful notes. *Young Children, 74*(3), 14-19. Retrieved from https://search.proquest.com/openview/d18258cca5cbb849e557233d04d05 8be/1?pq-origsite=gscholar&cbl=27755

Black, P. & Wiliam, D. (2018). Classroom assessment and pedagogy. *Assessment in Education: Principles, Policy & Practice,* 25(6), 551-575. DOI: 10.1080/0969594X.2018.1441807

Blessing, A. (2019). Assessment in kindergarten: Meeting children where they are. *Young Children,* 74(3), 6-12. Retrieved from https://www.naeyc.org/resources/pubs/yc/jul2019/assessment-in-kindergarten

Boss, S. & Larmer, J. (2018). *Project based teaching: How to create rigorous and engaging learning experiences.* Arlington, VA: ASCD

British Columbia Institute of Technology [BCIT]. (2010). *Classroom Assessment Techniques.* Retrieved from http://www.northernc.on.ca/leid/docs/ja_assesstech.pdf

Brookhart, S.M. (2013). *How to create and use rubrics for formative assessment and grading.* Arlington, VA: ASCD

Buck Institute for Education. (n.d.). Gold standard PBL: Essential project design elements. Retrieved from https://www.pblworks.org/what-is-pbl/gold-standard-project-design

CAST. (2019). *The UDL guidelines.* Retrieved from
http://udlguidelines.cast.org/?utm_medium=web&utm_campaign=none&utm_source=cast-about-udl

Chappuis, J. & Stiggins, R. (2019). *Classroom assessment for student learning* (3rd ed.). New York, NY: Pearson

Common Core State Standards Initiative. (2018). *What parents should know.* Retrieved from
http://www.corestandards.org/what-parents-should-know/

Cortiella, C. (2019). *No child left behind: Determining appropriate assessment accommodations for students with disabilities.* Retrieved from
http://www.ldonline.org/article/10938/

Dee, T., & Jacob, B.A. (2010). The impact of No Child Left Behind on students, teachers, and schools. *Brookings Papers on Economic Activity,* 149-207. Retrieved from https://www.brookings.edu/wp- content/uploads/2010/09/2010b_bpea_dee.pdf

Fisher, D. & Frey. N. (2010). *Guided Instruction: How to develop confident and successful learners.* Alexandria, VA: ASCD.

Grant, M. (2014). *A tale of two teachers: An analytical look at the co-teaching theory using a case study model.* Retrieved from
https://files.eric.ed.gov/fulltext/ED563448.pdf

Hendron, E. (2018). *What are multiple intelligences and how do they affect learning?* Retrieved from https://www.cornerstone.edu/blogs/lifelong-learning-matters/post/what-are-multiple-intelligences-and-how-do-they-affect-learning

Klein, A. (2015). *No child left behind: An Overview.* Retrieved from
https://www.edweek.org/ew/section/multimedia/no-child-left-behind-overview-definition-summary.html

Konen, J. (2017). *6 questions to tackle in using assessment in instruction.* Retrieved from https://www.teacher.org/daily/using-assessment-instruction/

Larmer, J., Mergendoller, J., & Boss, S. (2015). *Setting the standard for project based learning: A proven approach to rigorous classroom instruction.* Alexandria, VA: ASCD

Lew, M. & Nelson, R. (2016). New teachers' challenges: How culturally responsive teaching, classroom management, & assessment literacy are intertwined. *Multicultural Education,* Spring/Summer Issue 2016, 1-13. Retrieved from http://www.caddogap.com/periodicals.shtml

Mangione, P., Osborne, T. & Mendenhall, H. (2019). What's next? How learning progressions help teachers support children's development and learning. *Young Children,* 74(3), 20-25. Retrieved from
https://search.proquest.com/openview/acc0eaa91d1da10403249b1b39051013/1?pq-origsite=gscholar&cbl=27755

Marzano, R. (2006). *Classroom assessment and grading that work.* Alexandria, VA: ASCD.

McFarland, L. (2008). Anecdotal records: Valuable tools for assessing young children's development. *Dimensions of Early Childhood,* 26(1), 31-36. Retrieved from

https://www.researchgate.net/publication/316450939_Anecdotal_records_
Valuable_tools_for_assessing_young_children's_development

McMillan, J.H. (2018). *Classroom assessment: Principles and practice that enhance student learning and motivation* (7th ed.). New York, NY: Pearson

Mertler, C.A. (2014). *Introduction to data-driven educational decision making.* Alexandria, VA: ASCD

Metcalf, T. (2019). *What's your plan? Accurate decision making within a multi-tier system of supports: Critical areas in Tier 1.* Retrieved from http://www.rtinetwork.org/essential/tieredinstruction/tier1/accurate-decision-making-within-a-multi-tier-system-of-supports-critical-areas-in-tier-1

Meyer, A., Rose, D.H., & Gordon, D. (2014). *Universal design for learning: Theory and practice.* Wakefield, MA: CAST

Moss, C. & Brookhart, S. (2009). *Advancing formative assessment in every classroom: A guide for instructional leaders.* Alexandria, VA: ASCD.

Popham, W.J. (2017). *Classroom assessment: What teachers need to know* (8th ed.). New York, NY: Pearson

Reinholz, D. (2016). The assessment cycle: a model for learning through peer assessment, *Assessment & Evaluation in Higher Education,* 41(2), 301-315. DOI: 10.1080/02602938.2015.1008982

Roell, K. (2019). *How to create a rubric in 6 steps.* Retrieved from https://www.thoughtco.com/how-to-create-a-rubric-4061367

Shepard, L.A. (2018). Learning progressions as tools for assessment and learning. *Applied Measurement in Education, 31*(2), 165-174. DOI: 10.1080/08957347.2017.1408628

Spencer, S. (2009). *Classroom testing and assessment for all students.* Thousand Oaks, CA: Corwin.

Stein, E. (2016). *Elevating co-teaching through UDL.* Wakefield, MA: CAST Professional Publishing

Sztajn, P. & Wilson, P.H. (2019). *Learning trajectories for teachers: Designing effective professional development for math instruction.* New York, NY: Teachers College Press

Taylor, J.J., Buckley K., Hamilton, L.S., Stecher, B.M., Read, L., & Schweig, J. (2018). *Choosing and using SEL competency assessments: What schools and districts need to know.* Retrieved from http://measuringsel.casel.org/pdf/Choosing-and-Using-SEL-Competency-Assessments_What-Schools-and-Districts-Need-to-Know.pdf

Terada, Y. (2018). *Multiple intelligences theory: Widely used, yet misunderstood.* Retrieved from https://www.edutopia.org/article/multiple-intelligences-theory-widely-used-yet-misunderstood

VanDerHeyden, A. (2019). *Approaches to RTI.* Retrieved from http://www.rtinetwork.org/learn/what/approaches-to-rti

Villa, R.A., Thousand, J.S., & Nevin, A.I. (2013). *A guide to co-teaching: Lessons and strategies to facilitate student learning* (3rd ed.). Thousand Oaks, CA: Corwin

White, K. (2016). *Observation and assessment: If I saw it, does it count?* Retrieved from http://allthingsassessment.info/2016/09/09/observation-and-assessment-if-i-saw-it-does-it-count/

Young, N.D., Jean, E. & Mead, A.E. (2018). *The potency of the principalship: Action-oriented leadership at the heart of school improvement.* Wilmington, DE: Vernon Press

Young, N., Mumby, M., & Rice, M. (2019). *The Special Education Toolbox: Supporting Exceptional Teachers, Students and Families.* New York, NY: Roman & Littlefield.

Chapter 7

Staying on the Same Page:
Setting Classroom Expectations

Angela C. Fain, PhD, *University of West Georgia*

Successful collaboration among general educators and special educators requires effective classroom management. Classroom management translates into the procedures and routines teachers use to systematically manage the learning environment (Korpershoek, Harms, deBoer, vanKujik, & Doolaard, 2016). Too often, however, educators assume that the general school policies and classroom rules will be enough to manage the classroom setting on their own. The inclusive classroom setting is complex, comprised of a diverse group of students with a range of academic and behavioral abilities and life experiences.

As inclusive practices have increased in schools, collaborative relationships among individuals who work with students with disabilities has become essential (Asher & Nichols, 2016; Kellems, Springer, Wilkins, & Anderson, 2016). Students with disabilities are spending more time in inclusive classrooms (U.S. Department of Education, 2014), making co-teaching practices more common than ever. Classroom disruptions and noncompliance are among the most consistently challenging and frustrating behaviors teachers report they deal with on a daily basis (Alter, Walker, & Landers, 2013). Classroom management is more important than ever with increased numbers of students with emotional and behavioral difficulties (EBD) in the general education classroom (Epstein, Atkins, Cullinan, Kutash, & Weaver, 2008).

Collaboration vs Co-Teaching

Collaboration is a term used to describe an activity a person engages in with someone else. Key characteristics of collaboration identified by Friend and Cook (2016) include:

- voluntary participation - teachers may be assigned to work together, they cannot be forced to collaborate

- equal contributions – all contributions are integral to the collaborative effort and all teachers involved in the collaborative process must feel that each individual's contributions are equal

- shared goals – teachers must believe in the goal they are working on to collaborate successfully

- shared responsibilities for key decisions – teachers should be equal partners as decision makers

- shared accountability for outcomes – as shared decision makers, teachers must share responsibility for the outcomes of their decisions

- based on shared resources – each individual should contribute some resource

- emergent – as teachers work together more, they will gain more trust and respect for each other

Co-teaching is the shared instruction of a group of students, typically in one classroom setting (Friend, 2019). Co-teaching is a commonly used service delivery model used in schools, typically occurring with a general education teacher and a special educator, when there are a number of students with disabilities in the class and their academic and behavioral needs require the proficiency of the two teachers (Friend & Cook, 2016). In a typical co-taught classroom, the general educator's knowledge of the curriculum and standards combined with the special educator's understanding of student academic and behavioral strategies and interventions work together to create a very effective learning environment that will improve the learning of all children in the general education classroom (Fitzell, 2018).

Both the general education and special education teacher need to consider and discuss how they will share the roles of the classroom to manage the classroom; this includes the physical, instructional, and non-instructional spaces within the classroom (Fitzell, 2018). The general education and special education teacher need to be open to sharing responsibilities of instruction and classroom and behavior management of all students in the large group, not just individual students (Bouck, 2007; Scruggs & Mastropieri, 2017).

Too often, special education teachers are designated to instruct and manage the smaller group of students with disabilities in the general education setting while the general education teacher takes on the responsibilities of instructing and managing the larger group of students without disabilities (Scruggs, Mastropieri & McDuffie, 2007). Research has shown that special educators tend to take a subordinate role to general educators, especially in secondary levels with higher level content (Scruggs et al., 2007; Sweigart & Landrum, 2015).

Having one subordinate teacher is not an effective co-teaching strategy and can lead to many problems in the classroom (Murawski, 2010; Sweigart & Landrum, 2015). The general education and special education teacher have to collaborate on all aspects of classroom management to include the physical organization of the classroom, classroom climate, classroom routines for academic and nonacademic activities, behavior management such as rules and procedures and reinforcements, and the use of academic and nonacademic time (Fitzell, 2018; Friend & Cook, 2016).

Managing the Physical Environment

The physical environment includes the floor plan, walls, and lighting, the placement of the furniture that defines the seating arrangements and traffic flow, and visual displays on the walls. This should include a carefully designed seating plan that is conducive to student learning and accommodates individual student learning needs (Garwood, Harris, & Tomick, 2017). Students with visual impairments, for example, may need to be seated closer to the front of the classroom, near the board so they can view the instructional materials more easily. Teachers should consider how the high traffic areas such as the trash can, the pencil sharpener, the teacher's desk, the computer station, the book bag cubbies, to name just a few items, will impact the overall flow of the classroom. A student with attention deficit hyperactivity disorder (ADHD) may need to be seated away from high traffic areas and windows (Mastropieri & Scruggs, 2018).

Teachers should consider how they will decorate their classroom. Research has shown using visual prompts in the classroom can help support students (Carr, Moore & Anderson 2014; Kenworthy, Anthony, Alexander, Werner, Cannon & Greenman, 2014). Pictures with labels can be helpful for students with limited reading skills due to age, disability, or language differences (Ness & Middleton, 2012). Teachers love to cover their walls with stuff, whether it be content-related or encouraging and motivational posters; however, it is important not to over stimulate students with too much information on the walls. Students with disabilities can become easily distracted and lose their attention when they are overstimulated (Children and Adults with Attention Deficit/Hyperactivity Disorder [CHADD], 2019).

Establishing Expectations and Routines

A vital part of classroom management is the established expectations and routines for academic and nonacademic activities. Effective classroom management occurs when teachers create clear expectations (rules) and routines (procedures) for students (Friend & Cook, 2016). Teachers should decide on and establish 4-5 classroom rules (Gable, Hester, Rock, & Hughes, 2009).

Both teachers should model the expectations and routines for the students, provide opportunities for students to practice and receive feedback, and reinforce the expectations and routines until they are mastered (Chan, Graham-Day, Ressa, Peters & Konrad, 2014; Scott, Anderson, & Alter, 2012; Vaughn, Wanzek, Murray & Roberts, 2012). Routines should be established for entering the classroom, handing in homework, passing out papers, going to the bathroom, answering questions, getting the teacher's attention, making transitions, lining up to leave the classroom, fire drills, etc.

Managing classroom expectations and behaviors can be one of the most difficult tasks for any pair of co-teachers to tackle. Teachers have to actively problem solve how to manage and meet the behavioral needs of the students in the classroom (Friend & Bursuck, 2006). While many teachers have different classroom management styles, it is essential to agree on ways to address positive and negative behaviors. Teachers need to agree on a process for providing rewards and consequences to students.

Research has shown that when students are positively reinforced for desired behaviors such as following the rules, the behavior is more likely to occur again (Scott et al., 2012; Smith, Polloway, Patton, & Dowdy, 2008). Examples of reinforcement can include behaviour-specific positive praise, stickers, grades, points, charts/graphs, extra computer time, and tokens that can be used for classroom menu or prize box items. It is essential that both teachers take responsibility and equal part in establishing and reinforcing the rules and procedures of the classroom. Teachers can use classroom misbehaviors as opportunities to reteach skills (Scott et al., 2012).

Evidence-Based Strategies

All students benefit from the routines of good classroom management; however, students with disabilities may need specific classroom management strategies. Research has shown that when inclusive schools participate in successful collaboration, all students, including those with disabilities, demonstrate improved outcomes (Olson, Leko, & Roberts, 2016; Walsh, 2012). When classroom management is effective, students demonstrate improved achievement (Freiberg, Huzinec, & Templeton, 2009), higher rates of on-task behavior and lower disruptions (Lewis, Hudson, Richter, & Johnson, 2004). More importantly, when evidence-based classroom management strategies are used effectively in the classroom, students demonstrate higher engagement and achievement (Dunlap et al. 2010; Simonsen, Fairbanks, Briesch, Myers, & Sugai, 2008). Simonsen et al. (2008) described five "empirically-supported, critical features of classroom management" (p. 353) to include

1) Maximizing classroom structure and predictability – direct instruction, physical arrangement that minimizes distraction and crowding

2) Post, teach, review, monitor, and reinforce expectations – explicitly teach classwide/schoolwide expectations across settings, active supervision

3) Actively engage students in observable ways – provide varied opportunities for students to respond (OTRs), response cards,

4) Use a continuum of strategies to acknowledge appropriate behavior – positive behaviour-specific praise, classwide group contingencies, behavioral contracting, token economies

5) Use a continuum of strategies to respond to inappropriate behavior – error correction, performance feedback, planned ignoring, differential reinforcement, response cost, time-out from reinforcement

Providing Reinforcement

It is important for co-teachers to decide on a process for providing rewards and consequences to students. Inappropriate classroom behaviors that interfere with instruction and learning, impede social interactions with teacher and students, or endanger others are considered conduct problems (Mather, Goldstein, & Meyer, 2015). Talking out, not following directions, being out of one's seat, verbal aggression, and physical aggression are examples of inappropriate classroom behaviors. Study skill problems are considered behaviors that interfere with academic performance and progress and examples include failure to follow directions, failure to complete assignments, not paying attention, and poor time management (Mather et al., 2015).

In recent years, more attention has been placed on providing behavioral support to students who exhibit inappropriate classroom behaviors. Using this approach, emphasis is placed on ways the instructional environment can be manipulated to support, encourage, and develop appropriate behaviors (Simonsen & Myers, 2015). Teachers should focus on readjusting the physical environment, teaching replacement behaviors, and manipulating consequences to reduce or eliminate the unwanted behaviors.

It is important to remember that a behavior followed by a reinforcer is more likely to occur again (Simonsen & Myers, 2015). A student who receives teacher attention for raising their hand is likely to repeat this action the next time they would like the teacher to acknowledge them. This is an example of positive reinforcement. A student who turns in their homework to stop getting nagged by their teacher and parents is being negatively reinforced. The behavior is being followed by the removal of an unpleasant condition. Reinforcement is most effective when it is clearly associated with a specific behavior and presented immediately following the behavior (Simonsen & Myers, 2015).

Extinction is the removal of a reinforcer that has been accompanying a behavior in the past; for example, if a teacher is attending to a student who keeps calling out in class, the teacher should consider ignoring the student when they call out until they raise their hand. A punishment or consequence occurs when an aversive (unpleasant) event follows a behavior and might include verbal reprimands, points, time-out, and response cost. In time-out, a student is removed from an event that is reinforcing. Response cost is the loss of earned privileges (Webster, 2019).

Managing the Classroom Climate

The classroom climate is the tone, or climate, of the classroom. The classroom climate and the teacher's classroom management practices directly impact students' probability of achievement (Gage, Scott, Hirn, & MacSuga-Gage, 2018). Research shows a positive relation between teachers who implement higher rates of classroom management practices such as feedback and OTRs and higher rates of student engagement (Gage et al., 2018).

When co-teachers are able to work together and seamlessly teach and manage the classroom together, opportunities are created such as instructional and personal freedom, new role opportunities, and more support (Bouck, 2007). If one teacher is absent, for example, instruction can continue with minimal interruption. In addition, teachers can learn to accomplish more working together and assume different roles within the classroom.

Final Thoughts

Co-teachers will need to negotiate their roles as they plan together and work through situations in the classroom. When co-teachers disagree about behavior management, it is important to use effective communication strategies to discuss the issues (Scruggs & Mastropieri, 2017). Teachers should look for common ground and find ways to compromise and ensure that the needs of the student come first. Using formative assessments and data can be helpful when making decisions regarding discipline and individual student behavior plans (Scruggs & Mastropieri, 2017). Teachers should also use research-based strategies that support positive behavior changes, such as classroom and school-wide behavior management strategies.

Points to Remember

- *Classroom management refers to the procedures and routines teachers use to systematically manage the learning environment. The inclusive classroom setting is complex and comprised of a diverse group of students with a range of academic and behavioral abilities and life experiences.*

- *When inclusive schools participate in successful collaboration, all students, including those with disabilities, demonstrate improved outcomes. Likewise, when evidence-based classroom management strategies are used effectively in the classroom students demonstrate higher engagement and achievement.*

- *Co-teachers have to actively problem solve how to manage and meet the behavioral needs of the students in the classroom.*

- *Evidence-based classroom management strategies include direct instruction, explicit instruction, OTRs, response cards, planned ignoring, behavior specific positive praise, classwide group contingencies, time out from reinforcement, and many others.*

- *In recent years, more attention has been placed on providing behavioral support to students who exhibit inappropriate classroom behaviors. Using this approach, emphasis is placed on ways the instructional environment can be manipulated to support, encourage, and develop appropriate behaviors.*

- *Co-teachers will need to negotiate their roles as they plan together and work through situations in the classroom. When co-teachers disagree about behavior management, it is important to use effective communication strategies to discuss the issues.*

References

Alter, P., Walker, J. N., & Landers, E. (2013). Teachers' perceptions of students' challenging behavior and the impact of teacher demographics. *Education and Treatment of Children, 36,* 51–69. doi: 10.1353/etc.2013.0040

Asher, A. & Nichols, J. D. (2016). Collaboration around facilitation emergent literacy: Role of occupational therapy. *Journal of Occupational Therapy, Schools, & Early Intervention, 9*(1), 51-73. DOI: 10.1080/19411243.2016.1156415

Bouck, E. C. (2007). Co-teaching...not just a textbook term: Implications for practice. *Preventing School Failure, 51*(2), 46-51. DOI: 10.3200/PSFL.51.2.46-51

Carr, M. E., Moore, D. W., & Anderson, A. (2014). Self-management interventions with students with autism: A meta-analysis of single-subject research. *Exceptional Children, 81,* 28–44. DOI: 10.1177/0014402914532235

Chan, P. E., Graham-Day, K. J., Ressa, V. A., Peters, M. T., & Konrad, M. (2014). Beyond involvement: Promoting student ownership of learning in classrooms. *Intervention in School and Clinic, 50,* 105–113. DOI: 10.1177/1053451214536039

Children and Adults with Attention Deficit/Hyperactivity Disorder [CHADD]. (2019). *Classroom accommodations.* Retrieved from https://chadd.org/for-educators/classroom-accommodations/

Dunlap, G., Iovannone, R., Wilson, K., Kincaid, D., Christiansen, K., Strain, P., & English, C. (2010). *Prevent-Teach-Reinforce: The school-based model of individualized positive behavior support.* Baltimore, MD: Brookes.

Epstein, M., Atkins, M., Cullinan, D., Kutash, K. & Weaver, R. (2008). *Reducing behavior problems in the elementary school classroom. An IES practice guide.* Washington, DC: Institute of Education Sciences. Retrieved from https://ies.ed.gov/ncee/wwc/Docs/PracticeGuide/behavior_pg_092308.pdf

Fitzell, S.G. (2018). *Best practices in co-teaching & collaboration: The HOW of co-teaching – implementing the models.* Manchester, NH: Cogent Catalyst Press

Freiberg, H. J., Huzinec, C. A., & Templeton, S. M. (2009). Classroom management—A pathway to student achievement: A study of fourteen inner-city elementary schools. *Elementary School Journal, 110,* 63–80. DOI: 10.1086/598843

Friend, M. (2019). *Co-Teach! Building and sustaining classroom partnerships in inclusive schools* (3rd ed.) Greensboro, NC: Marilyn Friend, Inc.

Friend, M., & Bursuck, W. D. (2006). Including students with special needs: A practical guide for classroom teachers. Boston, MA: Pearson, Allyn, and Bacon.

Friend, M. & Cook, L. (2016). *Interactions: Collaboration skills for school professionals* (8th ed.) Upper Saddle River, NJ: Pearson.

Gable, R. A., Hester, P. H., Rock, M. L., & Hughes, K. G. (2009). Back to basics: Rules, praise, ignoring, and reprimands revisited. *Intervention in School and Clinic, 44*(4), 195-205.

DOI: 10.1177/1053451208328831

Gage, N. A., Scott, T., Hirn, R., & MacSuga-Gage, A. S. (2018). The relationship between teachers' implementation of classroom management practices and student behavior in elementary school. *Behavioral Disorders, 43*(2), 302.

DOI: 10.1177/0198742917714809

Garwood, J. K., Harris, J. D., & Tomick, J. (2017). Starting at the beginning: An intuitive choice for classroom management. *Teacher Education and Practice, 30(1),* 77-97.

Retrieved from https://www.researchgate.net/publication/316982528_Starting_at_the_Beginning_An_Intuitive_Choice_for_Classroom_Management

Kellems, R. O., Springer, B., Wilkins, M. K. & Anderson, C. (2016). Collaboration in transition assessment: School psychologists and special educators working together to improve outcomes for students with disabilities. *Preventing School Failure, 60,* 215-221.

DOI: 10.1080/1045988X.2015.1075465

Kenworthy, L., Anthony, L. G., Alexander, K. C., Werner, M. A., Cannon, L. M., & Greenman, L. (2014). *Solving executive function challenges: Simple ways to get kids with autism unstuck and on target.* Baltimore, MD: Paul H. Brookes.

Korpershoek, H., Harms, T., deBoer, H., van Kujik, M., & Doolaard, S. (2016). A Meta-analysis of the effective classroom management strategies and classroom management programs for educational practice: A meta-analysis of the effects of classroom management strategies and classroom management programs on students' academic, behavioral, emotional, and motivational outcomes. DOI: 10.3102/0034654315626799

Lewis, T. J., Hudson, S., Richter, M., & Johnson, N. (2004). Scientifically supported practices in emotional and behavioral disorders: A proposed approach and brief review of current practices. *Behavioral Disorders, 29*, 247–259. DOI: 10.1177/019874290402900306

Mastropieri, M.A. & Scruggs, T.E. (2018). *The inclusive classroom: Strategies for effective differentiated instruction* (6th ed.). New York, NY: Pearson

Mather, N., Goldstein, S. & Meyer, L. (2015). Understanding and managing challenging behaviors. In N. Mather & S. Goldstein, *Learning Disabilities and Challenging Behaviors: Using the Building Blocks to Guide Intervention and Classroom Management* (3rd ed.), (pp. 123-154). Baltimore, MD: Brookes Publishing

Ness, B. M., & Middleton, M. J. (2012). A framework for implementing individualized self-regulated learning strategies in the classroom. *Intervention in School and Clinic, 47*, 267–275. DOI: 10.1177/1053451211430120

Olson, A., Leko, M. M., & Roberts, C. A. (2016). Providing students with severe disabilities access to the general education curriculum. *Research and Practice for Persons with Severe Disabilities, 41*, 143-157. DOI: 10.1177/1540796916651975

Scott, T. M., Anderson, C. M., & Alter, P. (2012). *Managing classroom behavior using positive behavior supports.* Boston, MA: Pearson.

Scruggs, T. E. & Mastropieri, M. A. (2017). Making inclusion work with co-teaching. *Teaching Exceptional Children, 49*(4), 284-293. DOI: 10.1177/0040059916685065

Scruggs, T. E., Mastropieri, M. A., & McDuffie, K. A. (2007). Co-teaching in inclusive classrooms: A meta-synthesis of qualitative research. *Exceptional Children, 73*, 392–416. DOI: 10.1177/001440290707300401

Simonsen, B., Fairbanks, S., Briesch, A., Myers, D., & Sugai, G. (2008). Evidence-based practices in classroom management: Considerations for research to practice. *Education and Treatment for Children, 31*, 351–380. doi:10.1353/etc.0.0007

Simonsen, B. & Myers, D. (2015). *Classwide positive behavior interventions and supports: A guide to proactive classroom management.* New York, NY: Guilford Press.

Smith, T. E. C., Polloway, E. A., Patton, J. R., & Dowdy, C. A. (2008). *Teaching students with special needs in inclusive settings* (5th ed.) Boston, MA: Pearson/Allyn & Bacon.

Sweigart, C. A., & Landrum, T. J. (2015). The impact of number of adults on instruction: Implications for co-teaching. *Preventing School Failure, 59*(1), 22. DOI;10.1080/1045988X.2014.919139

U.S. Department of Education. (2014). *Thirty-sixth annual report to Congress on the implementation of the Individuals with Disabilities Education Act,*

2014. Washington, DC: Author. Retrieved from http://www.ed.gov/about/reports/annual/osep

Vaughn, S., Wanzek, J., Murray, C. S., & Roberts, G. (2012). *Intensive interventions for students struggling in reading and mathematics: A practice guide.* Portsmouth, NH: RMC Research Corporation, Center on Instruction.

Walsh, J. M. (2012). Co-teaching as a school system strategy for continuous improvement. *Preventing School Failure, 56*(1), 29-36. DOI: 10.1080/1045988X.2011.555792

Webster, J. (2019). *How response cost is used in school behavior management.* Retrieved from https://www.thoughtco.com/response-cost-in-behavior-management-3110361

Chapter 8

Co-Teaching in the Arena of
Social and Emotional Learning

Elizabeth J. Bienia, EdD, *Endicott College*
Nicholas D. Young, PhD, EdD, *American International College*
Gena M. Rotas, M.A., M.S.W., LICSW

Teaching is a craft. Like a craftsman, the teacher is continually learning skills, perfecting mastery and developing competence through their craft. Many professionals look for and find unique ways to explore the art of teaching by using their imagination, creativity, new strategies and skills, and exciting and motivating ideas that will foster growth and stimulation in the classroom (Boyd, 2019). Like an artist, who is working to idealize their vision and passion, the teacher is developing competence in planning the curriculum and executing lessons with care and purpose while maintaining a personal integrity that reflects ethical intentions. A passionate teacher who is in touch with delivering optimal opportunities for children to learn has a significant influence on the students' ability to flourish in the classroom and thrive in life (Jean & Rotas, 2019; Young, Jean & Citro, 2018; Young, Jean & Citro, 2019).

For someone who is eager to learn a craft, there might be a period of apprenticeship with a master carpenter, a seasoned potter, a talented glass blower, or a unique quilter in order to build the confidence and competence to venture out on their own. A talented and effective teacher seeks out a mentor to impart learning and the expertise it takes to continually perfect the art of teaching (Young, Jean & Citro, 2018). Teacher trainings often leave teachers wanting more in terms of being able to manage the classroom dynamics or how to best build relationships with their students. Teachers are expected to learn the skills of communication, relationship building, empathy, compassion, goal setting, group dynamics, and patience, all while trying to meet the demands of curriculum, assessments, evaluations and parents (Minahan, 2012). Co-teaching addresses the importance of having another craftsman in the classroom to support the personal and professional development of both teachers; therefore, they may be able to deliver a cooperative experience of the highest quality (Barshay, 2018).

In education today, we know that our most valued resources for learning are the educators who work directly with students. Education is all about relationships (Sparks, 2019). Children certainly remember who taught them and regardless if students perceive those educators as positive or negative, interpersonal relationships impact learning, self-esteem, self-worth and lifelong dreams. Building relationships is the thread that ties together the craft of teaching to the canvas of the classroom (Boyd, 2019). If the relationship between teacher and child is fundamental to success, then the relationship between co-teachers is vital to the harmony and productivity of the classroom.

In today's classroom, there is a different profile forming the picture of what it looks like to be in charge of a group of children who want to learn. The movement towards co-teaching in an environment that supports social and emotional learning gives education a powerful new perspective. Teachers enter the profession with enthusiasm, commitment and determination to make a significant difference in the lives of the children they work with (Austin, 2018). Unfortunately, this often transforms into a wave of teacher stress, burnout, attrition, discontent, compassion fatigue, resentment, confusion and abandonment of the passion that ignited careers (Austin, 2018; Berdik, 2019; Carr, 2018). By learning to address the stress and emotional struggles in their personal lives, teachers will find relief, hope, inspiration and a renewed enthusiasm to re-ignite and reboot their commitment to education (Austin, 2018).

In order to deliver a curriculum steeped in social and emotional learning, the teacher must be willing to consider the core competencies for their own growth and development (Jagers, Rivas-Drake, & Borowski, 2018). Social and emotional learning (SEL) is an undertaking of knowledge, attitudes, skills and strategies which help children and adults understand and manage their emotions (Jagers et al., 2018). With the guidance of social and emotional learning, adults and children learn the skills of positive goal setting, cultivating and displaying empathy for themselves and others, developing and sustaining healthy relationships and orchestrating responsible decision making (Gunn, 2018).

A primary consideration in this education of self includes self-awareness and self-management, which means learning the skills of self-care and emotional balance (Proulx & Schulten, 2019). Social awareness is another consideration, which refers to the ability to relate to others, especially the children in the classroom (Proulx & Schulten, 2019). If the relationship between child and teacher is critical, then the relationship between co-teachers is paramount.

Children learn by watching the adults in their world. Teachers model and practice the skills it takes to develop positive, meaningful, genuine, empathetic, sincere and productive interactions between adults in the classroom and with the children (Jean & Rotas, 2019). All of the efforts to promote social and emotional learning are designed to demonstrate compassion, understanding, acceptance and patience with others; thus, providing an environment in which children flourish (McLanahan et al., 2017). Research also reinforces the fact that teachers thrive personally when they engage in positive relationships with their students and their co-teachers (Austin, 2018; Sparks, 2019). Meaningful relationships foster a new sense of joy rather than anxiety in the classroom, all of which support learning (Sparks, 2019).

Social and Emotional Learning

There are many and varied ways to deliver a curriculum steeped in social and emotional learning (Durlak, Domitrovich, Weissberg, & Gullotta, 2015). Given the individuation in teachers, children and classrooms, a core competency has underscored the profession in an attempt to give some sense of consistence to the movement (Durlak et al., 2105). The social and emotional core competencies include, but are not limited to, self-awareness, self-management, social awareness, relationship skills, responsible decision making (Irving, 2018).

Awareness is a skill that is modeled and taught on an ongoing basis (Booth, 2017). Social and emotional learning is the space between each breath. When you pay attention to your own breathing, you notice there is a space between the in-breath and the out-breath (Hanh, 2017). Rarely do you even think about the flow of your breathing, it flows on its own. That breathing routine happens over and over throughout a lifetime. The space between breaths keeps the mechanism flowing similarly, social and emotional awareness fosters learning and relationships towards fluid and flowing connections (Hanh, 2017). Social and emotional learning addresses the stress that many teachers endure and offers skills and strategies to manage emotions, cope with that stress and build resiliency to continue to bounce back in the face of challenging circumstances (Berdik, 2019).

Layers of support and research indicate a growing movement towards an educational environment that addresses and supports the social and emotional needs of the children as well as the faculty enmeshed in the classrooms of today (DePaoli, Atwell & Bridgeland, 2017). There is valid consensus in the research that children deserve the foundational learning in social and emotional well-being and self-care, in order to thrive and flourish in life (Irving, 2018; Proulx & Schulten, 2019). New research continually validates the strengths of an individual who has had training, skills and practice in social and emotional learning.

Students who spend time learning about their emotional intelligence perform better academically, can cultivate improved and positive attitudes and behaviors, have the ability to build cooperative relationships with peers and adults, and can manage the landscape of their emotional lives with greater ease

(Brotto, 2018). Without being equipped emotionally and socially to navigate the tumultuous storms of inter-personal, intra-personal, inter-dependent and global relationships, our young people of today will be ineffective as the adults of tomorrow (Brotto, 2018).

Current educators, students, and families are witness to the reality of how social and emotional learning can transform a classroom into a powerful field for practicing the skills towards effective, efficient and significant learning (Brotto, 2018). Teachers who embrace social and emotional learning benefit as the children learn new ways to connect with each other, the adults who support them, and the school community (Pelligrino, 2018). These newly learned skills filter down into family life as well (Pelligrino, 2018). When social and emotional learning is the base for instruction so that children feel safe, cared for, comfortable while participating and free of unnecessary stress and pressure, everyone benefits. The results show that academic performance improves, while behavioral challenges diminish (Brotto, 2018; Pelligrino, 2018). Attitudes on the part of teachers and children reflect a growth mindset, peer relationships are enhanced, and everyone feels a deeper connection to the mission of school (Jean & Rotas, 2019). Most significantly, emotional concerns such as depression, anxiety, stress and social withdrawal are gently and tenderly reduced (Brotto, 2018; Frezza, 2018).

Co-Teaching is Like a Marriage

Co-teaching is first a proposal and then a marriage between two teachers. The intention of the union is to create a nurturing environment similar to the structure of a family. The emotional health of the family depends on the ability of the parents to be respectful of each other and aware that the children are watching (Taylor, 2016). The parents display and model positive behavior towards each other and encourage cooperation in their family (Murawski, 2017). A healthy and emotionally stable family takes into consideration the social and emotional needs of each member.

Like a marriage, co-teaching demands that the relationship between the adults be addressed first before establishing the learning environment. Co-teaching is not meant to be an arranged marriage where two individuals have no time and space to get to know each other (Taylor, 2016). Co-teaching will not work well if the teachers are expected, assigned or told to work together. Teachers who are assigned to work together and have not established a solid, compassionate, genuine and productive relationship, are in danger of setting everyone up for a difficult and risky experience (Taylor, 2016).

Co-teaching functions best when each individual teacher finds their own rhythm, identifies a personal style, and knows their own strengths and challenges before committing to the co-teaching classroom (Murawski, 2017). It is critical that administrators think seriously about providing adequate professional development. If offering a co-teaching arrangement between consenting parties, there needs to be time for scheduling, planning, debriefing on a regular basis with supportive feedback (Murawski, 2017). When it comes to assessments for teachers and children, an administrative team and a mentor need to be available for on-going coaching, constructive direction and encouraging feedback to ensure continued growth for children and teachers. (Murawski, 2017).

Building on the wisdom in the field of education, learning from colleagues who have successfully navigated a classroom with a co-teaching model is a powerful beginning for growth.

The first step in co-teaching is to build a relationship based on trust, respect, confidence, empathy and compassion (Carson, 2011; Kudo & Hartley, 2017). It is vital that each half of the teaching team gets to know the other and takes the time to understand what makes each an individual who is passionate about teaching (Carson, 2011).

Each educator must be aware of their own emotional landscape and determine the skills and strategies they need to employ to manage their own emotional well-being. When emotions are stormy, energized by frustration, anger, resentment or even sadness and shame, rational and reasonable thinking becomes foggy (Carson, 2011). Co-teachers who learn to employ stress-reducing strategies as simple as taking a few deep breaths positively impact the outcome of a challenging exchange.

Educators who can come back to a neutral state of being, keep communication moving forward and rather than trying to find blame, work together and constructively to problem solve (Samuels, 2015). The same is true for the students served by this twosome; therefore, helping children to bring themselves back to a neutral thinking space is a significant part of social and emotional learning. The benefits for the students, the classroom and the community are long-lasting.

There is a great deal of work involved prior to the delivery of the curriculum to students who will see, feel and identify the cultivation of trust you have built as a co-teaching team. The mutual respect you demonstrate and the caring for positive interactions will create a firm foundation for a sense of safety and support for new learning (Blackley, 2019). By building a trusting relationship as a team, co-teachers model the impact that social and emotional learning has on everyone. When teachers model trusting relationships between the adults in the room, students learn to develop trusting relationships with their teachers and their peers (Miller, 2019).

Attachment theory supports success in the classroom and in learning (McLeod, 2017). Fostering teacher-student relationships that are secure, trustworthy, safe, wrapped in mutual respect and an ongoing sense of connection are key to any well-run classroom. Making it comfortable and easy for students to seek help, advice and support as well as moments of condolence and tenderness support SEL and co-teaching simultaneously (Carson, 2011; Irving, 2018).

Strong, secure and authentic attachments to caring adults is a long-term, influential component in a child's life. The educators in a co-teaching relationship must first demonstrate a supportive and trusting relationship with each other, in order for students to establish the similar trusting relationship with teachers, equally (Bergin, 2009). Emotional and social regulation is critical to helping children establish behaviors that will nourish and support success in their lives.

The modeling of warmth, sensitivity and regulations of emotions between co-teachers leads to great benefits for the students watching (Bergin, 2009). Children learn what they see, not always what they hear. The young developing nervous system of children is constantly attuned to the non-verbal energies and nuances that take place between the adults in their experience (Shrier, 2014). Teachers who are talented in reading body clues, facial nuances, emotional energy and even moments that could cause stress for the student must be prepared to bring themselves back to a neutral position and offer guidance for others struggling through challenging emotions.

Co-Teaching Through the Lens of Social and Emotional Learning

Once co-teachers have established their personal relationship, the delivery of classroom cooperation and inspiration has the firm foundation needed to build an environment that demonstrates safety, understanding, acceptance, compassion, kindness, excitement for learning, joy and even fun (Slavin, 2014). The sense of safety becomes the powerful component for students who are struggling with past traumas, unsettling negative experiences due to their mental, physical and emotional challenges, fragile self-esteem, uncertain apprehension of schooling, confusing past history of abuse, uncertain feelings of acceptance and many other burdens children carry in their backpack of emotional struggles (Berdik, 2019; Minahan, 2019) Perhaps the co-teaching team will consider writing down the strategies and skills that will actually enhance a classroom steeped in emotional and social support (Minahan, 2019; Zakrzewaki, 2014).

The team might answer the following questions after genuine and authentic conversation:

- How do you talk to a child who is defiant and resistant to following directions?

- Where do you sit when confronting a child who has misbehaved and broken a rule or hurt someone?

- When do you offer advice, condolence, a listening ear or a soft smile?

- Why are nonverbal interactions more helpful with certain children?

- What are the nonverbal skills which ease the difficult interactions in stressful situations?

- Are you both aware of which children become easily upset?

- Can you both offer preventive measures to maintain order and safety for everyone?

- Do you have written plans to meet the social and emotional demands that are rarely addressed in the curriculum?

These are just some of the thoughts, concerns, issues, strategies and actions that need to be discussed, planned, written and referred to on a regular basis. With administrative support and enough time, co-teachers will be able to have the difficult and time-consuming conversations that will enhance learning for everyone (Minahan, 2019).

A math teacher is continually reinforcing their knowledge and skills in mathematics. The same holds true for a teacher who is willing to incorporate social and emotional learning into their teaching as they are committed to doing homework and improving their emotional and social skills for well-being (Lang, 2019). When teachers take care of themselves and demonstrate self-care and what it looks like in the classroom, their students learn to do the same. Collectively, everyone finds it easier to feel connected, cared for, safe, calm, cooperative and more comfortable sharing feelings and challenges (Nankin & Fenchel, 2019). Self-awareness, self-management, social awareness, relationships and responsible decision-making are the cornerstones for SEL and it all begins with teachers who are willing to address their own social and emotional well-being (Minihan, 2019).

Social and emotional learning starts with self-awareness. Co-teachers should consider incorporating mindfulness skills and stress reduction techniques into the schedule to address the needs of both adults and students (Graybiel, 2014). Practicing gratitude and kindness to help manage attitudes of hope, bolster self-esteem, identify positive thinking, and regulate the emotional landscape of being in the world help to keep the classroom calm (Minihan, 2019). Using language that reminds everyone to be caring, kind, encouraging, accepting and patient is another useful tool (Nankin & Fenchel, 2019). The skills of social and emotional learning deserve a place woven throughout the day and repetition of those skills ensures that good habits form and bad habits diminish (Graybiel, 2014).

Start at the beginning and explore your wishes, hopes and dreams as well as your fears, challenges and struggles (Yoder & Gurke, 2017). Having on-going conversations, open communication and relentless re-evaluations of what is happening between the teachers and the children is exactly what co-teaching demands (Stuart, 2018). Gunn (2018) offers the following questions to begin the difficult conversations that must occur if co-teaching is to be successful

- What does it take to build a classroom around social and emotional learning in a co-teaching arrangement?
- How do two individuals make an agreement to present a unified front when working with children?
- When does it make sense to join forces and insist that together the teaching team is better than being an island?
- Why would two teachers even want to consider co-teaching when it is difficult enough to manage one's own individual ambitions in the world of education?
- Who does the decision making?
- Who manages the discipline?
- Who delivers the content?
- Who keeps an eye on the children?
- Who assesses the learning?
- Who knows what happens next?
- Who picks up the pieces when something goes wrong?
- Who carries the belief that co-teaching will make a difference in the lives of the children and in the lives of the teachers?

Final Thoughts

It is necessary for each teacher to work individually on their co-teaching relationship - first building a trusting connection based on mutual respect and compassionate non-judgment. Educators who build a tender rapport with each other and get to know each other build a strong foundation and partnership. Co-teachers should commit to a 'tell-all attitude' that leads to the establishment of an environment of trust, acceptance, and harmony for both adults and students. Misunderstandings will happen; however, a strong commitment to patience, respect and problem solving will support all efforts to maintain a healthy and productive relationship.

When co-teachers talk openly about their preferred teaching and learning style(s) it helps to build a foundation of acceptance, tolerance, flexibility and curiosity towards each other. Asking questions such as 'What do you love doing?' 'How do you address misbehavior?' and 'What do you do when you are thrown off center?' will help to establish common ground and communication. As each half of the co-teaching pair finds ways to complement and encourage the other, planning and lesson implementation, as well as student contact and behavior management become more fluid (Yoder, & Gurke, 2017).

Co-teachers must be willing to explore their own strengths and weaknesses as a means to finding balance between two different personalities and supporting the other member of the team; thus, providing an experience steeped in growth and understanding. Each member of the pair must agree to share everything they know about the students in their care. Each educator might have specific goals and objectives for different students; however, together they know what is happening all the time and can see the long-term goals clearly.

Action makes things happen; therefore, formulating clear action plans that support the smooth flow in the classroom is necessary. Co-teachers should consider developing time for scheduling, discussing behaviors, how to deliver consequences, which assessments are relevant, what skills and strategies to use to reduce stress for everyone, and how to work to present a united front when making contact with parents and caregivers (Nankin, & Fenchel, 2019).

Co-teachers should make working together a collaborative experience rather than a competitive one. It is vital for the teaching pair to be aware of language, intonation, and use of supportive comments as a team to make things happen. The classroom becomes 'our classroom,' the children become 'our children,' and the lessons become 'our lessons.' Like the metaphor of a family, co-teachers want to appear as a unified team, with everyone in the same boat (Minahan, 2019)

Co-teachers are building a trusting relationship and have each other's back, making it somewhat safer to take risks to learn and grow as a professional. Realizing that they are not alone in the classroom and perhaps for the first time ever in their career, gives each half of the teaching pair a safety net and allows them to enjoy some of the original passion that catapulted them into the profession in the first place. This safety net also provides trust and flexibility by supporting the other member of the co-teaching team. Together, each member is learning to bend and be flexible as well as finding ways to bring motivation and excitement back into the lives of the students they serve.

Emotionally, it is vital that each member fills their bucket, takes care of themselves and depends on the other member for reminders about how to find and hold on to the elusive life-work balance. It is important to enrich personal well-being through a sharing of values, an individual's love and motivation for teaching, and why each member works so hard to mold and teach the students in their care (Berdik, 2019; Miller, 2019). Co-teaching, when planned and executed with intention has the ability to bring joy to the life of each educator; thereby showing students that life and learning can and should be fun and that cooperative teaching and learning is possible and profitable (Marston, 2018; Murawski, 2017; Blackley, 2019).

Points to Remember

- *There is an art to the craft of teaching, and especially co-teaching. Professionals are continually perfecting their skills in order to deliver a classroom and teaching that supports the success of children.*

- *On the job training for new teachers demands an understanding of what it takes to build positive relationships with children and coworkers.*

- *Co-teaching in the environment of social and emotional learning has stepped into the forefront of classroom design. Creating a co-teaching team can help reduce the strain and stress of the emotional demands in the dynamics of the classroom.*

- *Emotional and social awareness supports the relationship between co-teachers and children. Core competencies of social and emotional learning (SEL) include self-awareness, self-management, social awareness, relationship skills, and responsible decision making.*

- *Co-teaching is like a well-balanced marriage. Children learn what they see. Working together as equal partners to establish a co-teaching classroom takes great effort but offers great rewards.*

- *The relationships between co-teachers and students are critical to classroom and academic success.*

- *Educators should ask questions and consider guidelines to help develop an action plan that benefits everyone involved.*

References

Austin, V. (2018). Fostering growth in the classroom: culture and supports that make a difference. In N.D. Young, E. Jean, & T. Citro. *From Head to Heart: High quality teaching practices in the spotlight.* (pp. 147-164). Wilmington, DE: Vernon Press

Barshay, J., (2018). *The Hechinger Report: Two studies point to the power of teacher-student relationships to boost learning.* Retrieved from https://hechingerreport.org/two-studies-point-to-the-power-of-teacher-student-relationships-to-boost-learning/

Berdik, C. (2019). *The Hechinger Report: Future of learning: Fighting teacher stress.* Retrieved from https://hechingerreport.org/fighting-teacher-stress/

Bergin, C. & Bergin, D. (2009). Attachment in the classroom. *Educational Psychology in Review, (2009)*21, 141-170. DOI: 10.1007/s10648-00991040

Blackley, A., (2019). *8 Things Successful Co-Teachers Do: Co-teachers who take risks together, grow together.* Retrieved from https://www.weareteahers.com/co-teahing-tip/

Booth, R. (2017). *Master of mindfulness, Jon Kabat-Zinn: 'People are losing their minds, that is what we need to wake up to'.* Retrieved from https://www.theguardian.com/lifeandstyle/2017/oct/22/mindfulness-jon-kabat-zinn-depression-trump-grenfell

Boyd, M., (2019). Incorporating SEL as a new teacher. *Edutopia.* Retrieved from https://www.edutopia.org/article/incorporating-sel-new-teacher

Brotto, G. (2018). *The future of education depends on social emotional learning: Here's why.* Retrieved from https://www.edsurge.com/news/2018-06-04-the-future-of-education-depends-on-social-emotional-learning-here-s-why

Carr, T.A. (2018). *Joy in teaching: Building resilience, fight burnout, reclaim the joy.* Mount Vernon, IO: Throw Out the Box Publishers

Carson, D.S. (2011). *Understanding teacher's experiences in co-taught classrooms.* Retrieved from https://pdfs.semanticscholar.org/2d35/c8a777eb3842e20e1ba34ae2327470ee7620.pdf

DePaoli, J., Atwell, M., & Bridgeland J. (2017). *Ready to lead: A national principal survey on how social and emotional learning can prepare children and transform school.* Retrieved from https://files.eric.ed.gov/fulltext/ED579088.pdf

Durlak, J., Domitrovich, C., Weissberg, R., & Gullotta, T. (2015). *Handbook of Social and Emotional Learning: Research and Practice.* New York, NY: The Guildford Press

Frezza, D. (2018). *Four reasons why students - and teachers - need SEL embedded into school all day, every day.* Retrieved from https://www.edsurge.com/news/2018-09-04-four-reasons-why-students-and-teachers-need-sel-embedded-into-school-all-day-every-day

Graybiel, A. (2009). Habits, Rituals, and the Evaluative Brain. *Annual Review of Neuroscience 31*(1), 359-837. DOI: 10.1146/annurev.neuro.29.051605.112851

Gunn, J., (2018). *Bringing Social Emotional Learning into the Classroom.* Retrieved from https://education.cu-portland.edu/blog/classroom-resources/sel-content-classroom/

Hanh, T.N. (2017). *Thich Nhat Hanh on the practice of mindfulness.* Retrieved from https://www.lionsroar.com/mindful-living-thich-nhat-hanh-on-the-practice-of-mindfulness-march-2010/

Irving, D. (2018). *Social and emotional learning prepares students for life.* Retrieved from https://www.rand.org/blog/rand-review/2018/08/social-and-emotional-learning-prepares-students-for.html

Jagers, R.J., Rivas-Drake, D. & Borowski, T. (2018). *Equity & social and emotional learning: A cultural analysis.* Retrieved from https://measuringsel.casel.org/wp-content/uploads/2018/11/Frameworks-Equity.pdf

Jean, E. & Rotas, G. (2019). Fostering growth in the classroom: culture and supports that make a difference. In N.D. Young, E. Jean, & T. Citro. *Empathic teaching: Promoting social justice in the contemporary classroom* (pp. 13-30). Wilmington, DE: Vernon Press

Kudo, I. & Hartley, J. (2017). *Teaching (with) empathy and compassion in schools.* Retrieved from http://blogs.worldbank.org/education/teaching-empathy-and-compassion-schools

Lang, R.R. (2019). *Addressing teacher's social and emotional learning is key to comprehensive SEL implementation.* Retrieved from http://www.nasbe.org/press-releases/addressing-teachers-social-and-emotional-learning-is-key-to-comprehensive-sel-implementation/

Marston, N. (2018). *6 steps to successful co-teaching: Helping special and regular education teachers work together.* Retrieved from https://www.nea.org/tools/6-steps-to-successful-co-teaching.html

McLanahan, S., Currie, J.M., Haskins, R., Kearney, M., Rouse, C.E., & Sawhill I. (2017). Social and emotional learning. *The Future of Children: A Collaboration of the Woodrow Wilson School of Public and International Affairs at Princeton University and the Brookings Institution.* Retrieved from www.futureofchilden.org

McLeod, S. (2017). Attachment Theory. *Simple Psychology.* Retrieved from https://www.simplypsychology.org/attachment.html

Miller, K., (2019). *Top 11 benefits of self-awareness according to science.* Retrieved from https://positivepsychology.com/benefits-of-self-awareness/

Minahan, J. (2012). *Gap in teacher training.* Retrieved from https://www.huffpost.com/entry/gap-in-teacher-training_b_1452208

Minahan, J. (2019). Making school a safe place: Trauma-informed teaching strategies. *ASCD, 77*(2), p. 30-35. Retrieved from http://www.ascd.org/publications/educational_leadership/oct19/vol77/num02/Trauma-Informed_Teaching_Strategies.aspx

Murawski, W. (2017). *Successful co-teaching.* Retrieved from https://www.cec.sped.org/News/Special-Education-Today/Need-to-Know/Need-to-Know-CoTeaching

Nankin, I., & Fenchel, M. (2019). *Social-emotional learning matters…for students and teachers.* Retrieved from https://www.edsurge.com/news/2019-02-05-social-emotional-learning-matters-for-students-and-teachers

Pelligrino, J. (2018). Sciences of learning and development: Some thoughts from the learning sciences. *Applied Development Science.* DOI: 10.1080/10888691.2017.1421427

Proulx, N. & Schulten, K. (2019). *Empathy and resilience, responsibility and self-care: Resources for social and emotional learning from The New York Times*. Retrieved from https://www.nytimes.com/2019/01/23/learning/empathy-and-resilience-responsibility-and-self-care-resources-for-social-and-emotional-learning-from-the-new-york-times.html

Samuels, C. (2015). *Co-teaching for rookies: Building trust and looking at the big picture*. Retrieved from http://blogs.edweek.org/edweek/speced/2015/08/co-teaching_building_trust.html

Shrier, C. (2014). Young children learn by copying you! Retrieved from https://www.canr.msu.edu/news/young_children_learn_by_copying_you

Slavin, R.E. (2014). Instruction that sticks: Making cooperative learning powerful. *ASCD, 72*(2), p. 22-26. Retrieved from http://www.ascd.org/publications/educational-leadership/oct14/vol72/num02/Making-Cooperative-Learning-Powerful.aspx

Sparks, S. (2019). *Why teacher-student relationships matter: New findings shed light on best approaches*. Retrieved from https://www.edweek.org/ew/articles/2019/03/13/why-teacher-student-relationships-matter.html

Stuart, K. (2018). *3 practical resources to help teachers integrate SEL and academics*. Retrieved from https://www.edsurge.com/news/2018-06-25-three-practical-resources-to-help-teachers-integrate-sel-and-academics

Taylor, K. (2016). *Co-teaching: A story of arranged marriage*. Retrieved from http://angelsandsuperheroes.com/2016/04/18/co-teaching-a-story-of-arranged-marriage/

Yoder, N., & Gurke, D. (2017). Social and emotional learning Coaching toolkit: Keeping SEL at the center. Retrieved from https://www.air.org/sites/default/files/downloads/report/Social-and-Emotional-Learning-SEL-Coaching-Toolkit-August-2017.pdf

Young, N.D., Jean, E., & Citro, T.A. (2018). *From Head to Heart: High quality teaching practices in the spotlight*. Wilmington, DE: Vernon Press

Young, N.D., Jean, E., & Citro, T.A. (2019). *Acceptance, understanding, and the moral imperative of promoting social justice education in the schoolhouse*. Wilmington, DE: Vernon Press

Zakrzewaki, V. (2014). How Social-Emotional Learning Transforms Classrooms. Retrieved from https://greatergood.berkeley.edu/article/item/how_social_emotional_learning_transforms_classrooms

Chapter 9

Effective Co-Teaching and Collaboration for Linguistically Diverse Learners

Robert A. Griffin, EdD, *University of West Georgia*

Imagine stepping into a seventh-grade social studies classroom with 25 students from diverse linguistic backgrounds. The content area teacher is playing a vocabulary review game using key terms such as 'constitution' and 'independence' from yesterday's lesson on the American Revolution. Another teacher with a flipboard in hand jots down students who call out the correct term or definition. Afterwards, one of the teachers immediately pulls aside students who did not correctly identify the vocabulary to review the key terms while the other teacher provides an enrichment activity for those who demonstrated proficiency. This is one of many examples of how to navigate the distinct roles and responsibilities within a co-teaching setting. The students who are pulled aside for reteaching in this scenario, however, are multilingual learners whose limited schema related to American history may have contributed to their misunderstanding or misapplication of the content vocabulary from the previous lesson, and the teacher who provided this redelivery is a certified language acquisition expert or English to Speakers of Other Languages (ESOL) specialist. The students, however, are not aware of the distinct roles of these collaborating educators.

Achievement Gaps

Co-teaching is often viewed through the prism of special education with general education teachers collaborating with special education teachers in their classroom settings; however, educators should consider another sizable and growing subgroup of linguistically diverse learners in U.S. schools—multilingual learners (also referred to as English language learners [ELLs] or simply English learners).

Multilingual learners are among the fastest-growing subgroups of students in P–12 schools internationally and in the U.S. (Kieffer & Thompson, 2018; Premier & Parr, 2019), and they are the largest subgroup identified for learning support services (Counts, Katsiyannis, & Whitford, 2018). In 2015, roughly 4.8 million or 9.5% of all public school students in the U.S. spoke English as an additional language (McFarland et al., 2018), and demographers predict that by the year 2030, approximately 40% of U.S. students will be multilingual learners (Ardasheva, Tretter, & Kinny, 2012; Roseberry-McKibbin & Brice, 2019).

Academic performance among this rapidly-growing population of linguistically diverse students has consistently remained far below that of their monolingual peers (McFarland et al., 2018). The percentage of students who achieve proficiency in reading on the National Assessment of Educational Progress (NAEP) is on average 35–50 percentage points lower for multilingual learners than for native-English-speaking students (McFarland et al., 2018). In 2017, the achievement gap in reading between multilingual learners and their English-proficient peers on the NAEP was 37 points in fourth grade and 43 points in eighth grade (McFarland et al., 2018). In addition, the high school completion rate is 19 percentage points lower for multilingual learners (63%) compared with other students (82%) (McFarland et al., 2018; Sanchez, 2017). Given these vast achievement gaps, training educators to engage in meaningful, collaborative practices for a growing culturally and linguistically diverse student population has never been more urgent.

Co-Teaching in ESOL Settings

Over the last three decades, educators have made major strides in how they teach and support multilingual learners (de Oliveira & Yough, 2015; Shen & Byfield, 2018). In the past, ESOL teachers were considered solely responsible for the success of their English learners, and they often worked in isolation, pulling their students out of mainstream classes to deliver English language instruction (Tesol International Association, 2013).

With the advent of the Common Core State Standards (CCSS) and renewed emphasis on rigor, multilingual learners could no longer afford to be left outside of the mainstream classroom (Honigsfeld, & Dove, 2019). Research suggests that English learners who are pulled out to another classroom for extended periods of time become disconnected from the instructional experience and mainstream curriculum. As a result, achievement and self-efficacy for these students decline (de Oliveira & Yough, 2015; Dove & Honigsfeld, 2018).

An area that has received attention in recent years concerning ESOL instructional models is effective co-teaching for multilingual learners in mainstream classrooms (Bell & Baecher, 2012; Dove & Honigsfeld, 2018; Honigsfeld & Dove, 2019). When two teachers—one a language acquisition expert, the other a content expert—teach in tandem, instruction can remain rigorous, authentic, and meaningful.

The advantages of authentic collaboration extend far beyond the collaborating teachers. Student achievement also increases at greater rates in schools with cultures of collaboration (Ronfeldt, Farmer, McQueen, & Grissom, 2015). It is important, therefore, to compare co-teaching between a content area teacher and an ESOL specialist with other forms of co-teaching, particularly traditional push-in constructs. It is also vital to explore other issues and trends related to effective ESOL co-teaching.

Equal Roles and Responsibilities

The old English proverb "Two heads are better than one" (Heywood, 1546, n.p.) may seem cliché, but it is at the heart of what makes co-teaching so effective. Collaborating teachers should perceive each other as equally valuable contributors to the professional dialogue. Students, conversely, should see both teachers as equally responsible for their success. When roles are balanced, the colleagues will have an equal share in planning, instructing, and assessing (Peercy, Martin-Beltrán, Silverman, & Nunn, 2015). To foster dynamic professional partnerships, collaborating teachers should negotiate their roles and responsibilities early on because authentic collaboration must be organic and mutually beneficial (Hersi, Horan, & Lewis, 2016).

Beck and Pace (2017) note that "the secret to successful co-teaching is in the planning" (p. 42). During these vital planning sessions, content area teachers and ESOL specialists discuss classroom expectations, procedures, and their roles and responsibilities (Honigsfeld & Dove, 2019). This partnership begins with building mutual respect for one another and the co-teaching process. While general education teachers report feeling unprepared to teach multilingual learners (Huerta, Garza, Jackson, & Murukutla, 2019), co-teaching promotes mutual understanding and professional development for the content teacher as well as the ESOL specialist and is mutually beneficial for both collaborators if they are willing to foster a professional partnership.

In traditional push-in models where the content teacher assumes the lead role, the support teacher can easily become relegated to the role of an assistant (Dove & Honigsfeld, 2018). The very term 'push-in' implies that the support teacher elbows her way into the other teacher's classroom (Huynh, 2017). In reality, many ESOL teachers are expected to co-teach numerous preps, which detracts from their capacity for excellence; however, when collaboration centers on establishing ground rules for planning, instruction, and assessment, potential for co-teaching success is greater.

Particular emphasis should be given to finding ways of ensuring both teachers have equal responsibilities and roles within the classroom (Fitzell, 2018). The goal here is for the teachers to have parity and for students to perceive the two teachers as equally responsible for their success (Dove & Honigsfeld, 2018; Giles, 2018). The focus should be on shifting away from the isolationist sentiment of 'my classroom and my students' to the collaborative 'our classroom and our students.'

Content and Language Experts

Also important are the distinct but equal roles of the mainstream teacher as a content expert and the ESOL specialist as a language expert. ESOL specialists are trained in language development and can work with content teachers to make the coursework accessible to multilingual learners, whereas content teachers can provide ESOL specialists with content background knowledge to inform how they modify instruction for language learners (Maxwell, 2013). ESOL and content teachers can jointly examine results from the ACCESS for ELLs (WIDA, 2018) or similar state-mandated assessment of English language proficiency and state-mandated content assessments to design instructional strategies and assessment techniques at appropriate language and content levels.

The roles of the two teachers should complement one another. As the generalist teaches the content, the ESOL specialist teaches the academic language of the content, builds background knowledge, and connects content with language development (Echevarría, Vogt, & Short, 2018). The ESOL specialist, for example, can work with the content area teacher to write language objectives corresponding to the content objectives for the course (Echevarría et al., 2018). Going back to the opening example of the lesson on the American Revolution, if the content objective is 'Students will understand the major causes of the American Revolution,' a corresponding language objective might be 'Students will write a letter explaining the causes of the American Revolution.' To teach this language objective, the ESOL teacher could provide a cloze-writing graphic organizer and a key vocabulary list to support multilingual learners (Honigsfeld & Dove, 2019; Ponce, 2017).

Language Proficiency - not Disability

Distinctions exist between co-teaching in special education and ESOL contexts. Special education teachers refer to a student's individualized education plan (IEP) for details regarding the student's learning disability or special need, progress goals, and accommodations (Mastropieri & Scruggs, 2018). Similar to the process involved in writing an IEP, the ESOL teacher, in collaboration with other educators, is responsible for determining appropriate accommodations and modifications necessary to "level the playing field" (Beck & Pace, 2017, p. 78) and make the content accessible for multilingual learners.

It is worth noting here that the legal weight of an ESOL accommodations plan (referred to by different names in different states) is the same as an IEP. For multilingual learners, however, the focus is not on disability as language learners do not have a disability; rather, they are still developing proficiency in English (Dove & Honigsfeld, 2018). This situation is similar to a native English speaker being placed in a Japanese history class with only a cursory knowledge of the Japanese language. Accommodations and modifications would have to be made if the native English speaker would reasonably expect to be successful in the class; however, these modifications would not indicate anything about the English speaker's cognitive abilities, only that their proficiency in Japanese is still developing.

Differentiated Assessment

Differentiation is central to effective ESOL instruction, and it is equally important for effective assessment of multilingual learners (Beck & Pace, 2017; Echevarría et al., 2018). What is typically seen in push-in models is the content area teacher assessing 'his students,' the mainstream students, while the ESOL specialist pulls 'her students' out to deliver accommodations. Instead, both collaborating teachers should work together, capitalizing on the other's expertise, to design modified instructional strategies and assessments and deliver them in ways that draw the least amount of attention to the students themselves (Fitzell, 2018; Dove & Honigsfeld, 2017).

An example of this is when the language of an assessment may need to be modified to make it more accessible to multilingual learners. Most teachers, however, do not have the time or resources to create multiple versions of the same assessment. Two teachers working as a team may be able to make this best practice feasible (Fitzell, 2018). Opportunities for meaningful, ongoing formative assessment with both teachers sharing the responsibility of this type of assessment have already been explored. Just as students served through special education may require accommodations or modified assessments, so do multilingual learners (Roseberry-McKibbin & Brice, 2019; Shen & Byfield, 2018).

Models for ESOL Co-Teaching

Teachers are interested in how theory translates into practice and what they can do to effectuate student achievement. Equally sharing roles and responsibilities for multilingual learners in an ESOL co-teaching setting has a specific look and vibe. Dove and Honigsfeld (2018) have published numerous articles and books on effective collaboration between content area teachers and ESOL specialists. Building on the work of Friend and Cook (2017), one of their major contributions to this area has been their delineation of seven models of ESOL co-instruction.

The first three models involve one group of students—multilingual learners and native English speakers together—in one classroom setting (Dove & Honigsfeld, 2018). Models 4–6 involve two student subgroups arranged, depending on student need and teacher judgment, by language proficiency or content mastery, and Model 7 includes multiple student groups of three or more (Dove & Honigsfeld, 2018).

Within each model, the roles of the ESOL specialist and content area teacher are interchangeable and flexible. Neither teacher assumes the role of lead leader. What follows is a brief explanation with examples for each model; however, Dove and Honigsfeld (2018) caution that these models are not set in stone; rather, they are possibilities. Educators should use them interchangeably in short segments of time as appropriate for the students in their classes.

Model 1–3: One Student Group

The first model is commonly seen during traditional push-in time. One teacher serves as the lead teacher who delivers the lesson, while the other teacher moves throughout the classroom "teaching on purpose" (Dove & Honigsfeld, 2018, p. 57) or providing targeted support for individuals or small groups who are struggling. This model, while effective in short segments as needed, is traditionally what the less-effective push-in model has looked like with the ESOL specialist serving as an assistant or tutor (Giles, 2018; Premier & Parr, 2019). Dove and Honigsfeld (2018) caution against the prolonged use of this model.

The second model is a break away from the traditional push-in construct. Here the ESOL teacher and content specialist take turns delivering the content to the whole class; for example, the content area teacher may introduce the content objectives of the lesson while the ESOL specialist introduces the language objectives (Dove & Honigsfeld, 2018; Echevarría et al., 2018).

The third model is the example provided in the exposition to this chapter, in which one teacher teaches the whole group while the other assesses or observes the responses of the students (Dove & Honigsfeld, 2018). In the opening example, one teacher served as host for a vocabulary review game while her colleague recorded the students' answers (Ponce, 2017). The value of this model is that data is being collected in real time, which maximizes instructional time and allows more opportunities for ongoing formative assessment (Dove & Honigsfeld, 2018).

Model 4–6: Two Student Groups

With the fourth model, collaborating teachers divide the class into two groups and teach the same content (Dove & Honigsfeld, 2018). Not only does this configuration reduce the student-to-teacher ratio, but it is useful when utilizing different classroom resources. Teachers can instruct 12 students at the smartboard more skillfully than 25 or 30.

For models 5 and 6, teachers pull aside small heterogeneous or homogeneous groups, depending on individual student's needs, to either pre-teach or reteach content (Dove & Honigsfeld, 2018). In the fifth model, for example, one teacher may pull aside a small group to pre-teach vocabulary, which helps multilingual learners and struggling learners build background or schemata (Beck & Pace, 2017; Roseberry-McKibbin & Brice, 2019; Shen & Byfield, 2018). The other group could work on an enrichment activity, digging deeper but not moving forward and leaving the other group behind. Instead of preteaching, the sixth model involves one of the teachers working with a group to reteach as illustrated in the opening example (Dove & Honigsfeld, 2018).

Model 7: Multiple Student Groups

The last model involves three or more groups with both teachers circulating and monitoring the students and is commonly used for guided reading groups or learning centers Giving students opportunities to work collaboratively with their peers in small groups while receiving immediate feedback and support is an advantage to the seventh model (Dove & Honigsfeld, 2018).

Final Thoughts

Co-teaching is an effective support model in special education settings, and its effectiveness has now gained popularity in ESOL settings (Dove & Honigsfeld, 2018; Honigsfeld & Dove, 2019; Premier & Parr, 2019). Fostering inclusive learning environments where multilingual learners build their English proficiency while learning the core academic content of the grade level is a matter of equality and equity for linguistically diverse students. Using the principles discussed in this chapter, educators who are committed to professional growth and equitable teaching practices can collaborate in meaningful ways to co-plan, co-instruct, and co-assess multilingual and monolingual students. The benefits of collaboration between ESOL specialists and content area teachers are immeasurable and extend to all parties involved—communities, schools, teachers, and students.

Points to Remember

- *Multilingual learners are one of the fastest-growing subgroups internationally and in the U.S., yet their achievement falls far below their native-English-speaking peers.*

- *Co-teaching in ESOL settings is distinctive from other push-in forms of co-teaching in that students should not be able to distinguish between the ESOL specialist as a language expert and the mainstream teacher as a content expert.*

- *When both teachers learn to respect one another and develop parity of roles and responsibilities within the classroom, teacher effectiveness and student achievement are enhanced.*

- *Pedagogical differences should be expected and addressed professionally as soon as they arise to better foster mutually beneficial co-teaching partnerships.*

- *Using variations of the seven models of co-instruction allows both teachers to share distinct but equal roles within the classroom setting during instructional time.*

References

Ardasheva, Y., Tretter, T. R., & Kinny, M. (2012). English language learners and academic achievement: Revisiting the threshold hypothesis. *Language Learning, 62*(3), 769–812. https://doi.org/10.1111/j.1467-9922.2011.00652.x

Beck, C., & Pace, H. (2017). *Leading learning for ELL students: Strategies for success.* New York, NY: Routledge.

Bell, A., & Baecher, B. (2012). Points on a continuum: ESL teachers reporting on collaboration. *TESOL Journal, 3*(3), 488–515. https://doi.org/10.1002/tesj.28

Counts, J., Katsiyannis, A., & Whitford, D. K. (2018). Culturally and linguistically diverse learners in special education: English learners. *NASSP Bulletin, 102*(1), 5–21. doi:10.1177/0192636518755945

de Oliveira, L. C., & Yough, M. (Eds.). (2015). *Preparing teachers to work with English language learners in mainstream classrooms.* Charlotte, NC: Information Age Publishing.

Dove, M. G. & Honigsfeld, A. (2018). *Co-teaching for English learners: A guide to collaborative planning, instruction, assessment, and reflection.* Thousand Oaks, CA: Corwin Press.

Echevarría, J., Vogt, M., & Short, D. J. (2018). *Making content comprehensible for secondary English learners: The SIOP® model* (3rd ed.). New York, NY: Pearson.

Fitzell, S.G. (2018). *Best practices in co-teaching & collaboration: The HOW of co-teaching –implementing the models.* Manchester, NH: Cogent Catalyst Press

Friend, M., & Cook, L. (2017). *Interactions: Collaboration skills for school professionals* (8th ed.). Boston, MA: Pearson.

Giles, A. (2018). Navigating the contradictions: An ESL teacher's professional self-development in collaborative activity. *TESL Canada Journal, 35*(2), 104–127. doi:10.18806/tesl.v35i2.1292

Hersi, A. A., Horan, D., & Lewis, M. (2016). Redefining 'community' through collaboration and co-teaching: A case study of an ESOL specialist, a literacy specialist, and a fifth-grade teacher. *Teachers and Teaching: Theory and Practice, 22*(8), 927–946. doi:10.1080/13540602.2016.1200543

Heywood, J. (1546). *A dialogue conteinyng the number in effect of all the prouerbes in the Englishe tongue.*

Honigsfeld, A.M. & Dove, M.G. (2019). *Collaborating for English learners: A foundational guide to integrated practices.* Thousand Oaks, CA: Corwin

Huerta, M., Garza, T., Jackson, J. K., & Murukutla, M. (2019). Science teacher attitudes towards English learners. *Teaching and Teacher Education, 77*(1), 1–9. doi:10.1016/j.tate.2018.09.007

Huynh, Y. (2017). *Rethinking push-in pull-out (PIPO): The cause for sheltered co-teaching.* Retrieved from https://www.empoweringells.com/push-in-pull-out/

Kieffer, M.J. & Thompson, K.D. (2018). Hidden progress of multilingual students. *Educational Researcher, 47*(4). DOI: 10.3102/0013189X18777740

Maxwell, L.A. (2013). *ESL and classroom teachers team up to teach common core.* Retrieved from https://www.edweek.org/ew/articles/2013/10/30/10cc-eslteachers.h33.html

McFarland, J., Hussar, B., Wang, X., Zhang, J., Wang, K., Rathbun, A., ... & Bullock Mann, F. (2018). *The condition of education 2018* (NCES 2018-144). U.S. Department of Education. Washington, DC: National Center for Education Statistics. Retrieved from https://nces.ed.gov/pubs2018/2018144.pdf

Peercy, M., Martin-Beltrán, M., Silverman, R., & Nunn, S. (2015). "Can I ask a question?": ESOL and mainstream teachers engaging in distributed and distributive learning to support English language learners' text comprehension. *Teacher Education Quarterly, 42*(4), 33–58. Retrieved from https://pdfs.semanticscholar.org/1e93/9a67617be321a824be7ebb220d4c907773eb.pdf

Ponce, J. (2017). *The far reaching benefits of co-teaching for ELLs.* Retrieved from https://www.teachingchannel.org/blog/2017/01/20/benefits-of-co-teaching-for-ells/

Premier, J., & Parr, G. (2019). Towards an English as an additional language (EAL) community of practice: A case study of a multicultural primary school in Melbourne, Australia. *Australian Journal of Language and Literacy, 42*(1), 58–68. Retrieved from https://www.alea.edu.au/documents/item/1994

Ronfeldt, M., Farmer, S., McQueen, K., & Grissom, J. (2015). Teacher collaboration in instructional teams and student achievement. *American*

Educational Research Journal, 52(3), 475–514.
doi:10.3102/0002831215585562

Roseberry-McKibbin, C., & Brice, A. (2019). *Acquiring English as a second language: What's "normal," what's not.* American Speech-Language-Hearing Association (ASHA). Retrieved from
https://www.asha.org/public/speech/development/easl/

Sanchez, C. (2017). *English language learners: How your state is doing.* Retrieved from https://www.npr.org/sections/ed/2017/02/23/512451228/

Shen, X., & Byfield, L. (2018). Promoting English learners' willingness to communicate in content-area classrooms. *The Clearing House: A Journal of Educational Strategies, Issues, and Ideas,* 1–8.
doi:10.1080/00098655.2018.1541856

Tesol International Association. (2013). *Implementing the Common Core State Standards for English learners: The changing role of the ESL teacher.* Retrieved from https://www.tesol.org/docs/default-source/advocacy/ccss_convening_final-8-15-13.pdf?sfvrsn=8&sfvrsn=8

WIDA. (2018). *ACCESS for ELLs.* Retrieved from
https://wida.wisc.edu/assess/access

Chapter 10

Developing a Strong Co-Teaching Home-School Connection: Forging a Foundation for Success

Elizabeth J. Bienia, EdD, *Endicott College*
Nicholas D. Young, PhD, EdD, *American International College*

The importance of parental involvement - developing a family-school partnership - cannot be underestimated and has been the focus of extensive research for over 20 years (Jensen, 2011; National Education Association, 2011). The primary, overarching reason to develop such relationships is "to help all children succeed in school and later in life" (National Education Association, 2011, p. 91). As noted by O'Donnell and Kirker (2014), children whose families are engaged in the learning process and the school realize important pay-offs including better math and reading abilities, higher grades, improved employment after high school and higher pay grades when matched up to peers with families who were not involved (Young, Jean, & Mead, 2019).

Schools today must contend with the daunting challenge of effectively dealing with a growing array of student needs. Escalating cultural diversity and an ever-increasing number of students for whom English is a second language have changed the landscape of the modern classroom (Martin & Hagan-Burke, 2002). Hispanic (meaning Spanish-speaking) English Language Learners (ELL) students are the fastest-growing minority group in the United States (Martin & Hagan-Burke, 2002).

According to the National Center for Educational Statistics (2019), there were 4.86 million ELL public school students in 2016, representing 9.6% of all students - ranging from 0.9% in West Virginia to 20.2% in California. Of all ELL public school students, Spanish was the home language of 3.79 million, representing 76.6% of all ELL students and 7.7% of all public K-12 students (National Center for Educational Statistics, 2019). The dropout rate of Hispanics in 2014 was 9.5%, even more alarming is that the dropout rate of foreign-born Hispanics in 2014 was 19.9% (National Center for Educational Statistics, 2019).

The Migrant Policy Institute in 2014 (as cited by Johnson & Johnson, 2016) noted that Hispanic immigrants account for the vast majority of United States immigration. The next most commonly reported home languages were Arabic, Chinese and Vietnamese, representing 0.7% of all students (National Center for Educational Statistics, 2019). Considering that by 2060 Hispanics are predicted to make up 38% of all students between ages 3-14 - surpassing whites (33%) and African Americans (13%) - it is crucial that teachers engage all parents while recognizing and accommodating the cultural and language challenges this engagement may pose (Santiago, Taylor, & Galdeano, 2015).

Today's classrooms are a unique blend of environments, technology, and cultural diversity, with many students who have additional academic needs or for whom English is a second language and an ever-changing social-emotional dynamics (Martin & Hagan-Burke, 2002; Young, Jean, and Citro, 2018b). A growing number of students have a wide variety of learning and behavioral challenges and are ill-equipped to face the stresses of the classroom and the school (Martin & Hagan-Burke, 2002). These factors, and more, such as school culture, may cause stress and anxiety not only for the students, but for the parents as well.

Teachers and schools need to help parents understand the culture, dynamics and day-to-day activities, not only of the classroom, but also of the school and school system (Young et al., 2018b). Research agrees that making connections with families is the glue that strengthens student outcomes; therefore, "the more educators and parents share pertinent information regarding their shared student, the better equipped both will be to help that student achieve" (Young et al., 2018b, p. 107).

History of American Parent Involvement in Education - A Pendulum of Involvement

Educating a child was, historically, the prerogative of the child's parents. Children were educated privately, in the home, by the parents on subjects ranging from basic skills and work skills to discipline and instilling ethics and values (Hiatt-Michael, 2001). An older child may have received further education through a trade apprenticeship arranged by the parents. Parents had complete control over the education of their children, choosing what, where, when and how to teach their children (Hiatt-Michael, 2001). Public, formal education, even if available, was generally not utilized by parents. Parents had full control of children's education.

Initially, in America, a community's religious leaders created the first schools and parental educational choices were to school at home or send their children to private or religious schools (Hiatt-Michael, 2001). Control of these schools was later transferred to townships and governance was by parental lay boards, and by 1860 almost every state had a public school system (Hiatt-Michael, 2001). Required education was led by Massachusetts in 1852 with the passage of the first compulsory education law in America (Hiatt-Michael, 2001). Adoption of similar laws in other states was slow, by 1885 of the 38 states in existence then, only sixteen had enacted compulsory education laws (Hiatt-Michael, 2001).

These compulsory laws did little to motivate parents to send their children to school. In the nineteenth century, immigrant families needed their children to work to help the family survive - whether it be in a factory, a mine, or a mill earning wages, or laboring on the family farm (Hiatt-Michael, 2001). Economically, parents could not afford to send their children to school and lose their wages or their labor on the farm. Compelling parents to send their children to school - and give up their wages and labor - required truancy and compulsory school attendance laws that carried monetary penalties for refusal (Hiatt-Michael, 2001). Similar laws were eventually enacted in all states by 1918. Parental control and involvement in their children's education was effectively shattered by these laws (Hiatt-Michael, 2001).

Sensing the widening separation between parental control and the public schools, the National Congress of Mothers (NCM) and the Parent-Teacher Association (PTA) were founded in 1897 by Alice McLellan Birney and Phoebe Apperson Hearst (National PTA, n.d.). Schoff (1916), wrote that the NCM and PTA were "the first national movement to widen and deepen the influence of fathers and mothers...Neither parents nor teachers were in touch with each other and children suffered by lack of this mutual understanding - while the work of the teachers was greatly increased by lack of it" (p. 140). During the first part of the twentieth century the PTA connected home and school, opening an avenue for parental involvement in their children's education and "by the 1940s, parents of all social classes considered the monthly PTA meeting a mandatory community event" (Hiatt-Michael, 2001, p. 254).

The last four decades of the twentieth century were marked by greater parental involvement, particularly in attempts to effect changes in the increasingly bureaucratic public schools (Hiatt-Michael, 2001). These efforts included many landmark legal battles centered on equal opportunity for education for all children. The educational landscape was permanently changed by court actions initiated by parents. *Brown v. Board of Education of Topeka* in 1954 ruled that the racial segregation of children in public schools was unconstitutional (Duignan, 2019).

Serrano v. Priest (1971) resulted in court-ordered equalization of school funding (Hiatt-Michael, 2001). *Lau v. Nichols* in 1974 paved the way for bilingual education for non-English speaking students to ensure they received equal education (Bon, 2019; Stanford University, n.d.) and *Pennsylvania Association for Retarded Children v. Commonwealth of Pennsylvania* in 1971, required the Commonwealth to provide children with "free, public program of education and training appropriate to the child's capacity" (Disability Justice, 2019, n.p.) further clearing the way for equal access to free education for all children.

As part of President Johnson's "war on poverty," the United States Department of Education established the Elementary and Secondary Education Act (ESEA) of 1965 to provide quality and equality in education (Young, Jean & Citro, 2018a). Title 1 is the section of ESEA that distributes funds "to local educational agencies (LEAs) and schools with high numbers or high percentages of children from low-income families to help ensure that all children meet challenging state academic standards" (U.S. Department of Education, n.d., n.p.). When ESEA is reauthorized every five years, changes are made that represent the needs and desires of the public and administration.

The 2001 reauthorization - No Child Left Behind Act (NCLB) - provided a framework through which families, educators, and communities can work together to improve teaching and learning (U.S. Department of Education, 2004). The most recent reauthorization, known as the Every Student Succeeds Act (ESSA), "requires districts who receive federal funds to ensure outreach efforts to all families, implement programs and provide activities that directly involve families, and consult in meaningful ways with families on a variety of topics related to school and students" (Young et al., 2018b).

Both state education agencies (SEAs) and local education agencies (LEAs) are required to have written parent and family engagement plans as charged by the former NCLB and the current ESSA (Young et al., 2019). By January 2010, laws requiring the implementation of family engagement policies were enacted in 39 states and the District of Columbia (Mapp & Kuttner, 2013). One of several states to incorporate family engagement as part of its educator assessment system, Massachusetts made Family and Community Engagement the third of their four standards in their classroom teacher rubric (Massachusetts Department of Elementary and Secondary Education, 2018).

Among other requirements, this rubric states that the "teacher promotes the learning and growth of all students through effective partnerships with families, caregivers, community members, and organizations" (Massachusetts Department of Elementary and Secondary Education, 2018, p. 10). This inclusion of teacher accountability, and shared responsibility, in the school and home relationship "actively supports students both in and out of school and encourages best behaviors with a focus on academic success" (Young et al., 2018a, p. 12).

Importance of the Home-School Connection

Over 20 years of research has demonstrated the impact and importance of family involvement in a child's education (Jensen, 2011; Povey et al., 2016; National Education Association, 2011). Henderson & Mapp (2002) noted that the evidence is "consistent, positive, and convincing" (p. 7) that families have a major influence on children's achievement in school and through life; and that this relationship between family involvement and benefits holds true across "families of all economic, racial/ethnic, and educational backgrounds and for students of all ages" (p. 24).

Continual parental/family and school involvement has been found to have a protective effect on children, and the more families are involved and encourage their children's learning, the more their children are apt to thrive and succeed, as well as continue their education (Henderson & Mapp, 2002). The benefits of a solid parental/family/home and school connection or partnership are numerous and include:

- Higher achievement in reading and math
- Improved behavior at home and at school
- Improved school attendance and retention
- Better social skills, emotional development and adaptation to school
- More positive attitudes toward school
- Completion of more homework assignments
- Better work habits
- More academically independent
- Higher grade point averages and scores on standardized test or rating scales
- Enrollment in more challenging academic programs
- More classes passed and credits earned
- More likely to stay in school
- Have higher graduation rates
- Better employment after high school
- Increased pay rate as compared to peers whose families were not involved
- Increased rates of enrollment in and graduation from institutions of higher education

(Caplan, Perkins-Gough & McKinnon, 2001; Henderson & Mapp, 2002; Povey et al., 2016; Young et al., 2019).

Family-school partnership benefits are not limited to just to students. The other stakeholders, such as parents, teachers and administrators, also profit from a strong family-school connection. Parents benefit through the opportunity to partner with teachers and shape important decisions that enhance their children's success, consistent expectations, practices and messages about homework, increased opportunities to engage in home-learning activities, and increased knowledge of and access to schoolwide resources such as parent learning centers, homework hotlines, homework centers, parent workshops and home visits (Caplan et al., 2001, Young et al., 2018a).

Advantages for teachers who engage in home-school partnerships include closer communication with parents and a better understanding of parent expectations, which results in a better understanding of the student and an increased teacher ability to provide appropriate high- quality educational services for the students, an increased rate of return on homework, greater family involvement in home learning activities and increased parental support and cooperation (Mapp & Henderson, 2002; Young et al., 2018a).

Not surprisingly, mutually supportive and respectful family-school partnerships enhance teacher effectiveness and student success. School administrators, and hence the school and school system, also profit from successful home-school relationships through better communication between school and home, fewer complaints about inconsistent and inappropriate homework, better use of limited resources to link home and school, and an improved school climate as students see parents and teachers working together as partners. (Caplan et al., 2001, Mapp & Henderson, 2002; Young et al., 2018a).

According to Henderson and Mapp (2002), "when parents talk to their children about school, expect them to do well, help them plan for college, and make sure that out-of-school activities are constructive, their children do better in school. When schools engage families in ways that are linked to improving learning, students make greater gains" (p. 8). It is clear that the most impactful collaborative experience in which an educator can engage is partnering with families. A successful partnership will impart and enhance a school experience that is positive and beneficial for both the student and the family (Young et al., 2018a).

It is evident that "relationship-building should be a necessary component of every educator's repertoire" (Young et al., 2018b, p.107). This may be particularly important for families of different cultures, those speaking different languages or from other disadvantaged backgrounds. These families are at "greater risk of experiencing barriers to both forming partnerships with schools and engaging in their child's learning more generally" (Povey et al., 2016, sec. 2.2). These families, and others, may be unfamiliar with this type of partnership or collaboration with the school, making it difficult for them to understand classroom culture and the dynamics of the school (Young et al., 2018a). Building relationships with such families, even if only in the form of getting them to attend social events at school or volunteering, can help the parents/caregivers join or create supportive social groups, develop constructive, helpful and encouraging relationships with their children's teachers and other school staff, and begin to understand school culture and norms (Povey et al., 2016).

Family-School Partnership Frameworks

Parent/family-school involvement has numerous forms, which generally fall within two broad categories – those of school and home. The school component ranges from donating items or food for a classroom project, to chaperoning class field trips and attending parent-teacher conferences to advocating for their children and becoming involved with school governance (Epstein, 2019; Hansen, 1999).

Home-related activities include completing school paperwork (emergency card, permission slips, etc.), ensuring school attendance and timely arrival, making sure children are properly groomed, dressed appropriately, are well rested and fed, free from hunger (Hansen, 1999; Mapp & Kuttner, 2013). Of all the activities that occur at home, the most important aspect is academic readiness, which includes things the family can do to work with and encourage their children on school activities, homework, for example, and everyday learning activities such as shared reading (Epstein, 2019; Mapp & Kuttner, 2013).

According to Epstein (2019), a seminal expert on family-school partnerships, when teachers and administrators create more *family-like* schools, the uniqueness of each child is recognized, each child feels included and all families are welcomed - not just the easy to reach ones. In such a partnership, parents create more *school-like* families, where each child is also seen as a student and families emphasize the importance and value of school, homework and learning activities (Epstein, 2019).

Epstein (2019) developed a ground-breaking framework of six types of family involvement to help educators develop more comprehensive programs of school and family partnerships to include

1) parenting- help families establish home environments to support children as students,

2) communicating - design effective forms of school-to-home and home-to-school communications about school programs and their child's progress,

3) volunteering- recruit and organize parent help and support,

4) learning at home - provide information and ideas to families about how to help students at home with homework and other curriculum-related activities, decisions, and planning,

5) decision making - include families as participants in school decisions and develop parent leaders and representatives, and

6) collaborating with the community - coordinate resources and services from the community for families, students, and the school, and provide services to the community (Epstein, 2019).

Epstein's (2019) model led to several others, each taking what is believed to be the best parts and adding what each researcher thought was missing to improve the model.

Former Secretary of Education Arne Duncan, on April 8, 2014, announced the release (U.S. Department of Education, 2014) of a "framework for schools and the broader communities they serve to build parent and community engagement" (Brice, 2014, n.p.). This new framework, the Dual Capacity framework developed by Mapp and Kuttner (2013) and the U.S. Department of Education is a process to help teach school and administrators how to successfully engage parents and for parents to partner with their schools to enhance student achievement and create effective community engagement (Brice, 2014).

According to Mapp and Kuttner (2013), the Dual Capacity-Building Framework "should be seen as a compass...to chart a path toward effective family engagement efforts that are linked to student achievement and school improvement" (p. 6). The framework invites and compels a school community to create opportunities for all adult stakeholders - district staff, educators and family members "to develop the skills, knowledge, relationships, networks, sense of comfort, self-efficacy, and worldview to engage in effective family engagement" (Wood, Shankland, Jordan & Pollard, 2014, p. 2).

Mapp and Kuttner (2013) found that a true home and school partnership can only be built, and thrive, when both partners have the capacity to take on and connect in a partnership. Unfortunately, very often family engagement programs or projects focus only on providing information and training for families, not the educators. As families learn how to be more active in their children's education, educators are frequently left out of this part of the process (Mapp & Kuttner, 2013). This often leads to uncomfortable situations and increased tension as parents are met by an unreceptive and unwelcoming school climate and resistance from district and school staff (Mapp & Kuttner, 2013). To successfully build an effective family engagement program, programs need to enhance the capacities of not only families, but educators and administrators as well (Mapp & Kuttner, 2013). Capacity can be broken down into four components (Mapp & Kuttner, 2013).

Capabilities: Human Capital, Skills, and Knowledge (Mapp & Kuttner, 2013, p. 10). Young, Jean and Mead (2019) noted that "capabilities are the skills and knowledge that the community possesses that support engagement. These skills include cultural competency, ways to build trusting relationships, advocacy skills, language acquisition, and other skills necessary to support families' development" (p. 102). Families have the added responsibility to learn how to access knowledge about student learning and how their school and school system operates (Mapp & Kuttner, 2013).

Connections: Important Relationships and Networks—Social Capital (Mapp & Kuttner, 2013, p. 10). School staff and families need to learn to recognize and have access to social capital in schools, families and communities through social networks that have been built on trust and respect (Mapp & Kuttner, 2013). "These networks should include family–teacher relationships, parent–parent relationships, and connections with community agencies and services" (Mapp & Kuttner, 2013, p. 10).

Confidence: Individual Level of Self-Efficacy (Mapp & Kuttner, 2013, p. 10). School staff and families each need a sense of comfort and self-worth to engage in partnership activities (Mapp & Kuttner, 2013). Parents need confidence in their "skills and abilities to help their student with schoolwork, participate in school events, and be knowledgeable about decision-making processes" (Young et al., 2019, p. 109).

Cognition: Assumptions, Beliefs, and Worldview (Mapp & Kuttner, 2013, p. 11). Both school staff and families must be committed to working as partners (Mapp & Kuttner, 2013). It is crucial that staff believe in the value of such a partnership in improving student learning and that families truly consider themselves a partner in their children's learning. (Mapp & Kuttner, 2013). All stakeholders - educators, families and community – "must be devoted to understanding cultural differences and similarities and believe in the value of having diverse partnerships" (Young et al., 2019, p. 110).

These frameworks - and others - offer ways to encourage both families and educators to partner and be engaged in their children's education as family engagement is increasingly recognized as the "missing link in school improvement" (Wood et al., 2014, p. 1). Initiatives developed to create or improve family engagement, with the goal of improving student outcomes, will succeed only if they have buy-in, training and policy support from all levels of administration - from the district level to the classroom teacher (Wood et al., 2014).

Co-Teaching Tools for Connecting with Families

Engaging families reaps many benefits for students; they have improved school attendance, higher achievement in math and reading, higher test scores and grades, better social skills, higher high school graduation rates, as well as increased higher education enrollment and completion rates (Caplan et al., 2001; Henderson & Mapp, 2002; Povey et al., 2016; Young et al., 2018b; Young et al., 2019).

The benefits of a family-school partnership are not experienced solely by students, families also benefit - they have a better understanding of their children's classroom and school, including policies and procedures, and "they are more positive in terms of school satisfaction and are more likely to take on leadership roles at school, and are better able to help their student with work and the stresses associated with school" (Young et al., 2018b, p. 111). There are, however, stumbling blocks to this partnership. Often, regardless of the best efforts by school districts, "some educators do not believe that families have anything to offer and that it is easier if they do not include the family" (Young et al., 2018b, p. 111).

Past experience or personal biases may lead some teachers - as well as families - to be unwilling or unable to trust a particular person, family or other school group (Young et al., 2018b). Co-teachers who have insight into the history and importance of family-school partnerships - including some of the barriers - enhance their ability to communicate, to utilize tools and strategies and to work together (partner) with families (Young et al., 2018a).

The tools and ideas presented here will help set the groundwork for a successful partnership with the family and the co-teachers. These tools require co-teachers to plan in advance how they will share and coordinate the tasks and responsibilities. Establishing and nourishing a strong relationship requires both educators and the family to be equal partners and not just observers in the process. (Young et al., 2018a).

Communication. "Communication with families and communities must be viewed as a dynamic process - two way and mutually beneficial" (National Education Association, 2011, p. 49). A successful family-school relationship relies on effective communication that is respectful and clear. Educational jargon may be unfamiliar to families; indeed, they may be intimidated or too shy or hesitant to ask for clarification; therefore, educational jargon should be avoided or kept to a minimum and clearly explained to be understandable to families (National Education Association, 2011; Starr, 2017). Any terminology or material shared with families should be culturally sensitive (Martin & Hagan-Burke, 2002). Effective, positive communication that is two-way, respectful, mindful of cultural diversity, and free of educational jargon is vital to building a productive collaboration on behalf of the student - and conversely, communication that is one-way, disrespectful or oblivious to cultural diversity may well result in misunderstandings, increase hesitancy of the family to partner with educators and be an obstacle to developing an effective home-school partnership (Martin & Hagan-Burke, 2002).

First and early phone call home. A valuable tool to help build a good home-school relationship is the first phone call home. A positive phone call early in the school year, even before the school year starts or within the first couple of days, can establish a powerful, warm and friendly tone and can help create a strong bond (Aguilar, 2015; Young et al., 2018b). If unsure what to say in such a call, writing a script or a few simple prompts will be helpful. These might include basic items such as an introduction, sharing some information about the class, and asking for information about the student - these will help create a bridge with the home (Young et al., 2018b).

Co-teachers should share something good the student did or something else positive about the child, in advance of any issue that may occur later, as this can "breed positive feelings" (Boyd, 2017). Very often the only phone calls parents/caregivers receive from the school are reports of poor behavior, poor work or some other negative about their child, consequently some families may not answer the phone if they see the call is from the school (Boyd, 2017).

An added benefit to making an early, positive phone call is that if either of the educators need to call later to request support or share a negative situation/consequence the child earned, the family is more likely to answer the phone and listen because positive feelings were bred previously and a bridge had been built (Boyd, 2017). By focusing on the positive and a child's success, families are more willing to listen to an issue or problem situation and won't just expect to hear negative things (Graham, 2019).

Letter of introduction. Early in the year, even before school begins and prior to the Open house/Back to School night, co-teachers can start the year off on a positive note by sending home a letter that outlines the goals of the class for the year, perhaps a little bit about themselves and some simple classroom procedures and expectations (Young et al., 2018b). When writing to the family, use a phrase such as "Dear Families." Never assume all students have a traditional, nuclear family with a mother and father - today's families are extremely diverse and may well include other family or significant adults who may be in a caregiving role, or provide support for the student (Young et al., 2018a).

In a co-teaching classroom, this letter home may also include an explanation of co-teaching and which co-teaching techniques will most frequently be used in this class - one-teach, one assist or parallel teaching, etc. - with a simple and clear description of each of the techniques (Brendle, Lock & Piazza, 2017). Any communication sent to the family should always be signed by both teachers (Schwartz, 2018).

Home Visit. Connection and communication with families can be established in many ways; however, one of the most effective ways to create this connection is through a home visit. A home visit by an educator - or both educators in the case of co-teaching - will help establish a rapport with the parents/caregivers and offers an opportunity to learn about their family and community, as well as alleviate any "pressure on the parents to go to the school to be perceived as involved" (Johnson & Johnson, 2016, p. 111).

Home visits allow the educators to see things from the parents' perspective - to see the child and their school experience through their eyes (Johnson & Johnson, 2016). Educators who are open to meeting the parents on their own turf demonstrate a willingness to share authority, learn from their students' families and truly create a partnership with the family (Johnson & Johnson, 2016).

Open House - Back to School Night. This annual event has traditionally been a time for families to sit passively and listen to rules, classroom rituals and homework, attendance and behavior expectations; however, activities for the parents, offer parents ways to be actively engaged (EducationWorld, 2013; TeacherVision, 2019, Young et al., 2018b). Having note cards for parents to write questions on as they enter the room provide an opportunity for co-teachers to answer concerns on the spot without singling out a family. They can also be used to share things about the child. An exit ticket requesting some feedback about the evening and suggestions for other family events can also be useful to co-teachers (EducationWorld, 2013; TeacherVision, 2019, Young et al., 2018b).

Positive Meetings. Whether it is a parent/family conference or an individualized education plan (IEP) meeting, the tone should be positive and collaborative with open communication. Any meeting with educators can be very stressful for the family and "coming to the table with an open mind increases the chances for success and partnership" (Young et al., 2018b, p. 113). When in a co-teaching situation, attendance at all meetings by both teachers is vital and will help make a home-school partnership successful (Spencer, 2005). The co-teachers should decide in advance what role they will each take so that they do not foster misunderstandings or allow contradictions to occur during the meeting (Marston, 2019).

Meetings should have a definite beginning, middle and end. Allowing the family to speak first demonstrates that the educators genuinely take an interest in them and the student (Young et al., 2018b, p. 113). During the middle of the meeting, the educators share progress, both academically and behaviorally, as well as any concerns. Student work may also be viewed at this time, along with a time for the student, if in attendance, to speak and share their thoughts (Young et al., 2018b, p. 113). The end of the meeting should be focused on setting goals together and discussing ways the educators and the family can help the student achieve them (Young et al., 2018b, p. 113).

An IEP meeting can be even more stressful for the family, particularly when multiple educators and support staff may be in attendance (e.g., general education teachers, education specialists, counselors, psychologists, and administrators). A facilitator is essential during these meetings, and even more so when outside agencies may also be involved (Martin & Hagan-Burke, 2002).

It is essential for the facilitator to maintain a "positive mindset and open communication with the family" (Young et al., 2018b, p. 114). The facilitator, in addition to planning and leading these team meetings, should also serve as the 'point person' for contact for all team members, including the family. As the person of contact for all information and situations regarding the student, the facilitator is also in an "ideal position to head off potential problems early" (Martin & Hagan-Burke, 2002, p. 62).

'You Can' letters. Periodic letters home describing what the children are learning in their classroom will keep the family up-to-date and help them understand the work, as well as help them craft questions for the teacher if the student seems to be struggling. Including simple and tangible ideas for the family to help the student learn in this letter - under the heading of 'You Can' - will provide clarity for the family, as well as another opportunity to strengthen family engagement (Young et al., 2018b). Similar to the introductory letter, they should be respectful, culturally sensitive, mindful of the diverse types of families and languages spoken and free of educational jargon (Martin & Hagan-Burke, 2002).

Recruiting volunteers. Asking parents and other family members to volunteer for field trips or other classroom or school activities can increase parent/family involvement (Epstein, 2019). Volunteer activities may include reading to students, helping in the library, working one-on-one with struggling students, assisting with an afterschool program and many more activities (Epstein, 2019; Young et al., 2018b). Volunteering "enables families to share their time and talents to support the school, teachers, and students" (Epstein, 2019, p. 51).

Learning at home activities. These activities, which include homework assignments, "provide information and ideas to families about the academic work that their children do in class, how to help their children with homework, and other curriculum-related activities" (Epstein, 2019, p. 55). Interactive activities should be "designed so families and children will have interactions related to what they are learning" (Young et al., 2018b, p. 116). Learning at home activities will increase teacher-parent communication and parent-child conversations through the review of the child's schoolwork, monitoring of homework and general discussion of academics and future curricular activities (Epstein, 2019).

Technology. "Technology tools offer great potential for connecting home and school" (George Lucas Educational Foundation, 2011, n.p.). In today's world, it is not enough for teachers to just stuff newsletters and other communications into their students' backpacks. Increasingly, technology-based communication tools and social media provide parents with classroom and learning information and teachers with ways to share classroom and lesson information, pictures, homework assignments, translation services and much more (George Lucas Educational Foundation, 2011; Young et al., 2018b).

Technology provides an easy way for teachers to communicate with families via smartphones and email. Students can complete work online (Young et al., 2018a). Using an online application, other communication tools or social media, can provide a school or co-teachers with a powerful format through which information can be shared between school and family (Young et al., 2018a).

Final Thoughts

Schools today must contend with the daunting challenge of effectively dealing with a growing array of student needs. Today's classrooms are a unique blend of environments, technology, cultural diversity with many students with additional academic needs or for whom English is a second language, and ever-changing social-emotional dynamics (Martin & Hagan-Burke, 2002; Young, Jean, and Citro, 2018b).

The importance of parental involvement - developing a family-school partnership or home-school connection - cannot be underestimated and has been the focus of extensive research for over 20 years (Jensen, 2011; National Education Association, 2011). This research has clearly demonstrated the impact and importance of family involvement in a child's education, showing a positive connection between collaborative family-school partnerships and positive student outcomes which include higher academic success, lower rates of absenteeism, improved self-esteem, social skills, and work habits and increased graduation rates (Jensen, 2011; National Education Association, 2011; Povey et al., 2016; Young et al., 2018a).

Historically, the pendulum of parental involvement in a child's education has swung through the full arc - from full parental control to no control and back to parental involvement and control. Initially, when children were schooled at home, if they were taught at all, parents had full control. This was followed by the development of schools where parental control and involvement faded away to today, where parent and family involvement is now recognized as vital to a student's success and is mandated by law through various iterations of the Elementary and Secondary Education Act (ESEA) (Young et al., 2018a). By January 2019, laws requiring the inclusion of family engagement policies were enacted by 39 states and the District of Columbia (Mapp & Kuttner, 2013). In 2012, Massachusetts made Family and Community Engagement one of the standards on its Educator Rubric (Massachusetts Department of Elementary and Secondary Education, 2018).

There are numerous frameworks which provide suggestions and pathways that schools and educators can utilize to engage parents and families (Hansen, 1999; Epstein, 2019; Mapp & Kuttner, 2013). These frameworks require planning and commitment by the schools and educators in order to establish programs and environments that are welcoming, culturally sensitive and understandable for parents to comfortably participate in the learning of their children. (Young et al., 2018a).

Beyond the frameworks, there are many strategies and tools available to schools and co-teachers to encourage and help set the groundwork for a successful partnership with the family. Establishing and nourishing a strong relationship requires both the educator and the family be equal partners and not just observers in the process (Young et al., 2018a). A successful family-school relationship relies on effective communication that is respectful and clear.

Communication must be straightforward and educational jargon should be avoided (Starr, 2017). Two of the most valuable tools for co-teachers to employ are the first phone call home and the home visit. Both activities establish a robust rapport and create a strong bond and partnership with the family, which has the potential to improve student outcomes (Aguilar, 2015; Johnson & Johnson, 2016; Young et al., 2018b). Throughout the year, providing meaningful, open and respectful dialogue during family meetings engages both the families and co-teachers, and helps to build and strengthen an effective home-school relationship (Young et al., 2018b). Several other strategies, such as asking for volunteers, learning at home activities, and technology, also help to bring families and educators together (Epstein, 2019; George Lucas Educational Foundation, 2011; Young et al., 2018b).

Co-teachers who have insight into the history and importance of family-school partnerships - including some of the barriers - enhance their ability to communicate, to utilize tools and strategies and to partner with families, which "creates a winning combination for students and their families" (Young et al., 2018a, p. 117).

Points to Remember

- *The pendulum of family involvement has swung from full-control to no control or involvement, back to significant involvement and collaboration in children's education and with the schools.*

- *Family-school partnerships are now required by federal law and any school that receives public funds is tasked with finding and understanding the challenges that exist, creating policies and programs and, in turn, offer specific strategies and activities to encourage collaboration and build relationships between families and schools.*

- *Today's classrooms are a unique blend of environments, technology, cultural diversity, with many students for whom English is a second language or with additional academic needs and an ever-changing social-emotional dynamics.*

- *Co-teachers who have insight into the history and importance of family-school partnerships - including some of the barriers - enhances their ability to communicate, to utilize tools and strategies and to partner with families.*

- *Several frameworks aim at increasing family engagement to develop and enhance conditions to improve both student and family outcomes.*

- *Many tools are available to assist educators set the groundwork and build a successful partnership with families. Educators in a co-teaching environment will need to plan in advance how they will share and coordinate these tasks and responsibilities.*

References

Aguilar, E. (2015). The power of the positive phone call home. *Edutopia*. Retrieved from
   https://www.edutopia.org/blog/power-positive-phone-call-home-elena-aguilar

Bon, S. (2019). Lau v. Nichols. *Encyclopedia Britannica*. Retrieved from
   https://www.britannica.com/topic/Lau-v-Nichols

Boyd, R. (2017). Best practice_ positive parent phone calls. *Communicator*, *40*(8). Retrieved from https://www.naesp.org/communicator-april-2017/best-practice-positive-parent-phone-calls

Brendle, J., Lock, R., & Piazza, K. (2017). A study of co-teaching identifying effective implementation strategies. *International Journal of Special Education*, *32*(3), 538–550. Retrieved from
   https://files.eric.ed.gov/fulltext/EJ1184155.pdf

Brice, J. (2014). Department of education releases new parent and community engagement framework. *Homeroom, the Official Blog of the U.S. Department of Education.* Retrieved from https://blog.ed.gov/2014/04/department-of-education-releases-new-parent-and-community-engagement-framework/

Caplan, J., Perkins-Gough, D., & McKinnon, S. (2001). Strengthening the connection between school and home. *Essentials for Principals.* Retrieved from https://eric.ed.gov/contentdelivery/servlet/ERICServlet?accno=ED459521

Disability Justice. (2019). *The right to education.* Retrieved from https://disabilityjustice.org/right-to-education/

Duignan, B. (2019). Brown v. board of education of Topeka. *Encyclopedia Britannica.* Retrieved from https://www.britannica.com/event/Brown-v-Board-of-Education-of-Topeka

EducationWorld. (2013). *Open house: when first impressions matter.* Retrieved from https://www.educationworld.com/a_curr/curr272.shtml

Epstein, J.L. (2019). *School, family, and community partnerships: Your handbook for action* (4th ed.). Thousand Oaks, CA: SAGE

George Lucas Educational Foundation. (2011). *Home-to-school connections guide: Tips, tech tools, and strategies for improving family-to-school communication.* Retrieved from https://eric.ed.gov/contentdelivery/servlet/ERICServlet?accno=ED539387

Graham, E. (2019). 10 ideas for engaging parents: Educators share their best ideas for communicating and partnering with parents. *National Education Association.* Retrieved from http://www.nea.org/tools/56945.htm

Hansen, L.E. (1999). Encouraging parent involvement at home through improved home-school connections. Retrieved from https://eric.ed.gov/contentdelivery/servlet/ERICServlet?accno=ED430800

Henderson, A., & Mapp, K.L. (2002). A new wave of evidence: The impact of school, family, and community connections on student achievement. *National Center for Family and Community Connections with Schools.* Retrieved from https://www.sedl.org/connections/resources/evidence.pdf

Hiatt-Michael, D.B. (2001). Parent involvement in American public schools: A historical perspective 1642-2000. *Academic Development Institute.* Retrieved from http://www.adi.org/journal/ss01/Chapters/Chapter18-Hiatt-Michael.pdf

Jensen, D.A. (2011). Examining teacher's comfort level of parental involvement. *Journal of Research in Education, (21)*1, 65–81. Retrieved from https://eric.ed.gov/contentdelivery/servlet/ERICServlet?accno=EJ1098398

Johnson, E.J., & Johnson, A.B. (2016). Enhancing academic investment through home-school connections and building on ELL students' scholastic funds of knowledge. *Journal of Language and Literacy Education, (12)*1, 104–121. Retrieved from: https://eric.ed.gov/contentdelivery/servlet/ERICServlet?accno=EJ1100968

Mapp, K.L., & Kuttner, P J. (2013). *Partners in education: A dual capacity building framework for family-school partnerships.* Retrieved from http://www.sedl.org/pubs/framework/FE-Cap-Building.pdf

Marston, N. (2019). 6 steps to successful co-teaching: Helping special and regular education teachers work together. *National Education Association.* Retrieved from http://www.nea.org/tools/6-steps-to-successful-co-teaching.html

Martin, E. J., & Hagan-Burke, S. (2002). Establishing a home-school connection: strengthening the partnership between families and schools. *Preventing School Failure, (46)*2, 62-5. https://doi.org/10.1080/10459880209603347

Massachusetts Department of Elementary and Secondary Education. (2018).

Massachusetts model system for educator evaluation part iii: Guide to rubrics and model rubrics for superintendent, administrator, and teacher. Retrieved from http://www.doe.mass.edu/edeval/model/PartIII_AppxC.pdf

National Center for Education Statistics. (2019). *English language learners in public schools.* Retrieved from https://nces.ed.gov/programs/coe/indicator_cgf.asp

National Education Association. (2011). *The power of family school community partnerships.* Retrieved from http://www2.nea.org/mediafiles/pdf/FSCP_Manual_2012.pdf

National PTA. (n.d.). *History: Over 120 years strong.* Retrieved from https://www.pta.org/home/About-National-Parent-Teacher-Association/Mission-Values/National-PTA-History

O'Donnell, J., & Kirker, S. L. (2014). The impact of a collaborative family involvement program: Latino families and children's educational preferences. *School and Community Journal, 24*(1), 211-234. Retrieved from https://eric.ed.gov/?id=EJ1032271

Povey, J., Campbell, A.C., Willis, L.D., Haynes, M., Western, M., Bennett, S., Antrobus, E., & Pedde, C. (2016). *Engaging parents in schools and building parent-school partnerships: The role of school and parent organization leadership.* DOI: 10.1016/j.ijer.2016.07.005

Santiago, D.A., Taylor, M., & Galdeano, E.C. (2015). Fact sheet: Latinos in early childhood education. *Excelencia in Education.* Retrieved from https://www.edexcelencia.org/research/fact-sheets/latinos-early-childhood-education

Schoff, F. (1916). The national congress of mothers and parent-teacher associations. *The Annals of the American Academy of Political and Social Science, 67,* 139-147. Retrieved from https://www.jstor.org/stable/pdf/1013499.pdf

Schwartz, S. (2018). What it takes to make co-teaching work. *Education Week: Special Education: Practice & Pitfalls.* Retrieved from https://www.edweek.org/ew/articles/2018/12/05/what-it-takes-to-make-co-teaching-work.html

Spencer, T. (2005). Parental participation: co-teaching partners and families. *William & Mary School of Education.* Retrieved from https://education.wm.edu/centers/ttac/resources/articles/consultcollaborate/parentpartic/index.php

Stanford University. (n.d.). *Landmark US cases related to equality of opportunity in k-12 education.* Retrieved from https://edeq.stanford.edu/sections/landmark-us-cases-related-equality-opportunity-education

Starr, L. (2017). Activities to promote parent involvement. *Education World*. Retrieved from https://www.educationworld.com/a_curr/curr200.shtml

TeacherVision. (2019). Hosting a successful open house. Retrieved from https://www.teachervision.com/teacher-parent-collaboration/hosting-successful-open-house

U.S. Department of Education. (n.d.). *Parents prepare my child for school: Improving basic programs operated by local educational agencies (Title 1, Part A)*. Retrieved from https://www2.ed.gov/programs/titleiparta/index.html

U.S. Department of Education. (2004). *Parental involvement: Title I, part a: Non-regulatory guidance*. Retrieved from https://www2.ed.gov/programs/titleiparta/parentinvguid.doc

U.S. Department of Education. (2014, April 8). *FCE conference 2014 - Sec. of education Arne Duncan announces family-school partnership framework* [Video file]. Retrieved from https://www.youtube.com/watch?v=BR2e0HVKa4U&feature=youtu.be

Wood, L., Shankland, L, Jordan, C., & Pollard, J. (2014). How districts can lay the groundwork for lasting family engagement. *Southwestern Educational Development Laboratory [SEDL] Insights, (2)*2. Retrieved from https://files.eric.ed.gov/fulltext/ED593426.pdf

Young, N.D., Jean, E., & Citro, T.A. (2018). *From Head to Heart: High quality teaching practices in the spotlight*. Wilmington, DE: Vernon Press

Young, N.D., Jean, E., & Citro, T.A. (2019). *Acceptance, understanding, and the moral imperative of promoting social justice education in the schoolhouse.* Vernon Press

Young, N.D., Jean, E., & Mead, A.E. (2019). *From cradle to classroom: A guide to special education for young children.* Lanham, MD: Roman & Littlefield

Chapter 11

Professional Development for Partner Teachers: Learning the Skills to Work Together

Nicholas D. Young, PhD, EdD, *American International College*
Elizabeth J. Bienia, EdD, *Endicott College*

The U.S. Department of Education reported that in the fall of 2015, 95% of 6 to 21 year- old students with disabilities attended regular public schools. Of these students, 62.5% received the bulk of their instruction in the regular education classroom (U.S. Department of Education, National Center for Education Statistics, 2019). According to Faraclas (2018), regular education teachers reported that "they are inadequately prepared to instruct students with disabilities" (p. 524). As more schools implement co-teaching as a way to meet the needs of all students, professional development for both general education and special education teachers will be essential to the success of these partnerships (Shaffer & Thomas-Brown, 2015). As a group, educators are taught, primed and socialized to work and function in isolation; however, they must learn to collaborate to be successful in a co-teaching environment (Friend & Cook, 2016).

Ongoing professional development for both general and special education teachers is critical to the success of co-teaching and students with disabilities in those classrooms (Shaffer & Thomas-Brown, 2015). General education teachers are knowledgeable in content areas and curriculum and successfully deliver instruction to learners with varying needs (Miller & Oh, 2013); however, they require additional knowledge about students with disabilities and their unique educational needs (Friend & Cook, 2016).

Special education teachers are experts in instructional scaffolding, progressively moving their students to greater understanding, and utilizing multiple mediums to present information (Miller & Oh, 2013); however, they require additional knowledge about specific content and curriculum areas (Friend & Cook, 2016). In addition to these areas, to be successful co-teaching educators have a need for opportunities to build their knowledge of instructional strategies and methods for joint delivery of instruction, and skill development in program planning, communication and collaboration that will enable them to negotiate the roles and responsibilities in the co-taught class. (Friend & Cook, 2016; Friend, Cook, Hurley-Chamberlain, & Shamberger, 2010).

Beyond the teachers preparing to - or already participating in - a co-teaching classroom, there is another group of professionals for whom learning about co-teaching must be a priority (Friend et al., 2010). School administrators are "responsible for fostering growth among teachers and learning among students" (Faraclas, 2018, p. 538) and cannot successfully lead educators through this change in instructional strategy without fully understanding it, including the stresses and needs co-teaching places on the educators involved (Friend et al., 2010).

Principals and other school administrators are responsible for overseeing the day-to-day implementation of co-teaching, selecting and partnering teachers, arranging schedules, ensuring common planning time and addressing any program challenges that might arise (Friend et al., 2010; Texas Education Agency, 2018). They must also be able to explain co-teaching to parents and community members, as well as ensure the co-teaching initiative is accountable and sustainable (Friend et al., 2010). Professional development on co-teaching for administrators "could create a school environment in which co-teaching is more fully understood, more deeply valued and more appropriately supported" (Faraclas, 2018, p. 538).

Barriers to Effective Implementation of Co-Teaching

Neither general, nor special education teachers are prepared for co-teaching (Faraclas, 2018). Barriers to the implementation of co-teaching are numerous and include lack of training, lack of time for joint planning, lack of fidelity in implementation of co-teaching, differences in philosophies, limited resources, scheduling issues and lack of administrative support (Faraclas, 2018; Landrum, n.d.).

Professional development can address some of these issues. Training will improve individual teacher's instructional skills, planning and the performance of the co-teachers, as well as the fidelity of the classroom instruction (Faraclas, 2018). These enhancements to the classroom instruction and teacher collaboration should lead to improved student outcomes (Faraclas, 2018). Participation by school administrators will also increase support for co-teaching (Mizell, 2010).

Benefits of Professional Development

Merriam-Webster (2019) defines 'school' as "an organization that provides instruction, a source of knowledge [and] the students attending a school, *also*: its teachers and students" (n.p.). A school where both students and teachers learn is more "focused and effective" (Mizell, 2010, p. 18). Educators and school leadership who participate in professional development serve as role models for students, demonstrating that they value learning and believe it is important (Mizell, 2010). Schools that encourage and advance continued professional education promote the development of a culture of learning throughout the school and support the work and effort of educators as they endeavor to engage their students in learning (Mizell, 2010).

Students, regardless of their level of achievement, will learn and achieve more if their teachers participate in professional development (Mizell, 2010). It is difficult for a teacher to understand how each individual student learns, what might hinder their learning and how and which instructional techniques might improve their learning (Mizell, 2010). Professional development benefits students by providing educators with additional knowledge and instructional strategies to improve their teaching and help their students learn (Mizell, 2010).

School administrators also grow through reflection, studying, training and hard work, just as teachers do, and their learning supports both teachers' and students' learning (Mizell, 2010). School leaders who not only encourage, but also participate, in professional development can learn how to engage their teachers and staff and students in effective learning (Mizell, 2010). Through this engagement and support, the school develops into an institution of learning for all - teachers and students (Mizell, 2010).

Best Professional Development Practices for Co-Teaching

To optimize the effectiveness of professional development trainings, organizers should consider the ways adults learn (Croft, Coggshall, Dolan, Powers & National Comprehensive Center for Teacher Quality, 2010). According to Croft et al. (2010) "Adults learn best when they are self-directed, building new knowledge upon preexisting knowledge, and aware of the relevance and personal significance of what they are learning—grounding theoretical knowledge in actual events" (p. 8).

Several characteristics have been identified in providing effective professional development for educators (Darling-Hammond, Hyler & Gardner, 2017; Faraclas, 2018; Villegas, 2019). Training should be of sufficient duration, and ongoing, to allow time for participants to process and incorporate the information, ideas and practices, and to work through implementation and possible issues in their classrooms (Faraclas, 2018; Villegas, 2019). Conventional professional development that is periodic, intermittent, split into sections and disjointed "does not afford the time necessary for learning that is 'rigorous' and 'cumulative'" (Darling-Hammond et al., 2017. p. 15). Trainings that are longer in duration and are ongoing will have more of an effect on a teacher's practice and, as a result, a greater impact on student learning (Villegas, 2019).

Feedback. Beyond self-direction and active participation, adults require constructive feedback and opportunities to practice new skills (Villegas, 2019). Consequently, professional development trainings should be focused on tangible steps of instruction that are particularly pertinent and applicable to educators, include a combination of new information delivery, active participation with hands-on engagement with the new content, and time for the educators to discuss and try new techniques in their own classrooms (Croft et al., 2010; Villegas, 2019).

Active engagement. Professional development that actively engages participants in learning is effective in promoting and reinforcing learning and growth (Darling-Hammond et al., 2017). This active learning provides educators with opportunities to learn through a variety of approaches and through participation and practice (Faraclas, 2018; Villegas, 2019). Educators should have ample time and opportunities to engage in significant dialogue on the content and techniques they will use in their classroom (Villegas, 2019). Active learning, in contrast to traditional lectures, engages educators in the exercises, techniques and practices they are learning, serving to "provide deeply embedded, highly contextualized professional learning" (Darling-Hammond et al., 2017, p. 7).

Modeling. The use of models, modeling (an expert demonstrating the new technique) and demonstrations has been found to be successful at helping teachers understand a new instructional technique, promoting teacher learning and supporting student achievement (Darling-Hammond et al., 2017; Villegas, 2019). Other forms of active learning "help educators decipher concepts, theories, and research-based practices in teaching, modeling has been shown to be particularly successful in helping educators understand and apply a concept and remain open to adopting it" (Villegas, 2019, n.p.). Effective types of modeling include demonstrations, observation of peers, and video or written cases of teaching, among others (Darling-Hammond et al., 2017).

Collaboration. Professional development that utilizes effective collaboration can positively impact student achievement by allowing educators to learn together, share resources, problem-solve collectively and build a shared professional culture (Darling-Hammond et al., 2017; Villegas, 2019). Various forms of collaborative interactions can range from one-on-one or small groups to schoolwide groups to factions including external educators or other professionals (Darling-Hammond et al., 2017). In forming these groups, educators develop a community of support for one another's work and practice and "provide a broader base of understanding and support at the school level" (Darling-Hammond et al., 2017, p. 10).

Coaching. Coaching or expert support for teachers during the implementation of new content or techniques should be a part of any effective professional development training (Villegas, 2019). In coaching, one teacher - the expert - observes the other teacher's instruction methods and techniques to provide feedback on the delivery (Martino, 2016). Often this coaching is provided one-on-one in the teacher's own classroom (Darling-Hammond et al., 2017). According to Desimone (2011) "Some of the most powerful learning experiences occur in a teacher's own classroom, through self-examination or observation" (p. 29).

Teachers require tangible images and lucid descriptions that clearly demonstrate the application of the new instructional theories and techniques in their classrooms (Leko & Brownell, 2009). Coaching with repeated practice and feedback and with frequent opportunities for teacher and coach to discuss implementation and progress helps teachers relate their new knowledge to actual practice (Leko & Brownell, 2009). The utilization of coaching in professional development empowers teachers by instilling ownership, letting them take possession in their professional growth (Martino, 2016).

Planning. Teachers who plan to co-teach may have varied education, experiences and backgrounds and possess different and, possibly, contradictory perspectives on classroom management, instruction and assessment (Faraclas, 2018). While the content focus of professional development specifically for co-teaching training must include instruction on the basic six co-teaching instructional approaches (Friend et al., 2010), it must also include training in planning, instruction, classroom management, behavior management and assessment to foster parity between co-teaching partners and provide them with research-based strategies to effectively instruct all students (Faraclas, 2018).

Co-teachers who are able to effectively plan lessons together can maximize their instructional effectiveness. This planning includes co-planning lessons by contributing and combining the teachers' areas of expertise, accommodations and modifications required to meet the needs of all students and sharing equal responsibility for planning for all students (Faraclas, 2018). "Without co-planning time, co-teachers are forced to act independently, which completely undermines the co-teaching model" (Faraclas, 2018, p. 538).

Instruction training should provide strategies for the co-teachers to participate equally in the delivery of instruction, sharing of lead and support roles and the provision of specialized instruction for any student as needed (Faraclas, 2018). This instructional training should include training and practice in the six basic co-teaching approaches of one teach, one observe; station teaching; parallel teaching; alternative teaching; teaming; and one teach, one assist (Friend et al., 2010).

Classroom management. Classroom management incorporates the classroom structures and routines needed to establish a well-thought-out, controlled, and consistent approach to organizing teaching and learning tasks. Training in classroom management for the co-teaching classroom should present strategies to establish parity in the physical classroom, communication and relations with students and the management of daily classroom rules, routines and expectations (Faraclas, 2018).

Behavior management is essential to a well-run classroom and co-teachers need to work together to create and modify strategies to establish a consistent, cohesive and united approach to managing student behaviors and reduce interruptions and distractions to learning as a result of these behaviors (Faraclas, 2018). Training in behavior management for co-teachers should provide strategies to create "parity in the development and implementation of (1) positive reinforcement, (2) redirection of off-task behaviors and (3) reactive behavior strategies in their classrooms to reduce classroom disruptions and inappropriate behaviors expectations" (Faraclas, 2018, p. 530).

Co-teachers must collaboratively work to develop strategies for assessing student knowledge, comprehension and performance, monitoring their progress and modifying instruction to meet the needs of each student (Faraclas, 2018). Co-teaching assessment training must include strategies for the collection of data and other assessment activities, the monitoring of student efforts and responses and planning and implementation of modifications when student progress is unsatisfactory (Faraclas, 2018).

Final Thoughts

Professional development for teaching pairs and administrators is vital if co-teaching is to work in the classroom. An educator cannot magically walk into a room and become part of a pair, just as an administrator cannot walk into the school and ensure its success. The process is extensive and includes professional development that will ground the practice for teachers through the use of mentoring and real-time coaching. Administrators are tasked with providing the time needed to produce such a union as well as understanding the concepts that create the foundation of the co-taught classroom. When carefully woven together, the process becomes seamless and allows for administrators, teachers, and students to reap the rewards.

Points to Remember

- *Professional development for both general and special education teachers is critical to the success of co-teaching and students with disabilities in those classrooms.*

- *Professional development that leads to exceptional co-teaching provides numerous benefits for teachers and students regardless of ability or challenges.*

- *Ongoing professional development can ease barriers such as lack of time for joint planning, lack of fidelity in implementation of co-teaching, differences in philosophies, limited resources, scheduling issues and lack of administrative support.*

- *Effective professional development for co-teaching should include self-direction and active participation, constructive feedback and opportunities to practice new skills; be of sufficient duration and be ongoing; actively engage participants.*

- *Ongoing professional development should provide modeling, effective collaboration, coaching or expert support.*

References

Croft, A., Coggshall, J. G., Dolan, M., Powers, E., & National Comprehensive Center for Teacher Quality. (2010). Job-embedded professional development: What it is, who is responsible, and how to get it done well. *Issue Brief. National Comprehensive Center for Teacher Quality*. Retrieved from https://eric.ed.gov/?id=ED520830

Darling-Hammond, L., Hyler, M. E., Gardner, M. (2017). Effective Teacher Professional Development. *Learning Policy Institute*. Retrieved from https://learningpolicyinstitute.org/product/teacher-prof-dev

Desimone, L. (2011). *A primer on effective professional development*. Retrieved from https://pdfs.semanticscholar.org/c7b0/0ef4ad96ec3ed85914b5f0a64f6a73d36e04.pdf

Faraclas, K. (2018). A professional development training model for improving co-teaching performance. *International Journal of Special Education, 33*(3). Retrieved from https://files.eric.ed.gov/fulltext/EJ1196707.pdf

Friend, M. & Cook, L. (2016). *Interactions: Collaboration skills for school professionals* (8th ed.). New York, NY: Pearson

Friend, M., Cook, L., Hurley-Chamberlain, D., & Shamberger, C. (2010). Co-teaching: An illustration of the complexity of collaboration in special education. *Journal of Educational and Psychological Consultation, 20*, 9–27. DOI: 10.1080/10474410903535380

Landrum, K. (n.d.). *Co-teaching: Necessary components to make it work*. Retrieved from https://louisville.edu/education/abri/files/Co-teaching%20Webinar.pdf

Leko, M. M., & Brownell, M. T. (2009). Crafting quality professional development for special educators: What school leaders should know. *TEACHING Exceptional Children, 42*(1), 64–70. DOI: 10.1177/004005990904200106

Martino, M. (2016). Examining the impact of a coteaching professional development training on teachers and their students' achievement. *PCOM Psychology Dissertations*, 402. Retrieved from https://digitalcommons.pcom.edu/psychology_dissertations/402

Merriam-Webster Dictionary (n.d.). *School*. Retrieved from https://www.merriam-webster.com/dictionary/school

Miller, C., & Oh, K. (2013). The effects of professional development on co-teaching for special and general education teachers and students. *Journal of Special Education Apprenticeship*, 2(1). Retrieved from https://files.eric.ed.gov/fulltext/EJ1127783.pdf

Mizell, H. (2010). Why professional development matters. *Learning Forward*. Retrieved from https://www.learningforward.org/docs/default-source/pdf/why_pd_matters_web.pdf

Murawski, W. (2010). *Collaborative teaching in elementary schools. Making the co-teaching marriage work!* Thousand Oaks, CA: Corwin

Shaffer, L. & Thomas-Brown, K. (2015). Enhancing teacher competency through co-teaching and embedded professional development. *Journal of Education and Training Studies*, 3(3). DOI: https://doi.org/10.11114/jets.v3i3.685

Texas Education Agency. (2018). Co-teaching a how-to guide: Guidelines for co-teaching in Texas. *Texas Education Agency / Education Service Center*. Retrieved from https://projects.esc20.net/upload/shared/20984_CoTeaching_Updated_508.pdf

Villegas, P. (2019) Best practices in professional development. *NASA STEM Engagement & Educator Professional Development Collaborative*. Retrieved from https://www.txstate-epdc.net/best-practices-in-professional-development/

U.S. Department of Education, National Center for Education Statistics. (2019). *Students with disabilities, inclusion of*. Retrieved from https://nces.ed.gov/fastfacts/display.asp?id=59

Chapter 12

Relationships, Mentorship and Self-Renewal: Co-Teaching as a Vehicle for Personal and Professional Growth

Christine N. Michael, PhD, *American International College*

In the field of developmental psychology, the notion that the human lifespan can be broken down into "stages" that focus on specific developmental tasks that an individual must master has generally been accepted throughout modern history (Levinson, 1978). Sometimes viewed as phases or seasons (Levinson, 1978), these blocks of time served as the stepping-stones to further positive growth and development if individuals were able to master the key developmental homework built into each stage.

In the 1960s, theorists and researchers (Fuller, 1969; Gregorc, 1973; Katz, 1972) proposed that the lifecycle model could be applied in meaningful ways to the career cycle of educators. Later, in 1992, Fessler and Christensen developed the most comprehensive teacher career cycle model that included eight specific stages with developmental tasks built into each.

The Fessler and Christensen (1992) model led school leaders, supervisors, and higher education faculty to consider best practice in helping teachers navigate each step of the career cycle so that they could minimize challenges and maximize personal and professional development, avoiding burnout and disengagement along the way. Fessler & Christensen (1992) coined the term "enthusiastic and growing" (p. 138) for educators who were able to continuously develop and thrive even under changing school conditions.

Co-teaching can be an effective strategy for helping new teachers enter the profession and keeping veteran teachers in that enthusiastic and growing stage over their careers, which are becoming increasingly lengthier (Walker, 2018). It is important, therefore, to focus on explicating the stages of a teacher's life and the tasks inherent, considering how co-teaching can change shape and form at different points in a career, as well as what meaning can be derived from such an activity.

Conceptualizing the Teacher Life Cycle

Various ways of thinking about the human life cycle, particularly as it expanded in years, also influenced the ways in which scholars thought about career cycles. In the teaching profession, there are a number of prominent models, all of which share some commonalities.

Chickering: Seven Vectors of Identity Development

Interestingly, one of the earliest and most prominent models of emerging adult development would seem to have value in understanding the teacher career cycle as well. Chickering (1969) was one of the forefathers of the psychology of student development, which he crafted into his Seven Vectors of Identity Development and include Developing Competence in the interpersonal, intellectual and physical domains; Moving through Autonomy toward Interdependence; Developing Mature Interpersonal Relationships; Establishing Identity; Developing Purpose; and Developing Integrity.

One could argue that the novice teacher must pass through these same vectors in order to have a fulfilling career lifecycle. The novice is consumed with developing professional confidence and moving towards control over their classroom, curriculum, and meeting students' needs. This is aided when mature relationships can be formed, both with guides, faculty or mentors and, eventually, moving into collaborative relationships with colleagues, such as those found in successful co-teaching (Chickering, 1969).

With greater technical competence and more self-confidence, the teacher then can turn their attention to the formation of a professional identity that has goodness of fit for them. Later reflections, as in Katz's (1972) last two stages, permit the luxury of locating the purpose and pleasure within the work and developing integrity that will allow the teacher, at point of exit, to look back on their career with satisfaction and a feeling of a job well done.

Hunt: Conceptual Stages of Teacher Development

Hunt (1971) formulated a three-stage model of teacher development, with each stage being guided by an integral question. In the first stage, similar to Huberman's (1989) model, the question is 'How will I survive?'. The novice teacher is very respectful of authority and rules and does not have the ability yet to analyze or problem-solve in the classroom; therefore, novices have an external locus of control and few internal resources to deal with potential challenges (Hunt, 1971). These new teachers, Hunt (1971) wrote, do not have the ability to talk about teaching in the language of teachers yet. If things do not go smoothly in the classroom, they often blame others, or the students, rather than look inward.

In Hunt's (1971) second stage, the seminal question is 'How well is the class doing?'. Teachers still need a road map to guide them, but they are aware of the steps necessary in sound educational planning. While they still look outward to get a sense of what to do, they understand the theory of teaching, as well as the practical strategies for creating, delivering and assessing content (Hunt, 1971). Less fearful of survival, they are more flexible in their thinking and reception of feedback or critique.

The third stage is driven by the question 'How well is each student learning?' (Hunt, 1971). At this point, teachers are able to be original and creative, and can see the realities of different students' needs and meet them. In the classroom, the teacher is able to identify and solve problems, adapt to the unexpected, and embrace change (Hunt, 1971). They are comfortable with ambiguity and able to deal with controversy.

Katz: Developmental Stages of Teachers

Katz (1972) was interested in the concept of effective and meaningful professional development when he formulated his four-stage model. The stages consisted of survival, consolidation, renewal, and maturity, and like stage models of human development, each stage contained developmental tasks facing the teacher, implying different types of professional development would be necessary (Katz, 1972).

New teachers in the survival stage are consumed by wondering if they can make it through day-to-day life in the classroom. They are in need of direct and focused guidance in the areas of classroom management, instruction, and problem-solving (Katz, 1972; Nast, n.d.). Without such, they are at grave danger of leaving the profession (Mulvahill, 2019).

Mentoring and modeling that works is concrete, broken into small, applicable steps, easy to mimic, and situation-specific (Mekos & Smith, 2018). Survival-stage teachers exert more authority over their classrooms and feel lost without lesson plans or scripts to guide their practice (Katz, 1972). They are exceptionally fearful of failure and need encouragement and a toolbox of many tricks in order to stay afloat.

Consolidation stage teachers have weathered the storm that is the first year or two of teaching and now can advance from survival concerns to concerns about their students, especially those who may not be thriving in their classrooms (Katz, 1972). They can ponder questions about new resources, approaches, and individualized lessons that can help them reach all learners. Consolidation teachers can benefit from networking with others and with the exchange both of ideas and actual materials that they can try (Katz, 1972).

In the renewal stage, teachers have mastered their craft and are eager for new things to try out; they need stimulation in order to stay actively engaged in the profession, so they may take courses, attend conferences, engage in research, visit others schools or take part in exchanges, or expand roles to greater teacher leadership within their school (Katz, 1972). Consolidation teachers are internally-motivated; therefore, they are able to articulate their own annual professional goals and needs.

Maturity is a phase that allows the teacher to move well beyond the concerns of the classroom to reflect upon deeper questions of purpose, philosophy, and best practice within their profession. It is time to consider their values, how they can advocate for what they most strongly believe in and how they can become change agents. These are the teachers who make amazing mentors and guides since they have experienced all of the developmental stages themselves and can assist others in successfully navigating them.

Huberman: Career Development and Career Cycle Model

Huberman's (1989) teacher career cycle model was one of the earliest conceptualizations of what he called the "personal and organizational ecologies" (p. 33) of teachers' lives. As will be discussed in Fessler & Christensen's (1992) theory, personal influences resided in each educator's family, age and life stage, finances, culture, gender and wellbeing. At the organizational level, leadership styles, school culture, mandates and other required policy changes and participation in groups such as unions or affinity groups all held sway (Fessler & Christensen, 1992). Huberman's (1989) model included five different stages that were linked to a teacher's years of service.

The first stage of this model is the career entry stage; in it, the novice teacher, essentially, tries to keep their head above water (Huberman, 1989). There are many skills to master, among them classroom organization and management; curriculum development; building relationships with students and colleagues; navigating the complexities of the political and social cultures of one's school; practicing effective discipline; and rapidly building a "tool chest" of strategies to implement in an increasingly efficient manner (Greenberg, Putnam, Walsh, 2014). It is no wonder that so many career entry teachers exit the field within the first five years, especially if they are not surrounded by supportive colleagues (Morrison, 2019; Will, 2018).

Cruickshank and Callahan (1983) aptly describe the survival nature of this stage by mentioning that the distance that lies between a teacher's desk and the desks of his or her students is the longest psychological distance that novices have traveled in a brief time in their lives. Teachers in this stage almost never feel that they were adequately prepared to enter the classroom (Cruickshank & Callahan, 1983; Greenberg et al., 2014).

Being able to stick out the first three to five formative years, a teacher then moves into the stabilization period, where the educator moves the teacher from survival model to a greater sense of self-efficacy, as more and more decisions become routine (Huberman, 1989). The teacher also may lessen dependence on coaches, mentors, or other support systems and graduate to a greater sense of independence, autonomy, and competency (Tricarico, Jacobs & Yendol-Hoppey, 2013). With growing confidence and skill, a teacher is then able to experience their classroom from a different perspective (Huberman, 1989; Tricarico et al., 2013). Gone is the preoccupation with management and discipline of students, freeing the teacher to see students as individuals, respond to their needs, and establish genuine relationships that are so necessary to meaningful learning.

The third stage, which is called experimentation and diversification, takes up the next ten years of the teacher's life (Huberman, 1989). Assuming they have become confident and successful in the teaching role, the teacher then moves into greater professional and personal growth and satisfaction. They might experiment, conduct research, explore transdisciplinary teaching, or take on new roles within the school and community to include mentoring, co-teaching, seeking additional credentials, presenting, publishing, or taking on leadership positions (Mekos & Smith, 2018).

An interesting element of Huberman's (1989) model is that the third stage can also go in another direction---not that of fulfillment and growth; rather, what he calls stocktaking/interrogations. Here the teacher may evaluate their accomplishments to date and if that evaluation is not positive, they may be plunged into considering whether or not to remain in the profession (Mulvahill, 2019; Will, 2018). Teachers in such a stage of negativity or questioning are rarely willing to take on new roles, exhibit leadership, or interact with others in manners that enhance their growth; in short, such disgruntled teachers can be an institutional challenge or even liability (Huberman, 1989; Mulvahill, 2019).

The same duality that exists in the third stage of Huberman's (1989) model also occurs in the next stage, which occupies a decade or so. For teachers who are able to accept their career and find serenity by acknowledging that their youthful enthusiasm may have led them to believe they could change the world, or at least their classroom through sheer willpower, coming to appreciate small change, genuine teaching, and the value of relationships becomes rewarding and satisfying (Beasley, 2013). Teachers in acceptance and serenity are also aware that as they grow older and the age gap between themselves and their students widens, they can grow by opening themselves to the knowledge that their young charges can provide them.

Those teachers who can do nothing but cling to the past or lament the "good old days" of teaching are said to be in the conservatism stage; which Muhammad (2017) also calls the survivor stage. They resist new ideas, resort to what has worked for them before, and are often seemingly contemptuous of professional development or other new learning opportunities. The good thing is that it is possible for such teachers to rededicate themselves to the profession and reignite their passions, and often it is through gaining a valued role such as mentorship or co-teaching (Huberman, 1989).

The final stage of Huberman's (1989) model continues the divergent path concept, as disengagement from the profession can be either serene or bitter. The process of disengagement and the emotions attending it depend heavily on a number of factors. The first is whether the teacher feels personally satisfied with what has been accomplished in the field; this can be influenced by whether others have recognized and valued their work contributions (Huberman, 1989; Murphy, 2018). Those teachers who have found meaning and satisfaction in their careers are more likely to continue in roles such as mentorship (formal or informal), educational advocacy, writing, research, or other forms of disseminating the knowledge that they have garnered over their career (Murphy, 2018).

Fessler and Christensen: Teacher Career Cycle Model

In 1992, Fessler and Christensen authored the Teacher Career Cycle Model. Interested in factors that affect educators' continued personal and professional growth, meaning-making, and the satisfaction that they derived from their work, Fessler & Christensen (1992) noted that there were both external and internal influences on these variables. They further found that unlike rigid stage models, the career cycle was a dynamic, living model in which teachers might move in and out of various stages, even revisiting some of them more than once, based upon the influences from their personal and professional worlds (Fessler & Christensen, 1992). Such factors as changes in the family structure, health issues, life crises and even changing interests and values played powerful roles in how teachers experienced their work.

It is not difficult to see how personal and familial experiences impact job performance and satisfaction (American Psychological Association, 2019). At times, even joyful events such as the birth of a child, added stress to the work role. Caregiving responsibilities, such as caring for an aging parent, ill spouse, or in-law, burdened teachers at various points in their career, particularly in the trajectories of women's careers. Financial stressors, such as loss of income or new responsibilities, also played a role.

The same event, Fessler & Christensen (1992) argued, could be experienced very differently, turning it into a positive critical event or a negative life crisis for the educator. Having strong relationships, support networks, and adequate finances to bolster the teacher led to the ability to weather a storm, but their absence could tax them, leading to work-load stress or even distress that could affect health and wellbeing (Koepsell, 2018; Fessler & Christensen, 1992). Professional colleagues, a supportive boss, or a meaningful mentoring relationship all could serve as protective buffers when educators suffered a life stressor (Davey, 2015).

The authors point out that there are also internal traits that help or hinder teachers as they respond to life events. These are grounded in temperament, values, and attitudes that tend to color the outcomes of a life crisis (Xin et al., 2017). Those educators who are resilient are likely to frame such events as opportunities for growth and change and take stock of behaviors they have employed to help them overcome past life challenges (Moore, 2011). Reflecting upon their assets, educators are better able to thrive even in the face of adversity (Xin et al., 2017). If they have multiple meaningful roles in their lives, they are less likely to experience distress when challenged in one area of their personal or professional constellations (Fessler & Christensen, 1992).

Fessler and Christensen's (1992) eight-part model is a stage theory derived from data collection, built on norms arising from aggregate data collected and explains career stages in ways that can improve professional practice. It is critical to note, however, that this is not a linear model in that internal and external factors may prompt teacher movement in and out of different stages, even multiple times (Fessler & Christensen, 1992). Even a teacher who is enthusiastic and growing, for example, can move into career frustration or a period of minimal professional investment when confronted with a leadership style that is at odds with their own. On the other hand, frustrated or stagnant teachers can become enthusiastic when a new policy or a chance to mentor challenges and excites them.

There are many similarities between Huberman (1989) and Fessler and Christensen's (1992) models. Indeed, their first stage—preservice—corresponds with career entry in all aspects of its description (Huberman, 1989; Fessler & Christensen, 1992). The induction stage is truly a form of socialization that is necessary for newcomers in that they learn school culture, norms and expectations of the profession. The most common feeling among inductees is that they have not received as much preparation for 'real' teaching from their preservice training as they need to stay afloat (Loreman, Sharma, & Forlin, 2013).

Interestingly, even veteran teachers who undergo change (either willingly or by forced circumstances) experience this same array of feelings (Muhammad, 2017). This can occur in changes of location, grade level, academic subject they are teaching, or even moving to positions with greater leadership or responsibilities built in.

After preservice, the novice moves into a stage called competency building, in which they are driven to build the necessary skills, cognate knowledge, and application of that knowledge in order to feel confident in conducting the affairs of the classroom on a daily basis (Fessler & Christensen, 1992). Growth in the art of curriculum construction and implementation, the science of teaching, classroom management, efficient paperwork organization, and building relationships within and outside of the classroom are the stuff of competency building.

Fessler and Christensen (1992) believed that if teachers can master these competencies, their energies can turn from daily survival to a more automatic approach to daily routines; such freeing up of energies makes it more likely that they can find satisfaction in their work and avoid stress and potential burnout. It is easy to see how good co-teaching with a more experienced mentor can provide efficient transmittal of many of these skills to a newer teacher (Sachs, Fisher & Cannon, 2011). Teachers without such support are at higher risk for career frustration or exit.

The most evolved stage of being is the enthusiastic and growing stage (Fessler & Christensen, 1992). Teachers in this stage are not only extremely competent practitioners, they have also completely committed to their craft. They have passion for what they do and internal motivation to keep learning and growing (Barlin, 2010). Even remaining in the classroom, they are teacher leaders by virtue of their strong relationships with others, the respect they are accorded, and their positive approach to challenges (Barlin, 2010; Wolpert-Gawron, 2018).

Savvy leaders take advantage of these teachers' relational skills, enthusiasm and knowledge and use them as models and mentors for others (Wolpert-Gawron, 2018). They are ideal co-teachers because of their wealth of information, strong and positive sense of self, ability to get along with others, and wish to advance student achievement and school community (Barlin, 2010; Fessler & Christensen, 1992).

Career frustration, often termed burnout, is a period marked by teacher frustration, disillusionment, and disengagement (Fessler & Christensen, 1992). Many educators question their choice of career and many leave or simply dial back their energies and commitments to the role (Muhammad, 2017). This can be brought about by being overloaded, ill-suited for their current role, in mourning over lost roles, or feeling devalued. If the teacher was one of high quality in previous stages, they may be re-energized by being given a mentoring or co-teaching role; however, those who have never performed at a high level should not be placed in these important positions.

An individual who is experiencing career frustration can move in one of two directions, either choosing to exit the profession at this point in time or seeking out ways to recommit to the profession and recharge their professional batteries (Fessler & Christensen, 1992). Sometimes teachers who experience career frustration do so due to external obligations or challenges that grow to a level that they interfere with their professional performance. Counseling—either to help individuals transition to a new career or to support teachers in times of personal crisis—can be extremely valuable (Diaz, 2018). Other times, however, the mere fact of having daily encouragement and sharing the load with a co-teacher is the extra balm needed to help one through difficult times (Wolpert-Gawron, 2018).

Teachers who are said to be in career stability are running on autopilot (Fessler & Christensen, 1992). They have attained the cognate knowledge, skills, and relationships to fulfill their roles, which allows them to coast; yet, unlike enthusiastic and growing teachers, they are not motivated to continue professional growth nor to adopt leadership roles (Fessler & Christensen, 1992). Many are biding their time until retirement, having put in what they consider to be a long teaching career (Muhammad, 2017). They are in survival mode, knowing that there are likely to be new mandates and/or administrative changes and having endured long enough to believe they can outlast everything (Muhammad, 2017). In rare cases, the teacher may be just waiting to be invited into a new and meaningful role that acknowledges their expertise, and the smart leader may reach out to identify what that role could be.

Career wind down is the stage at which a teacher has decided to exit the profession; this decision can be experienced in two radically different ways (Fessler & Christensen, 1992). There are generally three trains of thought for these educators to include (1) the culmination of a satisfying career in which the individual feels they have made an impact, (2) a period of reflection, in which a sense of accomplishment, of having mattered, and (3) a bittersweet experience, either because the individuals feel they have received scant rewards or because of external forces, such as a layoff, lack of recognition, or forced resignation (Fessler & Christensen, 1992).

Similar to Erikson's (1994) stage of integrity vs. despair, career wind down can reflect both integrity and generativity in the case of those who have influenced the lives of students as well as the next generation of teachers, as in a mentoring or co-teaching situations. Without such meaningful relationships, however, it can be a time in which the teacher despairs over their career trajectory. The final stage of their model is actual career exit, which can come in a variety of forms (retirement, career change, involuntary departure, or even temporary, such as the birth of a child or a health issue). A teacher's level of engagement and professionalism at this point dictates whether schools will wish to continue to use the teacher's abilities in coaching, mentoring, volunteering, or consulting, or will part ways completely (Fessler & Christensen, 1992).

Steffy, Wolfe, Pasch & Enz: Advocacy Model

Steffy, Wolfe, Pasch and Enz (2000) have written one of the most widely-used models, the advocacy model, that professionalizes teaching by explicating a life cycle that consists of six different phases and

> calls to mind the image of a "teaching ladder" with six specific rungs. Those are termed novice; apprentice; professional; expert; distinguished; and emeritus. Born out of research on the life cycle, the model is based on the belief that "teachers who spend their careers in the classrooms have the capacity to maintain excellence for a lifetime…with the appropriate support (p. 2).

Steffy et al. (2000) wrote that this model is "both descriptive and prescriptive" (p. 2) in that it states what kinds of enrichment and support are needed at each distinct phase.

Steffy et al. (2000) stated that the model is not value neutral; rather, it is founded on strong beliefs that teachers are able to improve their practice when they are part of a community of inquiry. Excellent teachers have both internal and external factors influencing their growth. Internally, they are driven towards a mentality that is enthusiastic and growing, similar to Fessler and Christensen (1992). Yet external factors also have a profound influence on whether teachers thrive or flounder. School culture, leadership, training, personal relationships, and meaningful support and professional development are key (Steffy et al., 2000).

Novice teachers have been described in the other models and they are no different here (Steffy et al., 2000). They come to the profession either with formal higher education or some of the more innovative new models that recruit prospective teachers from the corporate and military domains and provide them with opportunities to translate former skills into classroom practice. Apprentices (induction stage) confront a difficult contrast between their idealistic dreams of how teaching might be and the realities of the classroom and the profession (Michel, 2013). Lasting the first two or three years of the teaching career, this phase is marked by the greatest percentage of educators leaving the field (Morrison, 2019).

Steffy et al. (2000) remarked that the majority of teachers in most schools are what they term professional teachers. These are the survivors of initial professional challenges—those who have forged bonds with their colleagues and students, found satisfaction in their daily work, and are willing to take on greater responsibilities in their role (Michel, 2013). They have grown in confidence and are at a point where they are more likely to take risks in the classroom and move beyond their personal level of comfort to try new things in the service of student achievement. While they are ideal teacher leaders, few wish to leave the classroom for administrative roles (Lumpkin, Claxton & Wilson, 2014). Professional teachers actively seek out opportunities for growth, reflection, and self-renewal (Darling-Hammond, Hyler, Gardner & Espinoza, 2017).

Expert teachers are what every administrator dreams their staff will be comprised of as they are the standard-bearers and they exert leadership within the school and its community even if they do not assume formal leadership roles (McNeel, 2019). They are focused on relational aspects of education, technical expertise, and they carve out time for study, research, and maintaining activities that nurture their own wellbeing (McNeel, 2019; Steffy et al., 2000).

Schools are fortunate indeed if they have a few distinguished teachers and Steffy et al. (2000) set aside this moniker for those who are compared to the general profession. This phase is reserved for those who are exceptionally gifted, who go beyond all expectations in technical expertise, and who are masters of their content and classroom management (Steffy et al., 2000). They may be seen as scholars and leaders within the field, taking on roles at the local, state or national level, adding to the Scholarship of Teaching and Learning through their applied scholarship, writing and presenting at conferences and acting as advocates and spokespersons for the profession (Felten, 2013). Continuing these practices after retirement makes an individual an emeritus teacher. They may have given up a formal position in PK-12 teaching; however, the trade-off is joining a higher education faculty, becoming a volunteer mentor, running for local school board positions, or serving on committees that deal with educational policy (Steffy et al., 2000).

How Co-Teaching Can Promote Positive Teacher Development

It is imperative that when considering co-teaching opportunities within an institution, the leaders (and teacher leaders) be very familiar with the models of the teacher career cycle in order to make the partnerships successful and to allow teachers to improve their practice, learn new techniques, reflect on their work and derive meaning and satisfaction from it. The National Staff Development Council [NSDC] (2008) designed a developmental chart to help mentors and coaches tailor support for the teachers they work with. The chart explicates the needs of teachers at different stages in their career development and offers stage-related, specific ways that mentors can be most effective, noting that while the stages are determined by one's years in teaching, specific teacher behaviors are more critical than years of experience in determining a teacher's stage of development (NSDC, 2008).

Killion & Harrison (2017) wrote of the ten roles that teachers can take on in contributing to their schools' success to include resource provider, instructional specialist, curriculum specialist, classroom supporter, learning facilitator, mentor, school leader, data coach, catalyst for change, and learner. These roles are intertwined in good co-teaching, which in turn benefits all participants—students and teachers alike.

Co-Teaching Provides Mentorship, Modeling and Support in the Early Years

There are myriad ways that co-teaching can serve as a catalyst for personal and professional growth and a buffer during the adverse circumstances that may affect an educator's life (Bullough, 2012). These may manifest themselves in different forms at different stages of the teacher's career cycle. All good co-teaching has the power to engage both parties in growth-enhancing experiences. Among these are emotional support, modeling, apprenticeship and mentoring, questioning, reflection, strengths-based practice, self-authorship, and leadership (Fitzell, 2018).

At the preservice, novice or induction stage, teachers need experiences that provide explicit modeling and guidance and need to see explicitly how book learning translates into actual classroom practice (Friend & Cook, 2016). They need to have instruction, classroom management, organization, assessment, communication, and relationship building modeled for them in a way that exposes them to best practice and allows them to ask questions and compare/contrast this with scholarly literature and research (Fitzell, 2018). New teachers need to understand how veterans perform and why they make the choices that they do. Strategies that minimize time and effort for routine tasks are particularly worthwhile as new teachers are continuously stressed by the demands of the profession (Sachs et al., 2011).

Given that the teaching profession loses the vast majority of educators within the first few years, co-teaching may be an incredibly valuable tool in retention (Morrison, 2019). A difficult task when transitioning into a new school, level of teaching or classroom, is learning the culture, expectations, mandates and protocols that inform them (Murawski & Lochner, 2018). This is where more veteran teachers can reduce the confusion and angst attending the transition and winnow out what matters most from what doesn't.

Novice teachers also benefit from having help in reviewing the specifics of the school and district expectations that directly affect their practice, such as curriculum guides or new initiatives or mandates (Fitzell, 2018). New teachers need to know how to locate resources, how to ask for help when they need it, and whom to seek out for the best advice on different challenges they may confront (Friend & Cook, 2016).

Many colleges and universities are adopting co-teaching as their preservice teacher model. As Graziano and Navarete (2012) of Nevada State College described their own implementation of co-teaching in a teacher preparation program:

> *For us, co-teaching served as both a teaching strategy in the classroom and a strategy for faculty development in our roles as teacher educators. The experiences that we gained from co-teaching provided rich opportunities for reflection on our teaching practices, ourselves as individuals, and our students' learning. These reflective opportunities allowed us to move beyond the practical application of "how to co-teach" into a "how to grow as a teacher and reflective practitioner* (p. 124).

Graziano and Navarete (2012) urged colleges and schools of education to offer incentives such as stipends and release benefits to faculty to practice co-teaching in their preparation programs and even York-Barr & Duke (2004) saw co-teaching as the logical next evolution in preservice teacher preparation.

Co-Teaching Relationships Support Acculturation and Lessen Environmental Stressors

Teachers' satisfaction and longevity over the career cycle are directly impacted by multiple factors from within the school as an institution. Everything from a school's leadership style, community relations, regulations and protocols, and the vitality of professional organizations and unions has a profound impact on teacher wellbeing and commitment to the mission (Wang, Li, Luo & Zhang, 2019). It's obvious that these factors can move teachers to enthusiastic dedication to the organization or disenchantment, negativity, and disengagement (Fessler & Christensen, 1992).

If teachers must navigate too many layers of bureaucracy, they are drained of the energy that they need to thrive (Wang et al., 2019). The more creative aspects of the role give way to the more mundane, depriving them of the very things that initially enticed them into the profession. Truly inclusive leadership can bolster teachers during times of change and challenge, while administrations that are seen as not genuinely respectful, relational, or trustworthy destroy the spirit of their staff (Pearson, 2012).

Teachers also are affected by issues of public trust and support; these can buoy or sink teacher esteem and satisfaction. If constantly operating under a cloud of criticism and negativity, teachers suffer a loss of motivation that may lead to stagnation, retreat, or exit (Ujifusa, 2019). This also is true of lack of financial support for schools where teachers cannot do what they know their students need because of monetary constraints (Ujifusa, 2019).

While not the magic solution to these contemporary stressors, co-teaching can be a buffer and a boon to teachers at various stages of the career. Novices benefit from having skilled and caring co-teachers help them acculturate quickly, focusing them on what the norms and necessities of the school culture requires (Fitzell, 2018). Co-teaching can provide a reciprocal infusion of hope and energy when one teacher may be struggling with professional or personal issues (Friend & Cook, 2016). Co-teachers may pool not only ideas but resources to best address their students' needs and the partnership may address the fact that teaching has often been called the loneliest profession (Strauss, 2013).

Co-Teaching Promotes Teaching with Developmental Intentions

Taylor, Marienau & Fiddler (2000) were the first to use the phrase "teaching with developmental intentions" (p. 31) when talking about adult learning. To the authors, 'intentional' means that impactful learning experiences must be constructed in a deliberate and thoughtful manner if they are to assist professionals in increasing their skills in the five dimensions of growth and development of their model. This model can be very helpful in thinking about co-teaching as a form of professional development and personal growth.

The first dimension, known as a dialogic process, is so-called for the reason that dialogue and learning are like processes where individuals are attempting to communicate effectively with one other (Taylor et al., 2000). This dimension recognizes the similarities between dialogue and learning. Doing so requires that each party must not only clearly articulate their own beliefs, they must also be able to hear and respect their partner's beliefs (Taylor et al., 2000). Dialogic learners are those who not only inquire about and respond openly to another's ideas and values but also simultaneously surface and question the assumptions that undergird their own philosophy and practice (Taylor et al., 2000). Co-teaching conducted in a supportive manner does just this.

Taylor et al. (2000) also wrote about helping learners to be in "dialogic relationship to oneself," (p. 32)—that is, able to see an individual's values and philosophies from multiple perspectives. This involves a process of self-scrutiny and reflection in which adults can uncover limitations in their own ways of thinking (Marzano, 2012). This is described as seeing personal experiences from both the 'inside out' and the 'outside in.' Classroom teaching is informed by a teacher's belief system; therefore, they must be aware of the implications of such a system. Teachers, it is argued, should pay attention to the familiar and not avoid the unfamiliar, expanding their capacity for critical self-reflection (Taylor et al., 2000). Co-teaching, under the best of circumstances, can prompt such self-scrutiny.

Just as Taylor et al. (2000) believed and Aguilar (2018a) concurred, the dimension of being a continuous learner prepares the adult to be more willing to take risks, accept cognitive dissonance as part of the learning process, and challenging oneself to be enthusiastic and growing over the career cycle.

Self-agency and self-authorship is the stage at which practitioners become the authors of their own stories, values, beliefs, and best practices and are necessary in order to operate with internal authority (Baxter-Magolda, 2008). Unexamined canon can give way to self-authored ways of being in the classroom.

Co-teachers and mentors can be extremely important in this self-authorship and self-agency development as their support, especially during the novice stage, can gently guide these new teachers in examining their values, beliefs and practices (Davidson, 2018; Fitzell, 2018). Through asking questions and actively listening, co-teachers can each engage in reflecting upon why they teach the way they do, the assumptions that underlie such practice, and other ways that such practice might be approached (Friend & Cook, 2016). By taking part in self-reflection, more veteran teachers can help empower newer ones to have increasing confidence and skill in greater self-authorship (Davidson, 2018; Marzano, 2012).

The last dimension of the model is termed 'connection with others' and is built through true communities of collaboration (Taylor et al., 2000). In such communities, boundaries between being connected to others and autonomy and individually-held beliefs and values are respectfully and supportively mediated in an ongoing fashion (Kaplan, 2012). Colleagues are now viewed as safe sources or sounding boards for trying out new theories, ideas or strategies.

Co-Teaching Provides an Apprenticeship that Initiates Teachers into the Profession

In times past, novices were mentored into the trades through apprenticeships that were guided by veteran masters who provided hands-on training (Dewey, 1997). Dewey (1997) postulated that students can only truly learn by practicing the craft that they sought to master. It was through the guidance of senior practitioners who, in Dewey's (1997) terms, initiated them into the traditions of practice. While guidance could be given in multiple forms, the student could only learn through direct, hands-on learning experiences that linked them to the means and methods of the craft and in turn showed them just how those means and methods were linked to end products. Students didn't learn, both

Dewey and Schön (1987) believed, through being told something; they had to experience it for themselves. Modeling and then practicing what they had seen modeled were effective ways to concretize essential skills and knowledge.

In order to meet the goals of providing education to stimulate reflective practice, promote positive human development, give practice in approaching problems of the "indeterminate zones" (Schön, 1987, p. 4), and help learners develop a more phenomenological stance in their work, supervision---viewed as ongoing professional education-- must pose real, meaningful dialogue about the clinical problems that the practitioner is encountering in the field.

These challenges require that clinical supervisors ponder the same questions of intentionality as do classroom professors and internship supervisors during the formal academic program (Schön, 1987). Such pondering about the supervisory role may serve as a vehicle for faculty's identifying current practices that attend to such needs, as well as critically examining areas for professional improvement (Marzano, 2012).

Many teacher preparation programs have adopted a co-teaching model for student teaching. Heck and Bacharach (2015/2016) characterize such models with the motto "off your seat and on your feet" (p. 25). The hallmarks of such a model are that student teachers are actively engaged from day one and the programs stress intentionality in all aspects of the relationship to include common language, planning, and implementation of co-teaching strategies (Heck & Bacharach, 2015/2016). The veteran teacher assists the novice in becoming Schön's (1987) reflective practitioner by guiding them through the difficult times of early practice and navigating the indeterminate zones that often baffle new teachers and undermine their confidence.

Through regular sessions of co-teacher reflection and refinement of practice, preservice teachers learn to value the reflective process and its link to the everyday classroom experience (Marzano, 2012). Heck and Bacharach (2015/2016) describe the tenets of a quality relationship in which

> Both teachers are involved in every aspect of planning and delivering instruction. Cooperating teachers provide modeling and coaching, explicitly sharing rationales for their instructional, curricular, and management decisions. They give teacher candidates time to develop and practice all aspects of teaching with support. As the experience progresses, pairs seamlessly alternate between leading and assisting with planning, instructing, and assessing (p. 25).

Co-Teaching Raises Cultural Awareness

MacDonald (1997) defined a multi-cultural encounter as any time that "two or more persons with different worldviews (ways of perceiving one's social environments) are brought together in a helping relationship" (p. 2). In teaching, this is always at least triadic, given that in any contemporary classroom, there are also the students' backgrounds to consider and their worldviews that are the product of such variables as gender, age, socio-economic status, race, ethnicity, religion, sexual orientation or physical/cognitive functioning (Hammond, 2014).

Aguilar (2018a) stressed the importance of cultural competence within any educational setting. Without it, there are no healthy school communities. According to Aguilar (2018a), there are three actions that teachers must take to expand their cultural competence to include knowing personal cultural identity, values and biases; knowing about the general role that culture plays in society and being aware of other cultures' ways of being; and being able to navigate differences effectively in action.

Co-teaching at its best allows educators to probe their own and their co-teacher's cultural background and beliefs and translate these into practice, sometimes intentional and sometimes unconscious; yet, these discussions must be delicate in nature and supportive of both members' worldviews if they are to be transformative (Fitzell, 2018). Co-teaching may bring together teachers who actually are from different countries and cultural traditions, or culture may be defined in educational terms that are derived from lessons ingrained in preservice training or other teaching experiences (Hammond, 2014).

Baber, Farrett, and Holcomb-McCoy's 1977 VISION model of culture can be adapted to co-teaching, coaching, and mentoring situations in that each component of the model provides valuable discussion between dyads. Articulated as a model for clinical supervision, it nevertheless addresses co-teaching situations well, as what might be discussed in observations of the supervisee and their clients can be recast in terms of teacher and their students (Baber et al., 1977). In particular, the 'V' and 'I' components have the most meaning for educators.

The 'V' of the model is centered on questions about values and beliefs—what is important to the teachers and why, what their beliefs are about such fundamental topics as human nature, social relations, and relationships between humans and the learning environment (Baber et al., 1977). 'I' relates to one's interpretation of their experience of teaching others and in being observed and coached—how an individual frames what's going on in both relationships (Baber et al., 1977).

Being able to understand each other's values and interpretive frameworks ensures that the teachers can then better structure the co-teaching relationship effectively, that in turn builds better communication within the pair (Conderman, Johnston-Rodriguez & Hartman, 2009). Preferences for verbal and non-verbal ways of communicating definitely should be shared and finding shareable ground that respects the goals of both is critical to co-teaching experiences that work (Fitzell, 2018).

Co-Teaching Helps Teachers Maintain the Reflection/Renewal Process

Steffy et al. (2000) put forth an advocacy model of teacher professional development differentiated by where each teacher is in the career cycle; yet, they agreed that the foundation of all personal and professional development relies upon two fundamental processes, those of reflection and renewal. As teachers commit themselves to growing in order to enhance student achievement in the academic and personal domains, they are forced to reflect on their practice.

Reflective teachers live in a state of constant re-examination of their teaching moments, both analyzing what they have tried and asking themselves the 'what if' questions. Similar to the action research process (Dick, 2000), they are engaged in questioning, generating fresh ideas for refining their practice, trying them out in real time, analyzing their success and reconceptualizing their practice again. As they do this, they are renewed personally and professionally; such experimentation keeps them engaged and excited (Marzano, 2012).

Most contemporary practitioners are challenged to find the time for such a process. Heck and Bacharach (2015/2016) argued that co-teachers must have time and shared that "if you don't co-plan, you won't co-teach. Co-teaching is not walking into the room and saying 'Hey, what are we doing today?'" (p. 28). The act of paired teaching must have an intentional structure that provides adequate time for both co-creation and authentic co-reflection (Heck & Bacharach, 2015/2016). Teachers who are new to the profession also may need to learn methods of reflective practice like taking reflective notes, using case studies, or employing journals or diaries (Fitzell, 2018).

Offering professional development that centers on research on reflective practice and providing concrete modeling and sharing how others have honed their reflective practice should become part of such development (Devlin-Scherer & Sardone, 2013; Mizell, 2010). This time must be held sacred, the authors opine. Beyond the co-teaching dyads, there are ways that professional learning communities and critical friends groups can nurture the reflection/renewal process (Bambino, 2002; DuFour, DuFour, Eaker, Many & Mattos, 2016).

Co-Teaching Transforms 'Meaning Perspectives'

Mezirow (1978) believed that undergoing new experiences could transform what he called "meaning perspectives" (p. 100) inherited from one's past history. When we undergo novel (or new) experiences, we are confronted with our own assumptions that have been derived from family of origin, culture, community, faith, occupation, or other factors (Vinney, 2019). When questioned about the validity of these assumptions, we may be at first defensive or protective of our ideas, beliefs and values, but with careful and supported scrutiny and the ability and willingness to listen to others' perspectives, we may come to modify or even radically change some of our assumptions, which, in turn, has implications for our practice (Mezirow, 1978).

This occurs in good co-teaching as colleagues or a mentor teacher and novice explore such things as what they believe to be best classroom practice, why they choose certain teaching or classroom strategies, and where various 'habits of mind' have come from (Kallick & Costa, 2008). Understanding their philosophies and their derivations and examining beliefs only can take place in supportive environments in which both teachers actively engage in constructive conversations and genuinely are interested in learning about one another (Mezirow, 1978). By stretching their thinking, co-teachers can advance as practitioners to a more expansive view of what may work with certain learners and in certain learning environments (Kallick & Costa, 2008).

Mezirow (1978) proposed that an individual's "perspective transformation" (p. 102) may occur in one or all of three dimensions (1) psychological - changes in how we understand the self, (2) convictional - revisiting values or belief systems, and (3) behavioral - making changes in how we live our lives. The most profound changes come from what he called a "disorienting dilemma" (p. 103) resulting from a life crisis or transition. For a novice teacher, this may be living daily within the realities of the classroom environment; for a veteran teacher, it may be having someone ask questions about why they do the things they do. Given that teachers rarely have the opportunity to observe each other in action, co-teaching may provide a valuable opportunity to have another colleague reflect on what they observed and listen to the rationale behind a teacher's actions as a way to problem solve and be reflective (Fitzell, 2018; Friend & Cook, 2016).

Needless to say, meaning perspectives will be transformed in a lasting way only when the parties involved feel safe in revealing themselves. Reilly (2015/2016) stressed the use of "reflective feedback" (p. 37) as a tool to promote partnership in co-teaching situations. It begins with the belief that the other wants to perform at as high a level as possible and is a capable practitioner. This stance involves focusing on strengths and assets that are present and building upon those.

The process begins with clarifying questions about a colleague's practice or to shared practices (Reilly, 2015/2016). Making all underlying assumptions transparent, the educator starts in a state of genuine curiosity about what has been observed. Reilly (2015/2016) urged co-teachers to:

> *State the value (or potential value) of the person you're talking with or the idea under consideration. With a value statement, you express what you value about the person you're addressing or the topic under consideration. You affirm a specific strength you've observed and make your own opinions about the topic or question explicit* (p. 37).

Reflective questions are then posed to stimulate critical thinking. These are posed to help both parties think deeply and creatively, to develop new connections among ideas, and to be open to other points of view. This practice aims at forging a dialogue and "engaging the other person in thinking about his or her practice and owning its effect on students" (Reilly, 2015/2016, p. 38).

Goodwin (2015/2016) reported that "when teachers were given guiding questions for their collaborative conversations and protocols for observing classrooms, peer coaching was more incisive and productive" (p. 82). Getting outside of an individual's comfort zones as a part of this process requires that there is follow-up support that focuses on adaptation of individual practice rather than the adoption of someone else's (Goodwin, 2015/2016).

Co-Teaching Enhances Self-Authorship

As teachers move away from daily survival mode and following the scripts of others, they need to become the authors of their own theories of best practice and belief systems. Co-teaching can augment this process through modeling different practices, strategies, and ways of being in the classroom and school community; however, self-authorship occurs at the point of competency or mastery, when the teacher can then pick and choose from among the different approaches and philosophies offered to them and land on a self-defined set of values and practices (Baxter Magolda, 2008). A skillful co-teacher/mentor working with a preservice or novice teacher gently probes to discover this mindset; with more veteran teachers, mutual conversation and exposure to new ways of seeing and being may prompt each to reconsider and perhaps refine their practice (Davidson, 2018; Fitzell, 2018).

Baxter Magolda (2008), who is considered one of the leading researchers on self-authorship, offered three questions that are seen as the seminal catalysts for movement to this stage (1) 'How do I know?', (2) 'Who Am I?', and (3) 'How do I want to construct relationships with others?'. In moving towards self-authorship, the learner (in this case, the teacher) graduates from following formulas, to the crossroads, to becoming the author of one's life, and finally to having an internal foundation (Baxter Magolda, 2007; 2008).

Passing through each stage moves the teacher away from externally-defined knowledge to truths and then truths-in-praxis that are self-derived (Baxter Magolda, 2007). This process can be helped or hindered by relationships with a co-teacher who supports the other, and engages in actions that involve questioning, active listening, reflection, goal-setting, and intentional planning (Fitzell, 2018). In such a process, the personal and the professional are melded into guiding principles (Baxter Magolda, 2008).

Drago-Severson (2009) purported that teachers, as adults who happen to be in a school setting, can only make meaning out of their teaching experiences based upon their developmental stage. That explains why a group of teachers going through the same experience—such as a school-based change or mandate—all will experience that change in different manners (Neubauer, Witkop & Varpio, 2019). Some may frame and interpret it in ways that are distressful, while others may interpret it in ways that result in no significant change or even in eustress or growth-enhancing stress. Personal responses will be based upon personal and professional stages and experience and it is important to understand this in co-teaching situations (Drago-Severson, 2009).

Drago-Severson (2009) believed that there were three fundamental ways of knowing to include instrumental, socializing and self-authoring. Instrumental knowing is defined as that which orients itself towards assuming that knowledge resides in external authority (Drago-Severson, 2009). This is the kind of concrete orientation of novice teachers who rely on organizational rules and those in supervisory roles and ranks for explicit direction; they are apt to be uncomfortable without expert advice and clearly-articulated procedures and protocols. Since they are treading water professionally on a daily basis, they can't really acknowledge multiple perspectives or ways of accomplishing the same educational goal; however, moving to the ability to do so is important to their growth, so supportive co-teaching relationships can ease the transition from a more external to a more internal way of seeing how to solve problems within the profession (Drago-Severson, 2009).

Socializing knowers are more able to reflect, think in an abstract manner, and be able to consider the views of others (Drago-Severson, 2009). This occurs as novices move into more self-efficacy and confidence; however, teachers in this status are also concerned by others' opinions and evaluation of them and their work and too often subordinate their own values and beliefs about best practice to meet what they believe others, especially those with more authority, want.

It is unfortunate that newer teachers' sense of self is usually relationally-derived to a large extent and conflict within those relationships is perceived as threatening. Co-teaching can help strengthen teachers who are socializing knowers if it is delivered skillfully because it creates the necessary guided opportunities that allow less-experienced teachers to clarify their own perspectives, values and beliefs and models how to hold firm to these even while engaging in dialogues of difference (Drago-Severson, 2009).

Drago-Severson's (2009) notion of self-authorship is that it is a process in which the teacher becomes able to generate their authentic values and take responsibility and ownership of seeking out what they need to grow and maintain professional enthusiasm. The teacher also can see the value in others' perspectives and beliefs and frequently can incorporate aspects of those diversities in ways that enrich their own professional practice (Fitzell, 2018).

Co-Teaching Raises the Status of Certain Teacher Populations

Kusuma-Powell and Powell (2015/2016) exposed the issue of teacher status in our schools, saying that such status affects not only individuals' self-concept, but whom students choose to see as having authority in the learning process. Students will gravitate towards those teachers that they perceive as the highest status and it is demonstrated that they will learn more efficiently and more widely with those high-status teachers (Kusuma-Powell & Powell, 2015/2016). The problem then becomes bringing a faculty into a community in which status and authority are equally shared.

Kusuma-Powell and Powell (2015/2016) believed that special needs students and those who are identified as their educational providers suffer the lowest status in our schools. As one school leader who was interviewed shared:

> *I never realized there was any expertise involved in learning support. I had thought of learning support teachers as kindly individuals who wanted to be helpful, but I didn't think there was a body of knowledge connected to the help they gave* (p. 65).

Involving special education and learning support teachers in co-teaching events raises their status, as the best-functioning teams require acknowledgement that there is reciprocity and egality in the relationship; therefore, both teachers are seen as experts but in different domains (Kusuma-Powell & Powell, 2015/2016). This can only be accomplished through equal planning of lessons and curricular units and making certain that the tasks each is assigned are viewed as equally valuable by both the teachers and the students. Fitzell (2018) reinforces these concepts by emphasizing that parity must be evident in all classroom practices and that language that clearly establishes teacher parity to students and other personnel is paramount in equal status.

Co-Teaching Broadens Teacher Identity

In well-designed co-teaching situations, each partner has the opportunity to stretch their identity by taking on new roles and developing new areas of strength (Friend & Cook, 2016). This can be a particularly powerful experience for teachers who often are marginalized such as those who work with special populations and less-experienced teachers or those who enter the profession via non-traditional routes as "people's identity influences their behavior and decision-making" (Kasuma-Powell & Powell, 2015/2016, p. 66).

If teachers identify with only one aspect of their identity—such as being a novice or being an advocate for special-needs students who cannot voice their own needs—they develop in a lop-sided manner and "limit their capacity to do other important work on behalf of students. [They also are left out of the opportunity to] facilitate, encourage, and structure professional learning for colleagues" (Kasuma-Powell & Powell, 2015/2016, p. 66).

While one might question how someone such as a novice might have important information to impart to veteran teachers, newer professionals may have recently studied research, theories or techniques. Those who come from the outside bring a fresh perspective on what the world of work needs from graduates, and teachers who work with special populations have valuable insights and perspectives that mainstream teachers may not be familiar with. In all cases, as Kasuma-Powell and Powell (2015/2016) point out that

> *teachers need opportunities to develop strengths in group facilitation. They need to be up-to-date in their reading and understanding of current research. They must be able to speak with authority and credibility and offer new understandings in ways that will be palatable to peers and colleagues* (p. 66).

Having the chance to do these things allows teachers to move towards greater self-authorship and identity formation.

Co-Teaching Bolsters Teacher Resilience

Aguilar (2018a) wrote extensively on building teacher resilience—a very necessary component of the teacher career cycle spread out over increasingly-longer numbers of years. Of importance, Aguilar (2018a) noted

> *resilience can substantially and dramatically increase our ability to manage the daily stressors and rebound from inevitable setbacks [and that it allows teachers to keep their] ears open to what we see and hear...[in addition, educators are able to] have difficult conversations-and if we aren't having difficult conversations in our efforts to transform*

schools, we're probably not making meaningful progress. Resilience will
bring communities and educators out of our silos and into healthy
camaraderie (p. 13).

Among the list of items on the list of habits of resilient educators are several
that are particularly enhanced by quality co-teaching relationships and include
knowing oneself, telling empowering stories, building community, being a
learner, celebrating and appreciating, and focusing on bright spots (Aguilar,
2018a). It is clear that good co-teaching promotes self- reflection, builds
community through support and acculturation, and promotes on-going
learning through a continuous exchange of ideas. Having another supportive
adult working alongside us can permit observations and feedback that we
would not have been able to access working solo (Fitzell, 2018).

Co-Teaching can be a Buffer and an Alert System to Teacher Stress and Burnout

Teacher mental health and wellbeing is an increasing concern in our schools
and a major reason for poor performance and exiting the profession (Harmsen,
Helms-Lorenz, Maulana & van Veen, 2018). Obviously, educational leaders and
other key personnel do not have the specific training to act in the role of mental
health counselors; yet, they often need to be able to assess the functioning and
wellbeing of their teachers on levels beyond just the professional realm
(Harmsen et al., 2018). Life issues and challenges bombard teachers every day
and not all are equipped to handle them well. Illness, grief, loss, role overload
and other factors can weaken teacher resilience; however, as most teachers
operate with such autonomy in their classrooms, their struggles may not be
witnessed, and thus their needs cannot be met (Harmsen et al., 2018).

Teacher mental health profoundly impacts student mental health, as leaders
look to their staff to model wellbeing in myriad ways. Job satisfaction,
performance, productivity, and longevity in the profession are also linked to
teacher mental and emotional health. Holmes (2016) reported that there is a
massive problem in this arena in schools in the United Kingdom where 84% of
educators report mental health issues and 81% of them blame their current
work conditions. Pickens (2015) noted that teacher mental health wanes as the
years go by and stress escalates, while Hsaing (2016) indicated that there is a
link between teacher emotional intelligence and compassion fatigue that leads
to lowered satisfaction and raised rates of burnout.

Aguilar (2018b) begs administrators, co-teachers and other coaches to

be aware of the signs of burnout in teachers. The Maslach Burnout
Inventory identifies three areas associated with burnout: emotional

exhaustion, depersonalization, and negative relation to personal accomplishment. In teachers, symptoms of emotional exhaustion include frustration, a lack of interest in teaching, a reluctance to try anything new, and blaming students or the institution for the lack of success. Depersonalization is marked by cynicism; poor attitudes toward students, colleagues, and the school itself; and growing isolation. Teachers on the road to burnout might not greet their colleagues, avoid sharing their classroom experiences, and neglect to socialize with colleagues. In terms of personal accomplishment, teachers on the edge don't set goals, seem uninterested in learning new things, and have low self-confidence.

Well-trained coaches need to know how to recognize these signs. It can be hard to spot teachers who are beginning to burn out, for the simple reason that they tend to hide their condition—or might not themselves be aware of what's wrong with them. Those supporting teachers need to know how to respond to symptoms of burnout, and prevent it, such as through building healthy, thriving staff communities. (Burnout isn't just about stress—it's also about loneliness and isolation.) (p. 29).

One emotional buffer is a supportive relationship with a significant other at the institution and a co-teacher can be that buffer. Co-teachers observe and communicate with one another in ongoing fashion; therefore, they are more apt to notice when their partner is exhibiting signs of distress (Aguilar, 2018a). It is not the role of the co-teacher to provide mental health counseling; rather, reaching out to their partner to lend an ear or acknowledge a difficulty can be extremely important. Building and maintaining trust between co-teachers is the foundation upon which meaningful relationships are formed (Fitzell, 2018). Without trust, co-teachers will not be willing to share personal concerns, nor will they be open to acting upon suggestions to seek out additional resources to bolster them during difficult times.

When forming teacher partnerships at any stage of the career cycle, teachers need access to professional development that openly discusses the implications of teacher wellbeing on performance, career satisfaction, student achievement, and personal and professional relationships (Mizell, 2010). Strategies such as those discussed in Aguilar's (2018a) book on teacher resilience, Haisman-Smith's (2017) article on teacher mental health, and Hsaing's (2016) research that more professional development must center on specific means to foster higher levels of teacher emotional intelligence need to be employed.

Final Thoughts

It is essential that schools consider their teaching staff from a developmental stance. Regardless of which of the conceptual models one uses—and there is much overlap and consonance among the most prominent models—the notion that teachers' career cycle experiences are linked to age and stage and can be growth-enhancing and satisfying or stagnant and frustrating is something that school leaders, higher education faculty, professional development experts, and teachers themselves must consider carefully. Being well-educated in the teacher career cycle and its implications is paramount.

There are many ways that co-teaching, in all its various forms, can inform best practice in nurturing personal wellbeing, promoting teacher growth, and enhancing professional practice at each stage of the teacher career cycle. The developmental challenges of different stages have been described above and strategies that co-teachers and mentors can use to support colleagues and mentees have been explicated.

Co-teaching holds much promise for improving teachers' performance, job satisfaction, collegiality, and longevity. This promise is made manifest, however, only when co-teaching is of the highest quality. Fitzell (2018) neatly summarized the components of quality co-teaching in this closing quote:

> *Co-teaching is two or more teachers working together to provide instruction, typically, to students in a heterogeneous inclusive setting Within a well-implemented co-teaching initiative, teachers plan together, instruct the class together, and collaborate....In a co-taught classroom that fully utilizes the talents of the two teachers and any other adult staff in the room, students are more likely to achieve high standards, to be successful, and to behave more appropriately than they would in segregated, pull-out, or self-contained classrooms* (p. 3).

The same outcomes are likely to be gained for teachers in a co-teaching relationship - greater achievement; higher standards; more success; higher self-esteem; greater technical competence; and more job satisfaction. Each of these outcomes is integrated into models of personal and professional development, and through co-teaching, the odds that teachers can become enthusiastic and growing and maintain high levels of enjoyment, engagement, and willingness to give back to their students and school community is worth any expenditure of time and effort to create meaningful teaching dyads.

Points to Remember

- *Many theorists and researchers have developed models of the teacher career cycle with distinct stages and developmental tasks inherent in those stages.*

- *These models postulate growth from a preservice and novice stage, to a competency-building stage, to a stage of mastery and an interest in growing within the teaching role to remain fully engaged and enthusiastic.*

- *Teachers make meaning out of their school-based experiences based, in part, on their developmental stage.*

- *All models acknowledge that in order for teachers to commit to a career in the classroom and derive satisfaction in their work they need specific supports and opportunities at each stage of their career.*

- *Quality co-teaching can support newer teachers in gaining knowledge and skills, learning school culture and protocol, and developing self-confidence and a sense of self-efficacy.*

- *Quality co-teaching can be a form of teacher leadership that allows more veteran teachers to share their skills and mentor others into the profession.*

- *Quality co-teaching can raise the status of marginalized teachers.*

- *The co-teaching relationship can promote adult development through critical reflection and reframing of meaning perspectives, especially through skillful and supportive questioning of both partners' philosophy, values, and preferred practices.*

- *Quality co-teaching enhances cultural competence when teachers learn to navigate conversations of difference in the service of student achievement and reciprocal understanding.*

References

Aguilar, E. (2018a). *Onward: Cultivating emotional resilience in educators.* San Francisco, CA: Jossey-Bass.

Aguilar, E. (2018b). Emotional resilience: The missing ingredient. *Educational Leadership, 75*(8), 24-30. Retrieved from http://www.ascd.org/publications/educational-leadership/may18/vol75/num08/Emotional-Resilience@-The-Missing-Ingredient.aspx

American Psychological Association. (2019). *Coping with stress at work.* Retrieved from https://www.apa.org/helpcenter/work-stress

Baber, W.L., Garrett, M.T., & Holcomb-McCoy, C. (1997). VISION: A model of culture for counselors. *Counseling and Values, 41*(3), 184-193. DOI: 10.1002/j.2161-007X.1997.tb00401.x

Bambino, D. (2002). Critical friends. *Educational Leadership,* 59(6), 25-27. Retrieved from http://www.ascd.org/publications/educational-leadership/mar02/vol59/num06/Critical-Friends.aspx

Barlin, D. (2010). *Better mentoring, better teachers.* Retrieved from https://www.edweek.org/archive/ew/articles/2010/03/23/27barlin.html

Baxter Magolda, M.B. (2007). Self-authorship: The foundation for twenty-first-century education. In *New Directions for Teaching and Learning, 109,* pp. 69-83. Retrieved from https://collab.its.virginia.edu/access/content/group/e4988829-79dd-4614-8f78-5f4de7aa2b32/Library/Articles/Magolda-2007-New_Directions_for_Teaching_and_Learning.pdf

Baxter Magolda, M.B. (2008). Three elements of self-authorship. *Journal of College Student Development,* 49(4), 269-284. Retrieved from https://muse.jhu.edu/article/241952

Beasley, T.A. (2013). *Influences contributing to the longevity of experienced teachers in the elementary, middle and high school settings.* Retrieved from https://pdfs.semanticscholar.org/d5f4/0390d188cbeb16e61d4f50a779b057b66fca.pdf

Bullough, R. (2012). Mentoring and new teacher induction in the United States: A review and analysis of current practices. *Mentoring and Tutoring: Partnership in Learning, 20*(1), 57-74. DOI: 10.1080/13611267.2012.645600

Chickering, A.W. (1969). *Education and identity.* San Francisco, CA: Jossey-Bass.

Conderman, G., Johnston-Rodriguez, S., & Hartman, P. (2009). Communicating and collaborating in co-taught classrooms. *Teaching Exceptional Children Plus, 5*(5), 2-16. Retrieved from https://files.eric.ed.gov/fulltext/EJ967751.pdf

Cruickshank, D.R., & Callahan, R. (1983). The other side of the desk: Stages and problems of teacher development. *The Elementary School Journal, 83,* 250-258. https://doi.org/10.1086/461315

Darling-Hammond, L., Hyler, M.E., Gardner, M. & Espinoza, D. (2017). *Effective teacher professional development.* Retrieved from https://learningpolicyinstitute.org/sites/default/files/product-files/Effective_Teacher_Professional_Development_BRIEF.pdf

Davey, L. (2015). *Helping a coworker who's stressed out.* Retrieved from https://hbr.org/2015/09/helping-a-coworker-whos-stressed-out

Davidson, D. (2018). *Teaching tips: Self-authorship & learning partnership models.* Retrieved from https://www.apscuf.org/wp-content/uploads/2018/07/bu_teaching_tips/TT_APSCUF_selfAuthorship_1.1.pdf

Devlin-Scherer, R. & Sardone, N. B. (2013). Collaboration as a form of professional development: Improving learning for faculty and students. *College Teaching, 61,* 30–37. https://doi.org/10.1080/87567555.2012.714815

Dewey, J. (1997). *Experience and education* (reprint). New York, NY: Touchstone Diaz, C.I. (2018). *The truth about teacher burnout: It's work induced depression.* Retrieved from http://psychlearningcurve.org/the-truth-about-teacher-burnout/

Dick, B. (2000). A beginner's guide to action research. Retrieved from www.aral.com.au/resources/guide.html

Drago-Severson, E. (2009). *Leading adult learning: Supporting adult development in our schools.* Thousand Oaks, CA: Corwin.

DuFour, R., DuFour, R., Eaker, R., Many, T.W. & Mattos, M. (2016). *Learning by doing: A handbook for professional learning communities at work* (3rd ed.). Bloomington, IL: Solution Tree Press

Erikson, E. (1994). *Identity and the life cycle.* W.W. Norton.

Felten, P. (2013). Principles of good practice in SoTL. *Teaching & Learning Inquiry: The ISSOTL Journal, 1*(1), 121-125. Retrieved from https://journalhosting.ucalgary.ca/index.php/TLI/article/view/57376/43149

Fessler, R., & Christensen, J.C. (1992). *The teacher career cycle: Understanding and guiding the professional development of teachers.* Boston, MA: Allyn and Bacon.

Fitzell, S.G. (2018). *Best practices in co-teaching and collaboration.* Manchester, N.H.: Cogent Catalyst Publications.

Friend, M. & Cook, L. (2016). *Interactions: Collaboration skills for school professionals* (8th ed.). New York, NY: Pearson

Goodwin, B. (2015/2016). Does teacher collaboration promote teacher growth? *Educational Leadership, 73*(4), 82. Retrieved from http://www.ascd.org/publications/educational-leadership/dec15/vol73/num04/Does-Teacher-Collaboration-Promote-Teacher-Growth%C2%A2.aspx

Graziano, K.E., & Navarete, L. (Spring, 2012). Co-teaching in a teacher education classroom: Collaboration, compromise, and creativity. *Issues in Teacher Education,* 109-126. Retrieved from https://eric.ed.gov/?id=EJ986819

Greenberg, J., Putnam, H., Walsh, K. (2014). *Training our future teachers: Classroom management.* Retrieved from https://www.nctq.org/dmsView/Future_Teachers_Classroom_Management_NCTQ_Report

Gregorc, A.F. (1973). Developing plans for professional growth. Retrieved from http://journals.sagepub.com/doi/abs/10.1177/019263657305737701

Haisman-Smith, N. (2017). The elephant in the (staff) room: Why we need to talk about teacher wellbeing. Retrieved from http://www.huffingtonpost.co.uk/nick-haismansmith/teacher-wellbeing_b_15335608.html

Hammond, Z.L. (2014). *Culturally responsive teaching and the brain: Engagement and rigor among culturally and linguistically diverse students.* Thousand Oaks, CA: Corwin

Harmsen, R, Helms-Lorenz, M., Maulana, R. & van Veen, K. (2018). The relationship between beginning teachers' stress causes, stress responses, teaching behaviour and attrition. *Teachers and Teaching: Theory and Practice, 24*(6). DOI: 10.1080/13540602.2018.1465404

Heck, T.W., & Bacharach, N. (2015/2016). A better model for student teaching. *Educational Leadership, 73*(4), 24-29. Retrieved from http://www.ascd.org/publications/educational-leadership/dec15/vol73/num04/A-Better-Model-for-Student-Teaching.aspx

Holmes, E. (2016). Why teacher mental health matters-and how to improve it. Retrieved from http://blog.optimus-education.com/why-teacher-mental-health-matters-%E2%80%93-and-how-improve-it

Hsiang, R. (2016). Teachers' mental health: The relationship of emotional intelligence in burnout and quality of life. Retrieved from https://pdfs.semanticscholar.org/9971/e6ba9c91f8c970658f1151110abf221144ce.pdf

Huberman, M.A. (1989). The professional life cycle of teachers. Teachers College Record, 91, (1), 31-57. Retrieved from https://eric.ed.gov/?id=EJ398425

Hunt, D. (1971). *Matching models of education: The coordination of teaching methods with student characteristics.* Toronto, Ontario: Ontario Institute for Studies in Education.

Kallick, B. & Costa, A.L. (2008). *Learning and leading with habits of mind: 16 essential characteristics for success.* Alexandria, VA: ASCD

Kaplan, M. (2012). *Collaborative team teaching: Challenges and rewards.* Retrieved from https://www.edutopia.org/blog/collaborative-team-teaching-challenges-rewards-marisa-kaplan

Katz, L.G. (1972). The developmental stages of preschool teachers. Retrieved from https://jstor.org/stable/1000851

Killion, J., & Harrison, C. (2017). *Taking the lead: New roles for teachers and school-based Coaches* (2nd ed.). Learning Forward

Koepsell, J. (2018). *Three ways to help your colleague through a crisis.* Retrieved from https://www.forbes.com/sites/juliekoepsell1/2018/08/05/how-to-help-a-colleague-through-a-crisis/#2518314c1f11

Kusuma-Powell, O., & Powell, W. (2015/2016). Lifting the status of learning support teachers. *Educational Leadership, 73*(4), 62-67. Retrieved from http://www.ascd.org/publications/educational-leadership/dec15/vol73/num04/Lifting-the-Status-of-Learning-Support-Teachers.aspx

Levinson, D. J. (1978). *The seasons of a man's life.* New York, NY: Ballantine Books.

Loreman, T., Sharma, U. & Forlin, C. (2013). Do pre-service teachers feel ready to teach in inclusive classrooms? A four country study of teaching self-efficacy. *Australian Journal of Teacher Education, 38*(1). Retrieved from https://files.eric.ed.gov/fulltext/EJ1008550.pdf

Lumpkin, A., Claxton, H. & Wilson, A. (2014). *Key characteristics of teacher leaders in schools.* Retrieved from https://dc.swosu.edu/cgi/viewcontent.cgi?article=1100&context=aij

MacDonald, G. (1997). *Issues in multi-cultural counseling supervision.* Retrieved from https://files.eric.ed.gov/fulltext/ED439341.pdf

Marzano, R.J. (2012). *Becoming a reflective teacher.* Bloomington, IN: Marzano Research Laboratory

McNeel, B. (2019). *Portrait of a turnaround principal.* Retrieved from https://www.edutopia.org/article/portrait-turnaround-principal

Mekos, T. & Smith, M. (2018). *Mentoring new teachers: A fresh look.* Retrieved from https://www.sreb.org/sites/main/files/file-attachments/mentoring _new_teachers_2.pdf?1516727553

Mezirow, J. (1978) Perspective Transformation. *Adult Education Quarterly, 28*, 100-110. http://dx.doi.org/10.1177/074171367802800202

Michel, H.A. (2013). *The first five years: Novice teacher beliefs, experiences, and commitment to the profession.* Retrieved from https://escholarship.org/uc/item/3cq6954m

Mizell, H. (2010). Why professional development matters. *Learning Forward.* Retrieved from https://learningforward.org/docs/default-source/pdf/why _pd_matters_web.pdf

Moore, W. & Hammond, L. (2011). Using education assistants to help pave the road to literacy: Supporting oral language, letter-sound knowledge and phonemic awareness in the preprimary year. *Australian Journal of Learning Difficulties, 16*(2), 85-110. http://dx.doi.org/10.1080/19404151003763029

Morrison, N. (2019). *Number of teachers quitting the classroom after just one year hits all-time high.* Retrieved from https://www.forbes.com/sites/nickmorrison/2019/06/27/number-of-teachers-quitting-the-classroom-after-just-one-year-hits-all-time-high/#20e9cd5360e5

Muhammad, A. (2017). *Transforming school culture: How to overcome staff division* (2nd ed.). Bloomington, IN: Solution Tree.

Mulvahill, E. (2019). *Why teachers quit.* Retrieved from https://www.weareteachers.com/why-teachers-quit/

Murawski, W.W. & Lochner, W.W. (2018). *Beyond co-teaching basics: A data-driven, no-tail model for continuous improvement.* Alexandria, VA: ASCD

Murphy, P. (2018). *Built to last: How to have a long teaching career.* Retrieved from http://teacherhabits.com/built-to-last-how-to-have-a-long-teaching-career/

Nast, P. (n.d.). *Resources toolkit for new teachers.* Retrieved from http://www.nea.org/tools/71139.htm

National Staff Development Council. (2008). *Chart the stages of teacher development.* Retrieved from https://learningforward.org/docs/leading-teacher/nov08_tool.pdf?sfvrsn=2

Neubauer, B.E., Witkop, C.T. & Varpio, L. (2019). How phenomenology can help us learn from the experiences of others. *Perspectives on Medical Education, 8*(2), 90-97. DOI: 10.1007/s40037-019-0509-2

Pearson, C.S. (2012). *The transforming leader: New approaches to leadership for the twenty-first century.* San Francisco, CA: Berrett-Koehler Publishers

Pickens, I. (2015). The brief wondrous life of teachers' mental health. Retrieved from https://www.psychologytoday.com/us/blog/revolutionary-thoughts/201509/the-brief-wondrous-life-teachers-mental-health

Reilly, M (2015/2016). Saying what you mean without being mean. *Educational Leadership, 73*(4), 36-40. Retrieved from

http://www.ascd.org/publications/educational-leadership/dec15/vol73/
num04/Saying-What-You-Mean-Without-Being-Mean.aspx

Sachs, G.T., Fisher, T., & Cannon, J. (2011). Collaboration, mentoring and co-
teaching in teacher education. DOI: 10.2478/v10099-011-0015-z

Schön, D.A. (1987). *Educating the reflective practitioner.* San Francisco, CA:
John Wiley & Son, Inc.

Steffy, B.E., Wolfe, M.P., Pasch, S.H., & Enz, B.J. (Eds.). (2000). *Lifecycle of the
career teacher.* Thousand Oaks, CA: Corwin Press, Inc.

Strauss, V. (2013). *Why teacher feel so alone.* Retrieved from
https://www.washingtonpost.com/news/answer-
sheet/wp/2013/08/19/why-teachers-need-free-coffee-at-school/

Taylor, K., Marienau, C., & Fiddler, M. (2000). *Developing adult learners:
Strategies for teachers and trainers.* San Francisco, CA: Jossey-Bass.

Tricarico, K.M., Jacobs, J. & Yendol-Hoppey, D. (2013). Reflection on their first
five years of teaching: Understanding staying and impact power. *Teachers
and Teaching: Theory and Practice, 21*(3), 237-259. DOI:
10.1080/13540602.2014.953821

Ujifusa, A. (2019). *10 big ideas: Teachers have trust issues.* Retrieved from
https://www.edweek.org/ew/articles/2019/01/09/teachers-have-trust-
issues.html?intc=EW-BIG-NXT

Vinney, C. (2019). *What is a schema in psychology? Definition and examples.*
Retrieved from
https://www.thoughtco.com/schema-definition-4691768

Walker, T. (2018). *Who is the Average U.S. Teacher?* Retrieved from
http://neatoday.org/2018/06/08/who-is-the-average-u-s-teacher/

Wang, K., Li, Y., Luo, W. & Zhang, S. (2019). Selected factors contributing to
teacher job satisfaction: A quantitative investigation using 2013 TALIS data.
Leadership and Policy in Schools. DOI: 10.1080/15700763.2019.1586963

Will, M. (2018). *5 things to know about today's teaching force.* Retrieved from
http://blogs.edweek.org/edweek/teacherbeat/2018/10/today_teaching_forc
e_richard_ingersoll.html

Wolpert-Gawron, H. (2018). *Every teacher needs a mentor.* Retrieved from
https://www.edutopia.org/article/every-teacher-needs-mentor

Xin, Y., Wu, J., Yao, Z., Guan, Q., Aleman, A., & Luo, Y. (2017). The relationship
between personality and the response to acute psychological stress.
Scientific Reports, 7(16906). DOI: 10.1038/s41598-017-17053-2

York-Barr, J., & Duke, K. (2004). What do we know about teacher leadership?
Findings from two decades of scholarship. *Review of Educational Research,
74*(3), 255-316. DOI: 10.3102/00346543074003255

About the Authors

Nicholas D. Young, PhD, EdD

Dr. Nicholas D. Young has worked in diverse educational roles for more than 30 years, serving as a teacher, counselor, principal, special education director, graduate professor, graduate program director, graduate dean, and longtime psychologist and superintendent of schools. He was named the Massachusetts Superintendent of the Year; and he completed a distinguished Fulbright program focused on the Japanese educational system through the collegiate level. Dr. Young is the recipient of numerous other honors and recognitions including the General Douglas MacArthur Award for distinguished civilian and military leadership and the Vice Admiral John T. Hayward Award for exemplary scholarship. He holds several graduate degrees including a PhD in educational administration and an EdD in educational psychology.

Dr. Young has served in the U.S. Army and U.S. Army Reserves combined for over 35 years; and he graduated with distinction from the U.S. Air War College, the U.S. Army War College, and the U.S. Navy War College. After completing a series of senior leadership assignments in the U.S. Army Reserves as the commanding officer of the 287th Medical Company (DS), the 405th Area Support Company (DS), the 405th Combat Support Hospital, and the 399th Combat Support Hospital, he transitioned to his current military position as a faculty instructor at the U.S. Army War College in Carlisle, PA. He currently holds the rank of Colonel.

Dr. Young is also a regular presenter at state, national, and international conferences; and he has written many books, book chapters, and/or articles on various topics in education, counseling, and psychology. Some of his most recent books include *Maximizing Mental Health Services: Evidenced-Based Practices that Promote Emotional Well-Being* (2019); *Masculinity in the Making: Managing the Transition to Manhood* (2019); *The Burden of Being a Boy: Bolstering Educational and Emotional Well-Being in Young Males* (2019); *The Special Education Toolbox: Supporting Exceptional Teachers, Students, and Families* (2019); *Sounding the Alarm in the Schoolhouse: Safety, Security and Student Well-Being (2019); Creating Compassionate Classrooms: Understanding the Continuum of Disabilities and Effective Educational Interventions* (2019); *Acceptance, Understanding, and the Moral Imperative of Promoting Social Justice Education in the Schoolhouse* (2019); *Empathic Teaching: Promoting Social Justice in the Contemporary Classroom* (2019); *Educating the Experienced: Challenges and Best Practices in Adult Learning* (2019); *Securing the Schoolyard: Protocols that Promote Safety and Positive Student Behaviors* (2018); *The Soul of the Schoolhouse: Cultivating Student Engagement* (2018); *Embracing and Educating the Autistic Child: Valuing Those Who Color Outside the Lines* (2018); *From Cradle to Classroom: A Guide to Special Education for Young Children* (2018); *Captivating Classrooms: Educational Strategies to Enhance Student Engagement* (2018); *Potency of the Principalship: Action-Oriented Leadership at the Heart of School Improvement* (2018); *Soothing the Soul: Pursuing a Life of Abundance Through a Practice of Gratitude* (2018); *Dog Tags to Diploma: Understanding and Addressing the Educational Needs of Veterans, Servicemembers, and their Families* (2018); *Turbulent Times: Confronting Challenges in Emerging Adulthood* (2018); *Guardians of the Next Generation: Igniting the Passion for Quality Teaching* (2018); *Achieving Results: Maximizing Success in the Schoolhouse* (2018); *From Head to Heart: High Quality Teaching Practices in the Spotlight* (2018); *Stars in the Schoolhouse: Teaching Practices and Approaches that Make a Difference* (2018); *Making the Grade: Promoting Positive Outcomes for Students with Learning Disabilities* (2018); *Paving the Pathway for Educational Success: Effective Classroom Interventions for Students with Learning Disabilities* (2018); *Wrestling with Writing: Effective Strategies for Struggling Students* (2018); *Floundering to Fluent: Reaching and Teaching the Struggling Student* (2018); *Emotions and Education: Promoting Positive Mental Health in Students with Learning* (2018); *From Lecture Hall to Laptop: Opportunities, Challenges, and the Continuing Evolution of Virtual Learning in Higher Education* (2017); *The Power of the Professoriate: Demands, Challenges, and Opportunities in 21st Century Higher Education* (2017); *To Campus with Confidence: Supporting a Successful Transition to College for Students with Learning Disabilities* (2017); *Educational Entrepreneurship: Promoting Public-Private Partnerships for the 21st Century* (2015); *Beyond the Bedtime Story: Promoting Reading Development during the Middle School Years* (2015); *Betwixt and Between: Understanding and Meeting the Social and Emotional Developmental Needs of Students During the Middle School Transition Years* (2014); *Learning Style Perspectives: Impact Upon the Classroom* (3rd ed., 2014); and *Collapsing Educational Boundaries from Preschool to PhD: Building Bridges Across the Educational Spectrum* (2013); *Transforming Special Education Practices: A Primer for School Administrators and Policy Makers* (2012); and *Powerful Partners in Student Success: Schools, Families and Communities* (2012). He also co-authored several children's books to include the popular series *I am Full of Possibilities*. Dr. Young may be contacted directly at nyoung1191@aol.com.

Angela C. Fain, PhD

Dr. Fain has worked in the field of special education for the past 20 years. She received her PhD and M.Ed. in special education at Georgia State University, as well as a B.S. in Therapeutic Recreation. She earned national certification as a Nationally Certified Therapeutic Recreation Specialist (TRS) and worked as a therapist for several years with children who had severe emotional/behavioral disorders (SEBD) and/or autism. Dr. Fain has worked in some of the most restrictive educational environments that students with disabilities are served, as both a TRS and special education teacher. She worked as a clinical instructor at Georgia State University while earning her doctorate and at the University of North Georgia while concurrently serving as an assistant professor. She is now an assistant professor at the University of West Georgia.

Dr. Fain is a regular presenter at state, national, and international conferences and she is an active board member of Learning Disabilities Worldwide. She has authored several book chapters and articles on various topics in special education ranging from classroom management to successful academic interventions for students with disabilities.

Teresa Citro, PhD

Dr. Citro is the Chief Executive Officer, Learning Disabilities Worldwide, Inc. and the Founder and President of Thread of Hope, Inc. She is a graduate of Tufts New England Medical School and Northeastern University, Boston. Dr. Citro has co-edited several books on a wide range of topics in special education, she co-authored a popular children's series *I Am Full of Possibilities*, and she is the co-editor of two peer review journals dealing with special education issues.